AMERICAN KARMA

QUALITATIVE STUDIES IN PSYCHOLOGY

This series showcases the power and possibility of qualitative work in psychology. Books feature detailed and vivid accounts of qualitative psychology research using a variety of methods, including participant observation and fieldwork, discursive and textual analyses, and critical cultural history. They probe the vital issues of theory, implementation, interpretation, representation, and ethics confronting qualitative workers. The mission of this series is to enlarge and refine the repertoire of qualitative approaches to psychology.

GENERAL EDITORS
Michelle Fine and Jeanne Marecek

Everyday Courage: The Lives and Stories of Urban Teenagers
Niobe Way

Negotiating Consent in Psychotherapy
Patrick O'Neill

Flirting with Danger: Young Women's Reflections on Sexuality and Domination
Lynn M. Phillips

Voted Out: The Psychological Consequences of Anti-Gay Politics
Glenda M. Russell

Inner City Kids: Adolescents Confront Life and Violence
in an Urban Community
Alice McIntyre

From Subjects to Subjectivities: A Handbook of Interpretive and
Participatory Methods
Edited by Deborah L. Tolman and Mary Brydon-Miller

Growing Up Girl: Psychosocial Explorations of Gender and Class
Valerie Walkerdine, Helen Lucey, and June Melody

Voicing Chicana Feminisms: Young Women Speak Out on and Identity
Aida Hurtado

Situating Sadness: Women and Depression in Social Context
Edited by Janet M. Stoppard and Linda M. McMullen

Living Outside Mental Illness: Qualitative Studies of Recovery in Schizophrenia
Larry Davidson

Autism and the Myth of the Person Alone
Douglas Biklen
With Sue Rubin, Tito Rajarshi Mukhopadhyay, Lucy Blackman, Larry Bissonnette,
Alberto Frugone, Richard Attfield, and Jamie Burke

American Karma: Race, Culture, and Identity in the Indian Diaspora
Sunil Bhatia

AMERICAN KARMA

Race, Culture, and Identity in the Indian Diaspora

SUNIL BHATIA

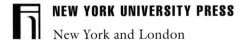

NEW YORK UNIVERSITY PRESS
New York and London

NEW YORK UNIVERSITY PRESS
New York and London
www.nyupress.org

Library of Congress Cataloging-in-Publication Data
Bhatia, Sunil.
American karma : race, culture, and identity in the Indian diaspora /
Sunil Bhatia.
p.   cm. — (Qualitative studies in psychology)
Includes bibliographical references and index.
ISBN-13: 978-0-8147-9958-1 (cloth : alk. paper)
ISBN-10: 0-8147-9958-2 (cloth : alk. paper)
ISBN-13: 978-0-8147-9959-8 (pbk. : alk. paper)
ISBN-10: 0-8147-9959-0 (pbk. : alk. paper)
1. East Indian Americans—Social conditions. 2. East Indian
Americans—Ethnic identity. 3. Immigrants—United States—Social
conditions. 4. United States—Ethnic relations. 5. United States—
Emigration and immigration. 6. India—Emigration and immigration.
I. Title.
E184.E2B497 2007
305.800973—dc22   2007007864

New York University Press books are printed on acid-free paper,
and their binding materials are chosen for strength and durability.

Manufactured in the United States of America
c 10 9 8 7 6 5 4 3 2 1
p 10 9 8 7 6 5 4 3 2 1

For Anjali and Amit and Anusha

Contents

■   ■   ■   ■

Acknowledgments

I owe this book to the intellectual, emotional, and moral support of my family, friends, colleagues, and students. At Connecticut College, I am thankful to my colleagues Peggy Sheridan, Michelle Dunlap, Jennifer Fredricks, Mike James, and Sandy Grande for creating a warm, supportive, and intellectually engaging "culture of work" in the department. In particular, I am deeply grateful to Peggy Sheridan for being a steady mentor and friend through the various phases of my career. It has been my good fortune and privilege to be a part of this department that she created with her vision and labor of love. The R. F. Johnson, Hodgkins, and Opatrny Summer Funds from Connecticut College granted me the opportunity to conduct my extensive fieldwork and interviews with the participants of the local Indian diaspora. I also extend my thanks to Mary Howard, whose keen editorial eye immeasurably refined and refocused my writing. I am thankful to my students—Mridula Swamy, Jessica Philips, and Rebecca Fagan—for working as dedicated research assistants for this research project. In particular, I want to thank Mridula and Jessica for giving such meticulous help with transcription, photocopying, editing, and coding. The input given by students from my ethnography courses in HMD 201 and HMD 406 played a crucial role in refining and transforming the arguments in my book project.

Above all, the magnanimity of the Indian immigrant community in southeastern Connecticut made this book possible. I owe a great debt to my participants, who welcomed me into their homes and patiently allowed me to interview them. My deepest thanks goes to them for sharing their life stories as immigrants. Over several cups of *garam chai and namkeen* snacks, they eagerly shared with me their narratives and their interpretations and experiences of their migrant life in the United States. I express my deepest and sincere thanks to Barun Basu, who played the role of gatekeeper and connected me with several families who were willing to be interviewed for this project. I am very grateful to Adesh and Gayatri Saxena for making sure that my fieldwork and ethnography were successfully completed. Their hospitality, openness, generosity, and friendship made this project much more than just another research activity. They were my intellectual partners in the community, and their compassionate support and insightful interrogations pushed me to clarify even more the findings of the ethnography. I am sincerely thankful to Jasgit and Ranjana Bindra for their advice, friendship, and support of this book project. A very special thanks to Usha and Avinash Thombre for supporting this project and setting up numerous contacts with several members of the diaspora.

I hope that I have been able to convey in some "authentic" way a slice of the rich, unsettling, varied, and complex cultural lives of the participants in this study. This book is about Indian migrants: their family conversations, their expressions of identity, and their ways of interpreting the worlds they inhabit. However, in the process of making sense of their lives, I have learned a little more about my own migrant journey, and I thank them for enabling me to see my own history through their everyday lives.

I am immensely grateful to my teachers at Clark University: Nancy Budwig, Michael Bamberg, Bernie Kaplan, Jaan Valsiner, and Jim Wertsch. I would also like to acknowledge the intellectual support provided by Hubert Hermans, Ingrid Joseph, and Hank Stam. I owe a great deal of intellectual debt to the works of scholars outside my discipline, such as Alejandro Portes, Vijay Prashad, Susan Koshy, Sunaina Maira, Sandhya Shukla, Kamala Visweswaran, and Mary Waters.

My conversations and lively discussions with Ram Mahalingam were important to shaping the basic architecture of this book. Ram's critical engagements with this project through all its phases and transformations added depth to its theoretical and methodological foundations. Ruma Sen, the "maha maa/godmother" of my kids, became a sounding board for my unfinished ideas—she carefully listened to my ideas, challenged my assumptions, and provided beneficial suggestions about the organization of the book. I am grateful for her friendship, her passion for Hindi movies, and her constant encouragement.

I am very thankful to Michelle Fine and Jean Marecek for choosing to make this book a part of the book series Qualitative Methods in Psychology. Their editorial suggestions and incisive comments on earlier drafts helped tighten my arguments and claims. I thank the anonymous reviewers for their insightful suggestions and helpful comments. In particular, I am very thankful to Jennifer Hammer for her exceptional skills as an editor—she nurtured and kept the project moving by making extremely thoughtful suggestions through several drafts of the manuscript. She offered systematic feedback on the manuscript and helped bring this book to fruition.

This book would not have been completed without the loving support of my wife, Anjali. She has listened patiently and given intellectual and critical feedback on almost every small and big component of this book. I am extremely grateful for her unwavering support for this project right from its inception to the end. My debt to her is enormous. I found the courage to launch this book project because of her faith in my abilities, and I thank her for always being such a steady and strong force in my life.

My twin children, Amit and Anusha, were born just as I was about to begin my fieldwork and interviews. During all the years that I have spent researching and writing this book, my children have been a constant source of joy and an appealing distraction. I developed, expanded, and wrote this book as I watched my children grow from infancy to their preschool years. Their loud and loving presence has been a constant backdrop for this project.

I also want to take this opportunity to thank my mother, Sabita Bhatia, and my brother, Sanjeev Bhatia, for their love and support. Finally, my deepest gratitude goes to Radha aunty, my mother-in-law, for taking care of my children. The endless hours of labor that she devoted to providing love, care, and support to my family allowed me to dedicate my time to completing this project.

Introduction

The displacement of millions of migrant laborers, refugees, and professionals from the postcolonial Third World to the First World and the formation of numerous migrant "ethnic enclaves" were among the most important defining features of the twentieth century. Given that currently one-fifth, or 20 percent, of all children in the United States are immigrants (Hernandez 1999), questions related to acculturation and identity are central to the field of psychology. Furthermore, today, questions about migration and the construction of identity are paramount, as the number of immigrants in the United States rapidly increased in the 1990s to "nearly a million new immigrants per year" (Suárez-Orozco and Suárez-Orozco 2001, p. 55). These "new" immigrants present a dramatically different demographic picture from that of the previous great wave of immigration at the turn of the last century. In 1890, more than 90 percent of immigrants to the United States were European, whereas in 1990, only 25 percent of migrants were European, 25 percent were Asian, and 43 percent were from Latin America (Rong and Preissle 1998). This striking shift can be largely attributed to the changes in immigration laws in the 1960s, when several racially motivated "exclusion acts" were eliminated in order to meet the demands of the U.S. labor market (Mohanty 1991). These new immigrants often must struggle with

asymmetrical cultural positions, racially charged situations, and an oppressive political rhetoric.

In her memoir, Meena Alexander, a poet of South Asian origin, reflects on her ethnicity as an Indian American and states that she is a
woman "cracked by multiple migrations," with many selves born out of
broken geographies (1993, p. 3). Her narrative foregrounds the struggles
with self and identity that many middle-class professional immigrants face
as they try to find a place in contemporary U.S. society. On one hand,
historical conceptions of class, race, and ethnicity all intermingle in different ways to shape Indian American and South Asian identity in the
United States (Bahri 1996). But on the other hand, Indian Americans
have used a particular set of agentive "immigrant acts," as Lisa Lowe
(1996) termed them, to craft their own identities and build public discourses of how they want to be seen by the larger American public.

American Karma shows how the suburbs have become the site for reconstructing and negotiating one's identity and personhood. In particular, I explore how first-generation, professional, middle-class Indians have
been inserted into the racial dynamics of American society and transformed into "people of color." Visweswaran argues that when talking
about South Asian racial formation, we need to find out how Indian
Americans construct an identity that goes beyond defining them as marginalized minorities or passive victims. For example, she observes that it
is indeed accurate that Indian Americans have been assigned a racial category by the majority, but she also emphasizes that "South Asians have
actively negotiated and sought to alter those designations over time.
For where there is assignation, there is also assertion" (1997, p. 6). Both
Koshy (1998) and Visweswaran (1997) believe that studies of Indian
American racial and ethnic identity must examine the complexities, contradictions, and conflicts found in the space between the acts of deliberative assertion expressed by the Indian American community and the acts
that position and situate them as having fixed racial identities.

This book describes how professional, middle-class Indians living in a
northeastern suburb of the United States understand the racial and cultural labels created by their white neighbors and coworkers. On one level,
I show how the larger, majority culture uses these terms, labels, and categories to define and frame the identity of the Indian migrants as other,

and I also examine how they counter these labels of otherness. On another level, I show how the terms and conditions under which issues related to diversity and difference are negotiated in the diaspora. The skin color, *bindis,* saris, food, gods and goddesses, and "thick accents" of the professional Indians in this book become the vehicles through which their sense of difference is articulated by their suburban neighbors and coworkers. How do the participants in my study reinterpret these markers of difference, such as brown skin, accent, *bindi,* or sari? How do they represent and package their sense of difference in the diaspora?

This book, *American Karma,* charts the journey of the post-1965 Indian migrants to the United States. In particular, I show that these middle-class migrants acquired their educational and linguistic capital in India and were remade and remanufactured as successful migrants in America. Although they earned their values, skills, and basic education in India, it was their tryst with America, or their "American Karma," that put them on a pathway to becoming a "model minority."

The participants deflected these narratives of otherness by repositioning their differences in the language of sameness and universal humanity. What are the competing cultural meanings that shape immigrants' narrative of racial difference in the United States? How do these middle-class Indians move between those voices that assign them labels of difference and those that assert their own meanings? Despite the racism and discrimination, why do most middle-class Indians use categories of sameness, universality, and color-blind meritocracy to construct meanings for their racial identities? The acts of assignations and assertions that I examined show that many professional Indians deal with this contradiction by both acknowledging their racial and cultural differences and placing them in the background. How should we understand this contradiction? How do these professional, elite, transnational migrants understand their racial designation as nonwhite people or "people of color"? How do members of the Indian professional diaspora collectively represent their sense of identity? How does their status as "elite" professionals affect their understanding of being both privileged and marginalized minorities?

The strategic assertions of the participants in my study—whether called strategies of justification, denial, deflection, resistance, or acceptance—can be construed as deliberative acts of agency. By agency, I do not mean a person working from outside the system who acts on the world with a free will and as a rational agent. Rather, agency here is acts of assertion played out in everyday cultural practices in which the agent is both enabled and constrained by the larger political and cultural forces. Through these and other strategies, the participants try to control how they, and others, view their differences.

Another equally important objective of this book is to contribute to the field of cultural psychology by showing how concepts such as diaspora and transnational migration have forced us to redefine the meaning of culture, identity, community, cultural difference, and development. In turn, these concepts have important implications for understanding how individuals reconstruct the meaning of their identities in the wake of migration, departures, homelessness, exile, and the formation of postcolonial diasporas.

We live in an age in which transnational immigration, border crossings, and global media are proliferating at an increasing rate. Discussions about the self—which are intensified by issues of race, gender, class, sexuality, ethnicity, and nationality—challenge the grand narratives of the stable, bounded, contained, and Cartesian self. This book provides a new theoretical framework for rethinking how postcolonial migrants maintain, resist, and reinvent their identities in the midst of enormous cultural change and conflict. Acquiring knowledge about issues of self and identity becomes critical in the face of the sweeping demographic changes in the United States and Europe where encounters with diverse histories, languages, religions, and ethnicities have become central to the daily lives of many urban, metropolitan cultural spaces.

In *American Karma,* the concept of diaspora falls within the vision of cultural psychology by offering new ways of thinking about and imagining the concept of culture and identity. I analyze ethnographic data from the Indian diaspora to show how otherness is reconstructed and revoiced in diverse cultural contexts. Drawing on ethnographic methods, I use participant observation and interviews to discover how diasporic families reinterpret the physical and emotional terrain of self, other, and home as they move back and forth between cultural locations. I asked open-ended questions during my interviews with the participants so as to gain insights into how the self moves among the various cultural and racial positions and how the participants negotiate their sense of being both accepted and marginalized by American society.

Methodology: Fieldwork and Interviews

I used ethnographic methods to collect and analyze my data. My ethnographic study was organized around two questions: (1) What kinds of racial and ethnic meanings were assigned to the middle-class diaspora, and (2) how did the Indian migrants make sense of those terms and labels assigned to them? I am a member of an Indian community of the suburbs of southeastern Connecticut and simultaneously have been doing the ethnography of the children and families of this local Indian diaspora. In one sense, my fieldwork is what Visweswaran (1994) calls "home work." For instance, I was invited to the homes of my participants in order to socialize with them on weekends. But after interacting as a member of the community, I quickly got into an ethnographer's mode, observing, conversing, and asking my participants questions about their experiences at work and in their everyday lives. I also asked their children about their experiences at school and in the community. On occasion, they responded to me by mimicking the Indian accent or sharing with me their racialized experiences as one of a few brown girls in a predominantly white school. Throughout the study, my roles as both a member of the community and an ethnographer were congenial, but on other occasions they seemed to raise concerns about my mode of inquiring about my very own people. My own self-reflexivity regarding these two roles was not just bound up with issues of power and representation but were also closely linked to ethical issues such as trust, friendship, self-disclosure, and vulnerability. For example, the community positioned me as a member of the Indian diaspora, and I was often invited to various local events such as Diwali dinners, Temple *pujas*,[1] family dinners, *desi* Christmas parties, children's birthdays, and many other community events. Similarly, some caregivers in the community elevated my position to "our very own" Indian professional developmental psychologist, who is studying and analyzing issues related to "our" own children.

My fieldwork lasted for sixteen months, between February 2000 and June 2001. Then from August 2001 to January 2002, I conducted in-depth interviews with thirty-eight first-generation Indian migrants. Most of my participants worked for the local ABC Computer Company and lived in the mostly white suburbs of East Lyme and Old Lyme, Connecticut. During my fieldwork, I socially interacted with my participants at their homes and engaged in everyday practices of having dinner, talking, negotiating, arguing, teasing, and having ordinary conversations. I took notes and made mental observations, which I periodically recorded in a file. I recorded some of the detailed notes about the scenes of social interactions, and sometimes I made very brief comments and notes about people, their experiences, and my reactions to the events.

Being a member of the community in which I was conducting research meant that the boundaries of "home" and "field" intersected and became blurred (Amit 2000; Gupta and Ferguson 1997; Knowles 2000; Okeley and Callaway 1992). Throughout the ethnography, I was very aware of my position as an "insider" and its implications when I interacted with the participants in my study. Critical perspectives on ethnography increasingly urge ethnographers to be aware of the various positions that they occupy in relation to their participants (see Bochner 1997; Conquergood 1991; Goodall 2000; Marcus 1998). Observing such critical and reflexive approaches, I show how the narratives and tales of the home/field were incorporated into the stories and identities of the researchers themselves. Such an approach rests on the belief that psychological knowledge about issues of identity, culture, and migration becomes more meaningful when viewed as a shared production between home and the field, the researcher and the researched, the transnational participant and the transnational researcher. There is now a good deal of literature in anthropology stressing the dilemmas of working in a field where home is situated in the field and the investigator's social positioning and autobiography is intertwined with constructing boundaries with participants in the field (Amit 2000; Gupta and Ferguson 1997; Raj 2003). The theorizing of the interconnections between home and abroad, home and field, and "bringing the field home" stem from the larger debate on issues of method and modes of inquiry in the social scientist.

This seven chapters of this book are as follows: Chapter 1, "American Karma: Race, Place, and Identity in the Indian Diaspora," lays out the principles on which my book is based and describes the ways in which the Indian middle-class professional community speaks about their bodies, accents, cultures, and selves as being racialized and marked as different. Chapter 2, "Qualitative Inquiry and Psychology: Doing Ethnography in a Transnational Culture," begins by locating this study in the contemporary debates examining the role of qualitative methods in psychology and related disciplines. In particular, I explain the significance of using qualitative/interpretive methodologies to study the interface between culture and identity in transnational settings. I argue that there now are quite a few groups of researchers in psychology who do not work with the "brute data" approach but instead draw on qualitative methods to study the stipulatory, context-bound, historically grounded notion of the agent and the world.

This chapter documents the ethnographic tools that I used in this study. I explain how I formulated the research questions and how I made the first contact with the participants. I also explain how I used participant observation and in-depth interviews to examine how diasporic families and their children reinterpret the physical and emotional terrains of self, other, home, nation, and "Indian culture" as they move back and forth between multiple cultural locations. I map out the dilemmas of doing ethnography in one's own community and show why such a methodological approach is deeply self-reflexive and contributes to the growing body of knowledge in the area of qualitative inquiry/methods. Open-ended, in-depth, narrative interviews with the participants provided insights into how the dialogical self moves between the various cultural positions and how it negotiates its sense of simultaneously being in two distinct cultural spaces.

In Chapter 3, "Des-Pardes in the American Suburbia: Narratives from the Suburban Indian Diaspora," I use the concepts of diaspora and transnationalism to show how migration, travel, and the increasing contact zones between cultures and people have created transnational communities across the metropolitan suburbs of the United States. These suburban diasporic communities are part of the second wave of new, non-European migration to the United States and are important sites for studying personhood and identity. I show how members of the diaspora maintain an identification with home, build an imagined community in the new world, and reinvent traditions and identity as they move between conflicting cultural spaces. I specifically show how the Indian diaspora in the United States was created out of two incongruent histories.

The first wave of migration came when the Punjabi Sikhs made their home in California by working as farmers and low-wage laborers. I chart their journey from the villages of Punjab to California and show how they evolved from a community of outcasts to a community of landowners and skillful businessmen. I also document the second wave of migration to the United States. This history begins with the arrival of the professional, well-educated, and highly skilled migrants who came to the United States after 1965. My accounts of these two divergent histories of Indian migrants show that the selfhood of migrant identity is intertwined with such sociocultural factors as colonialism, immigration, and the racialized, state-sponsored laws of the host society. These two histories of Indian migration show the contradictory and shifting meanings associated with identity, culture, and difference in the Indian community.

I use narrative and stories from the Indian diaspora to show how these immigrants' middle-class social positions at home, fluency in the English language, and a highly advanced education in postcolonial educational system in India prepared them for very successful professional careers in the United States. One of the aims of this chapter is to sketch the history of Indian migration in the United States to show how the Indian migrant's evolving conception of self is tied to America's discourse about the racial and multicultural "other." This history also illuminates the ways in which discourses of otherness shaped the path of Indian migration and citizenship.

In Chapter 4, "Saris, Chutney Sandwiches, and 'Thick Accents': Constructing Difference," I analyze the narratives of difference recounted in the Indian diaspora in a suburb of Connecticut. I examine how otherness is created by analyzing how the Indian community is assigned meanings of difference. In particular, I use a dialogical model of self to show how the voices of the larger majority culture help shape the racial and cultural identity of the Indian diaspora in the United States. I demonstrate that three types of dialogicality of otherness are created by the friends and coworkers of these Indian immigrants. These three forms of dialogicality—generic otherness, marked otherness, and disruptive otherness—are assigned to them by the larger majority culture. In this chapter, I analyze the stories of otherness and difference from the point of view of the Indian migrants.

In particular, I show how the "brown bodies" of Indian immigrants and cultural artifacts, such as saris, *bindis,* nose rings, gods, goddesses, "Indian culture," "Indian atmosphere," and their "thick accents" become the materials through which their otherness is constructed. The participants suggested, for example, that questions by their colleagues or friends like "Where are you from?" and "When are you going back home?" act as a destabilizing force that questions their sense of home and their belongingness "here." Furthermore, I show how the accents of the Indian participants are racialized in their everyday lives, and I examine the indirect pressures that they face from their employers to transform their "thick accents" into "thin accents." In this chapter, I explore how parents become aware of their own sense of difference through their children's experiences of disruptive, painful, and alienating forms of otherness. Children often are racialized at school when they are neglected by their teachers and subjected to racial slurs by their schoolmates on the playground or in the lunchroom. In this chapter, I also look at the story of how neighbors pressured an Indian family to leave a gated community by bringing legal charges against them.

Chapter 5, "Racism and Glass Ceilings: Repositioning Difference," shows how the members of the Indian diaspora respond to their assignations of difference. In particular, I explain how the participants negotiate their status as "people of color" in the American multicultural society. This chapter examines the various types of dialogicality that the participants use to understand their difference. I describe how members of the privileged Indian diaspora deal with their status as "brown people": How do they come to terms with their status as successful "others"? How do they negotiate their sense of difference at home and work? How do they reposition their markers of difference, such as their accents, *bindis,* and saris? What kind of discourse do they use to choose an identity for themselves? How do they repackage their racial and ethnic identity in the face of discrimination and intolerance?

In this chapter, I demonstrate that the participants of the local diaspora use three forms of dialogicality to reconstruct meanings about their otherness: (1) assertions of sameness, (2) assertions of individual merit, and (3) assertions of universality. I use narratives and stories from the Indian diaspora to show how these migrants use the language of universal humanity and human nature to talk about their racist experiences and barriers at work, such as glass ceilings and quotas. Instead of counteracting assignations of otherness by invoking language of structure, inequality and racism, they attempt to reposition their sense of self as equal to that of the white majority. Specifically, I illustrate how many Indian participants invoke the rhetoric of color-blind meritocracy to support their careers and their belief that color, race, and class are extraneous to the construction of their identity. In my interviews, the participants gave specific examples of racism and discrimination in India and Europe to show that they are part of human nature and the participants are better off in America than any in other part of the world.

Chapter 6, "Analyzing Assignations and Assertions: The Enigma of Brown Privilege," provides the conceptual and analytical framework to analyze the voices of assignations and assertions produced by the suburban Indian diaspora. Why do these participants invoke universal humanity and human nature to reject the assignations of racism and discrimination? I analyze these responses by locating them in the context of model minority discourse. I show how the professional, middle-class Indians have internalized their status as belonging to one of the most successful migrant communities in the United States. Their sense of self is tied to the public announcement of their model minority status and is equal to that of middle-class, white America.

This chapter shows how the participants use the model minority discourse to show that they possess cultural strategies to deal with the labels of otherness thrust upon them. This chapter uses incidences from the history of Indian migration to the United States to illustrate why the participants in the Indian diaspora are ambivalent about their racial identity, allowing them to be "separate but equal" to their white neighbors, coworkers, and friends. An essential part of the strategic identification with the model minority is that these Indian immigrants believe that their educational qualifications, material wealth, work ethic, and success at work not only can protect them from being different but also can grant them the same kinds of privileges that many whites enjoy in this society. Furthermore, I show that many Indian migrants want to be able to choose to invoke the type of symbolic ethnicity that Waters describes in her 1990 study on ethnic options.

This chapter uses a dialogical approach to understanding how Indian migrants living in diasporic locations negotiate their multiple and often conflicting cultural identities. I use the concept of voice to articulate the different forms of dialogicality in these transnational migrants' acculturation experiences. In particular, I contend that it is important to think of acculturation of these Indian migrants as essentially a contested, dynamic, and dialogical process.

Chapter 7, "Imagining Homes: Identity in Transnational Diasporas," is my conclusion, in which I broaden the concept of culture in psychology by means of diaspora theory. I argue that psychology should be expanded by placing in its archive those issues related to the formation of diasporas, such as race, representation, and conflict. I show that the formation of transnational diasporic cultures have led to the creation of new forms of identity and community and that this theorizing of culture must pay attention to concepts of race, colonization, class, and power. To conclude, I show how the meaning of home in the Indian diaspora is embedded in dual cultures and spaces by drawing on such concepts as racial ambivalence, acculturation, culture, and development.

1

■　　■　　■　　■　　■　　■　　■　　■　　■

American Karma

Race, Place, and Identity in the
Indian Diaspora

I remember one significant moment in my ethnographic research when I asked Rani,[1] a first-generation Indian who has lived in America for the last three decades, to define "American culture." Acknowledging that it was difficult, Rani quickly rattled off two points as though she had thought about them for a long time.

> American culture, as I understand, stands for individuality, but it doesn't really know what individuality is. It says we are nonconformist, but it is the most conformist. It says that we are very free, but I think you can have freer opinions in a "Third World" country such as India than you can . . . over here.[2]

Her second point emphasizes that the description of American culture changes in accordance with the culture being discussed: white culture or minority culture. I asked Rani to elaborate on and clarify this distinction. She answered, "Yes, it's the majority white culture. So either you're part of it, or you're not part of it. If you're white, you're part of it. If you're not white, then you're not part of it."

Rani's oversimplified definition of American culture is racialized through the asymmetrical power relationships between white and non-white groups, majority and nonmajority cultures, and "First World" and "Third World" countries. Framing the concept of culture and identity in terms of power, race, identity, and belongingness, Rani sees American culture through her own marginal eyes and describes it as a culture that excludes her. It is made up of a center where she does not belong. Her brown skin, gender, Indian accent, *bindi*,[3] sari, and cultural rituals reflect a culture that is not part of the majority. Rani's view of American culture as being synonymous with whiteness is an attempt to define it as made up of contested codes, symbols of power, and clearly marked boundaries and locations.

Rani's effort to see culture through a racial lens has forced psychologists to rethink how they define culture, community, and identity in a world where international borders are becoming porous and where travel and migration between geographical spaces are commonplace. But Rani's negotiations of self are filtered through the prism of race and nationality. These kinds of identity negotiation are commonplace in the migrant communities of, for example, Mexican Americans, Arab Americans, Chinese Canadians, Turkish Germans, French Maghrebi, and British Indians across the First World metropolitan areas.

There is a small, but growing, body of research being done on the formation of racial and cultural identity in the post-1965, middle-class Indian diaspora in the United States (Bhattacharjee 1992; Ganguly 1992; Gibson 1988; Helweg and Helweg 1990; Khandelwal 2002; Kumar 2000; Maira 2002; Maira and Srikanth 1996; Prashad 2000; Purkayastha 2005; Rangaswamy 2000; Rudrappa 2004; Shukla 2003; Visweswaran 1997). Similarly, a few scholars in Britain are exploring the South Asian identity and its complex intersections between race and ethnicity (Bhachu 1993; Brah 1996; Hutnyk and Sharma 2000; Raj 2003; Vertovec 1999; Werbner and Modood 1997). Susan Koshy writes that a "significant amount of research so far has been produced by literary scholars, but much empirical, and ethnographic work in anthropology, sociology, and history remains to be done on South Asian American racial identification" (1998, p. 287). My ethnographic study of the Indian diaspora builds on this research, especially on South Asian racial and cultural identity. In particular, I show how the Indian middle-class professional community regards the various ways in which their bodies, accents, cultures, and selves are racialized and marked as different. What kinds of narratives do they construct to understand their racial assignation? This book captures the lived experiences of diaspora and the contradictory and conflicting voices making up their identities.

The Indian Diaspora in Yankee Land

In what ways is the "Indianness" imported from the diaspora tied to the geography and the physical space of the homeland? How are these cultural importations of self and identity reconstituted in the diasporic space by their contact with suburban America? Approximately 1.7 million Indians live in the United States, and according to the 2000 U.S. census, the Indian American community is one of this country's fastest-growing immigrant communities. From 1990 to 2000, the number of Indian Americans grew by 106 percent, compared with the average 7 percent growth rate of the general population, and is the fastest-growing Asian American community.

Questions about the construction of "Indian identity" in the Indian diaspora are inevitably tied to questions about how India is incorporated in the imagination of the diasporic community. The migrant community imagines and stitches together diverse notions of "Indianness," which are shaped by the members' class positions back home, nostalgia, memories, emotions, and longing for the original *desi*[4] nation and culture of their homeland.[5]

By all accounts, the 1965 Immigration and Nationality Act fundamentally changed the background of Indians migrating to the United States. Within a very short time, Indian migrants in the United States changed from being "pariahs to elite" (Rangaswamy 2000, p. 40). Unlike the first wave of the Punjabi Sikh diaspora, the second wave of Indian migrants were highly skilled professionals, trained as medical doctors, engineers, scientists, university professors, and doctoral and postdoctoral students in mostly science-related disciplines like chemistry, biochemistry, math, physics, biology, and medicine. Prashad writes that between 1966 and 1977, 83 percent of Indians who migrated to the United States were highly skilled professionals composed of about "20,000 scientists with PhD's, 40,000 engineers, and 25,000 doctors" (2000, p. 75). These professional Indians have made their "home" in suburban diasporas in town and cities all across America.

One such Indian diaspora can be found in the suburbs of southeastern Connecticut and is the subject of this ethnographic study. With the passage of the Immigration and Nationality Act in 1965, the class and socioeconomic backgrounds of the second wave of Indian migrants changed significantly. Instead, the post-1965 Indian migrants who participated in this study come from middle-class families who use their economic success and wealth to overcome the hardships often associated with low-skilled, migrant labor. Their membership in competitive, exclusive professions such as medicine and engineering put them in the company of some of the most elite members of American society. Their economic success, educational accomplishments, and membership in professional societies have propelled them straight into Connecticut's middle- and upper-class suburbs. Since the 1960s, these migrants have lived in small cities and suburbs of southern Connecticut, such as Groton, Ledyard, East Lyme, Norwich, Norwalk, New London, Old Lyme, and Waterford.

Most of the professional Indians who participated in this ethnography lived in the suburban town of East Lyme and were part of the post-1965 highly skilled, professional migrants. Of the thirty-eight first-generation men and women whom I interviewed, twenty-six had PhD's and the rest had master's or an equivalent professional degree. The majority worked at a large multinational company called ABC Computer Corporation,[6] in various professional positions as directors, computer scientists, chemical engineers, biochemists, mid-level managers, and directors.

The members of the local diaspora who were not affiliated with the computer company were university professors, medical doctors, architects, school counselors, teachers, and social workers. There also was a group of women who had advanced degrees in the sciences but had decided to become full-time caregivers. Almost 80 percent of the families I interviewed were dual-income families with yearly earnings between $65,000 and $200,000. It is important to mention that the Indians in southeastern Connecticut are not very different from Indians in other middle-class communities across America.

Many of the professional Indian migrants who came to the United States after 1965 were medical doctors who took the Educational Council for Foreign Medical Graduates (ECFMG) exams that allowed them to work as interns and residents in U.S. hospitals. While doing research on the history of Indian migrants in New York, Khandelwal found that in one month in 1965, about two thousand Indian doctors were preparing to take the ECFMG exams so they could work in U.S. hospitals. She notes that from "1961 to 1968, 67% of Indians employed in the United States were in professional categories, and from 1969–1971, the figure jumped to 89%. Ninety-three percent of Indians who migrated to the U.S. in 1975 were 'professional/technical workers'" Furthermore, the "situation was so serious in the late 1960s that the Association for Service to Indian Scholars was formed to persuade Indian professionals to return home" (Khandelwal 2002, p. 93).

Most of the Indian professionals that I interviewed initially came to the United States determined to go back to India to "serve" the needs of the country. But once they earned an advanced doctoral degree, they were able to move quickly into the workforce and postponed indefinitely their return home. In some cases, the men made their first trip back home to find a wife, whose family members had arranged for them to meet. Most of the men in my study married professional Indian women with educational skills that could be used to obtain a good job in the United States. These women had advanced doctoral degrees in medicine, computer science, chemistry, and counseling, but they entered the United States as the wives of professional Indian men. A few of these women, however, came to the United States in the 1970s and 1980s to study in graduate school and then found their partners there. Generally, both the men and women of the diaspora had had a solid undergraduate education in the sciences and engineering at prestigious, competitive universities in India, which prepared them to meet the challenges of graduate school in the United States.

Destiny's Children: "After I Joined IIT . . . There Was No Other Option"

Many of the Indian professionals in my study had their basic training in engineering at prestigious Indian universities like the Indian Institute of Technology (IIT). Indeed, many now look back and marvel at the good science and engineering education they received in India. I asked Kishore, who worked at the ABC Computer Company and had graduated from one of the IIT universities, "What was unique about the IIT education in India?" Kishore told me that IIT provided a very good foundation and basic training in science, engineering, and mathematics. He admitted that graduate school in America was easy for him.

> I had a very good sort of fundamental basis, for the education. To me, graduate school was very easy, so I really didn't have to stretch too much in order to get the A grades and, you know, to do well. I think in those things, I probably lived up to the expectations that I might have had for myself coming out of India.

The exportation of these brilliant minds from India to the United States also was documented in an episode of CBS's *60 Minutes* in June 2003. As Leslie Stahl, who oversaw the feature, explained, "Put Harvard, MIT and Princeton together, and you begin to get an idea of the status of IIT in India." She pointed out that IIT has an extremely rigorous curriculum and that IIT graduates are known to be exceptional chemical, electrical, and computer engineers. With an acceptance rate of less than 2 percent, IIT is now one of the most competitive schools in the world. Stahl noted that not only is IIT's reputation impressive, but most of its graduate students go on to have illustrious careers in the United States. "While some of the IIT grads stay and have helped build India's flourishing high-tech sector, almost two-thirds—up to 2,000 people—leave every year, most for the U.S." Vinod Khosla, the founding executive officer of Sun Microsystems, graduated from IIT about thirty years ago. In the *60 Minutes* program, he proudly announced to American viewers that IIT graduates had played a major role in the software development of blue-chip companies like Microsoft, Intel, IBM, and Sun Microsystems.

In India, the status of IIT among middle-class families is almost mythical.[7] Accordingly, students who pass the IIT entrance tests are seen as geniuses who are guaranteed instant success. Since the rise of the city of Bangalore as a global hub of software development and a provider of low-cost technological services and call centers, IIT has begun to acquire a global brand name. IIT undergraduates are seen as destined to work and succeed in America. Over the decades, the massive exportation of IIT graduates—the cream of the crop—to the United States has also been the subject of much controversy. Toward the end of the *60 Minutes* feature, Stahl emphasized that the "brain drain" from India had hurt its economy and research and development and had benefited the United States. Although the participants in my study also were aware of the "brain drain" issue, for them there was no other option but to migrate to America.

Anil, a fifty-one-year-old IIT graduate whom I interviewed, came to the United States in the 1980s.

I:[8] I came to America because . . .

A: I don't know, I went to IIT, I don't know if you . . .

I: Of course!

A: And pretty much everybody came . . .

I: You went to IIT, Madras?

A: Yes, so in 1984 that was one of the things you did, and I came. So after the time I joined IIT, I never thought I'd come to the United States because I never thought about what happens afterwards. After I joined IIT, it was almost, you know . . . there was no other option.

I: Yeah, in fact I've heard that.

It is interesting that Anil felt he had no options in India after he graduated from IIT. In fact, he told me that out of his graduating class of twenty-eight chemical engineers, about twenty-two came to the United States in the mid-1980s.

Anil emphasized that the IIT system made it very easy to be admitted to graduate school in the United States. "It never occurred to me not to come, but I cannot say I came here because of my love for chemical engineering or something." After IIT, Anil got his PhD from a well-respected engineering school in Massachusetts and then moved on to a multinational computer company in Norwich, so he could get his green card and become a permanent legal resident in the United States.

The personal stories of the post-1965 migrants in this book show that before they arrived in the United States, they already had amassed enough cultural and linguistic capital to succeed here. In one sense, their career paths and life trajectories in the United States had already been determined in India. Their educational stopovers at places like Yale, Stanford, University of California, University of Michigan, Indiana University, and Rutgers ensured that they would be able to compete for the best jobs in the most competitive organizations and multinational companies in the United States. Their middle-class upbringing in India, their excellent foundations in the sciences, their fluency in English, and their good work ethic propelled them into an elite segment of U.S. society. Many of these university graduates had grown up being "America conscious" and knew what they needed to do to get into U.S. graduate schools. While it is true that their individual qualities—such as intelligence, merit, and hard work —ensured their passage to the United States, their social-class positions, world-class undergraduate education in science and engineering, and fa-milial networks also had a great impact on their decision to come to study in the United States.

Cultural Identity and Model Minority Status

The success story of the post-1965 migrants of the Indian diaspora makes them model minorities in the United States, and the language of the model minority discourse becomes the yardstick by which the Indian im-migrants measure their relatively rapid success in America. In this vein, Koshy observed, "The model minority position has increasingly come to define the racial identity of a significant number of South Asian Ameri-cans; it depends on the intermediary location of a group between black and white and holds a particularly powerful appeal for immigrant groups" (1998, p. 287). Many Indian immigrants were consumed by their own success story as a model minority in the United States, and the American public and politicians also conferred this status on the Indian community (Khandelwal 2002).

One point that many South Asian academics made is that the myth of model minority, which positions the Asian community as a highly quali-fied, professional, and successful group of immigrants, also can work against them. Both professional and nonprofessional Indian immigrants tend to be ambivalent about the racial and ethnic discrimination they face at work and in their daily lives, an ambivalence also experienced by other members of the Asian American diaspora. Kibria writes:

> The model minority stereotype has a highly fluid and multidimensional set
> of meanings. I found my second-generation Chinese and Korean American
> informants to be struggling at times to resist the label of model minority,

to ward off its limitations and dangers; they considered it part of their experience of racial marginality in the dominant society. But they also drew on the model minority stereotype in affirmative ways, in their efforts to make sense of and define the position of Asian Americans within the racial hierarchy of United States. (2002, p. 132)

One important part of this model minority discourse is that it reifies the idea that through hard work, family values, and educational qualifications, some migrant communities are able to rise above their circumstances. The statement by the former senator Phil Gramm, that Indian Americans represent the best and the brightest that the United States has to offer, reinforces the mistaken assumption that professional, well-to-do Indians have the same economic and educational opportunities that individuals from other ethnic and minority groups do.

Some Americans use such statements about the cultural and material achievements of Indian migrants to make unfair comparisons between Asian American communities and black America. According to Prashad,

These are not only statements of admiration. Apart from being condescending, such gestures remind me that I am to be the perpetual solution to what is seen as the crisis of black America. I am to be the weapon in the war against black America. . . . The struggles of blacks are met with the derisive remark that Asians don't complain; they work hard—as if to say that blacks don't work hard. (2000, pp. 6–7)

This book shows that the model minority story shaping the identity of so many professional Indian immigrants in the United States does not take into account that the lives of well-educated Indian migrants begin from a different starting point than that of other minorities. The model minority discourse, as Prashad observes, is "based on deliberate state-selection and not on based on cultural or natural selection" (2000, p. 4). That is, the successful "acculturation" or "assimilation" of professional Indian immigrants in the U.S. workforce is based on a special provision of the 1965 Immigration and Nationality Act, which allows the entry of only a few, highly qualified, transnational migrants educated in postcolonial schools and universities.

Race, Culture, Ethnicity, and Transnational Migration

In the last decade, many prominent scholars of migration studies have pointed out that the canonical "straight-line" and linear assimilation theory proposed by Warner and Srole (1945) and Gordon (1964) is not relevant to the contemporary patterns of non-European migration. For example, in identifying their various flaws, Alba and Nee (2003) write that these old theories of assimilation are formulated on the assumption that assimilation in American society is successful when ethnic groups "unlearn" and abandon their the cultural practices and rituals. This model of acculturation is defined as "unlineal acculturation—where the bargain was straightforward: please check all your cultural baggage before you pass through the Golden Gate" (Suárez-Orozco and Suárez-Orozco 2001, p. 160). People became assimilated in American society when they erased their cultural identity, unlearned their ethnic cultural practices and beliefs, and accepted the core values of mainstream American culture. The core "American culture" that immigrants were expected to adopt was the middle-class, white Anglo-Saxon Protestant culture. In these old models of acculturation, becoming American was clearly associated with becoming "white." In the last two decades, however, the racial and ethnic demographic profile of American mainstream society has changed significantly with the rapid migration of people from the Caribbean, Latin America, and Asia. Hispanics and Asians are now the largest minority population in California, and the ethnic and racial makeup of many American cities are changing as well.

In regard to the rapid migration of people from non-European countries, Alba and Nee ask an important question: "How then should assimilation be defined, given the prospects for a more racially diverse mainstream arising from large-scale migration of non-Europeans?" (2003, p. 11). Similarly, other scholars of migration, such as Suárez-Orozco and Suárez-Orozco, write that in regard to the migration of non-European, non-English-speaking people, the "incantation of many observers—acculturate, acculturate, acculturate—needs rethinking," that "the first issue that needs airing is the basic question of 'acculturating to what?'" (2001, p. 157).

Some scholars of migration have reconceptualized canonical theories of straight-line assimilation theory by incorporating in their theoretical construct issues related to contemporary ideas, such as boundary cross-ings, race, and transnational activities. An important aspect of this non-linear process of acculturation emphasizes the individual and collective choices that immigrants make when constructing meanings about their ethnicity (Alba and Nee 1997, 2003; Barkan 1995; Gans 1992). For ex-ample, Herbert Gans proposed a "bumpy-line" theory of migration, ar-guing that "the line will not necessarily 'decline' into final and complete acculturation" (1992, p. 175). Even though many critics of the old mod-els of assimilation have found deficiencies in the assimilation theories, some scholars believe that "there is still a vital core to the concept, which has not lost its utility for illuminating many experiences of contemporary immigrants and the new second-generation" (Alba and Nee 2003, p. 9). Although these theorists support the relevance of the assimilation model to explain contemporary migration, they also acknowledge the validity of pluralist and transnational theories of acculturation.

Other prominent scholars of migration have formulated an alterna-tive theory of acculturation. These scholars have incorporated the trans-national aspects of current migration by proposing concepts such as "segmented assimilation" (Portes and Zhou 1993; Zhou 1997), "trans-national communities" (Portes 1996), "transnational social fields" (Glick Schiller, Basch, and Szanton Blanc 1995), "transnational villager" (Levitt 2001), "transnational attachments" (Rumbaut 2002), "transnational life" (Smith 2000), and "assimilation without accommodation" (Gibson 1988). All these terms refer to the ways in which the experiences of the new first- and second-generation immigrants are shaped by the back-and-forth movement between multiple homes and societies, communication between the home and host cultures via media and technology, commer-cial linkages and financial remittances between the sending and receiving societies, racial encounters and discrimination in the host society, the cul-ture of the inner city, the presence of a social network across borders, and the immigrant communities' emphasis on preserving their home culture. In particular, Suárez-Orozco and Suárez-Orozco stress the psychosocial experiences associated with migration and how the majority of children of these non-European immigrants and "people of color" come to "expe-rience American culture from the vantage point of poor urban neighborhoods. Limited opportunities, ethnic tensions, violence, drugs, and gangs characterize many of these settings" (2001, pp. 157–58).

Portes (1997) points out that the experiences of the children of European immigrants in the early part of the twentieth century cannot be used as a guide to study the experiences of the new, mostly non-European second-generation immigrants. For example, Portes and Zhou outlined three possible acculturation pathways for second-generation migrants:

> One of them replicates the time-honored portrayal of growing accultura-
> tion and parallel integration into the white middle-class; a second leads
> straight into the opposite direction to permanent poverty and assimilation
> into the underclass; still a third associates rapid economic advancement
> with deliberate preservation of the immigrant's community's values and
> tight solidarity. (Portes and Zhou 1993, p. 82)

Many of these scholars who propose an alternative model of assimilation work within the transnational framework and have looked especially at the acculturation experiences of the "new second-generation" migrants in the United States (Levitt 2001; Portes, Guarnizo, and Landolt 1999; Waters 1999).

Glick Schiller, Basch, and Szanton Blanc called attention to two important implications related to transnational migration and the creation of diasporas. The first implication is concerned with the way in which the concept of culture, race, and ethnicity needs to be "unbound" (1995, p. 9). They argue that in most of the social sciences, analyses of "immigrant populations, their patterns of social relations and systems of meanings have continued to be enmeshed within theories that approach each society as a discrete and bounded entity with its own separate economy, culture and historical trajectory" (Glick Schiller, Basch, and Szanton Blanc 1995, p. 6). The second implication relates to the ways in which the members of the diasporic community negotiate their dual identities as they go back and forth between multiple homes, languages, and cultures and the ways in which family connections become the site for transnational flows and global capitalism, flexible citizenship (Ong 1999), culture and citizenship (Faist 2000), and the hybridization and creolization of cultures (Hannerz 1992).

Transnational has become an umbrella term with several meanings and multiple definitions. In *The Changing Face of Home: The Transnational Lives of the Second Generation*, Peggy Levitt and Mary Waters take a broad view of transnational migration, emphasizing the need to explore "how social actors construct their identities and imagine themselves and the social groups they belong to when they live within transnational social fields and when they can use resources and discursive elements from multiple settings" (Levitt and Waters 2002, p. 9).

My book on the first-generation, middle-class, transnational Indian diaspora draws on the insights of a wide array of scholars of transnational migration (Alba and Nee 2003; Basch, Glick Schiller, and Szanton Blanc 1994; Portes, Guarnizo, and Landolt 1999; Portes and Zhou 1993; Suárez-Orozco and Suárez-Orozco 2001; Waters 1990, 1999; Zhou 1997). Although many of these scholars have addressed issues related to the children of immigrants or the "new second generation" in the United States, their scholarly insights into contemporary migration theories are relevant also to understanding the acculturation struggles of the first-generation participants of my study. In particular, the work of sociologist Mary Waters (1990, 1999) has been useful in analyzing how, as social actors, first-generation Indian immigrants construct and reconstruct meaning about their race and ethnicity.

"Symbolic Ethnicity" in the Indian Diaspora

In *Ethnic Options*, Waters asks, "What does claiming an ethnic label mean for white middle-class Americans?" (1990, p. 147). Drawing on Herbert Gans's 1979 work, Waters suggests that third- and fourth-generation whites have a symbolic identification with their ethnicity: ethnic identity is symbolic and a matter of personal choice and does not have much influence on their everyday lives.

> It does not for the most part, limit choice of marriage (except in almost all cases to exclude non-whites). It does not determine where you will live, who your friends will be, what job you will have, or whether you will be subject to discrimination. It matters only in voluntary ways—in celebrating holidays with a special twist, cooking a special ethnic meal (or at least call-

ing a meal by a special ethnic name), remembering a special phrase or two in a foreign language. (Waters 1990, p. 147)

Furthermore, Waters argues that even though ethnicity does not play a significant role in many Americans' daily lives, they nonetheless enjoy the privilege of choosing their ethnic ancestry and feeling special as a result of it. Symbolic ethnicity is attractive and appealing to most white Americans because it is rooted in two incongruent belief systems. One is the deeply held belief in belonging to a community, and the other is the idea of individualism.

I use several conceptual schemes to analyze the contradictory, multiple, and layered responses of the members of the Indian diaspora. One of these, the concept of symbolic ethnicity, is a heuristic device I use to analyze the multiple, conflicting, and shifting identities of the Indian migrants. Waters's concept of "symbolic ethnicity" allows me to show why the participants in my study wanted the privilege of attaching their own meaning to their Indian ethnicity. Indian migrants counter their assignations of otherness by invoking the discourse of sameness, equality, and universal humanity to define their sense of identity. Their assertions of self, through the frame of universal humanity, do not mean that they are erasing their ethnicity or sense of "being Indian." Rather, they want to invoke their Indian ethnicity without having to feel that displaying their Indianness will have negative costs. They believe that discourses on model minority and universal humanity will protect them from being seen as the other and will lessen the racism and prejudice toward them.

In contrast to her work on white ethnics, Waters shows how Caribbean immigrants and their children living in the United States construct their identities by incorporating both their racial identity as blacks and their ethnic identity as West Indians or Jamaicans. Most of the respondents in Waters's study were not choosing between a racial and ethnic identity but were involved in complex, multilayered negotiations with all dimensions of their identity. Such an ongoing negotiation required identifying with and distancing themselves from black Americans.

The current power relations in the United States are such that the West Indians face a very particular situation shaping their identity choices.

Assimilation implies becoming black Americans, who have traditionally been the most stigmatized and abused people in American history (along with American Indians). If anyone has an incentive to maintain loyalty to another country or to maintain a transnational identity, these West Indians do. (1999, p. 329)

The participants of my study live in a transnational community and are labeled "people of color," but they clearly are ambivalent about their racial identity and make certain ethnic and racial choices in understanding their identity. These Indian migrants, like the Caribbean participants in Waters's study, have an ambivalent relationship with their "brownness" or their racial identity.

It is important to mention here the clear differences between how Caribbean and Indian migrants are inserted in the racial stratification of the United States. Most Indian professionals are middle class, live in suburban America, and are not subject to the structural inequalities of low wages, racism, and violent neighborhoods experienced by many Caribbean immigrants. However, there are some parallels in how both these groups of migrants come to terms with their racial and ethnic identity. On one hand, the Indian migrants are very proud of their Indian ethnicity and heritage. On the other hand, they invoke the discourse of sameness and universal humanity to distance themselves from their racial and ethnic identity. They realize that certain costs associated with being "Indian" are painful and hurtful and that invoking the discourse of sameness is meant to establish equivalence with the white majority. My study demonstrates that the members of the transnational Indian diaspora are more comfortable with a cultural identity than a racial identity because their insertion in the transnational diaspora has transformed them from being Indian to being "people of color."

Critiquing the Concept of Transnational Migration

Although the scholarship on transnational migration has given us an understanding of how new migrants move between social fields and live with multiple identities, homes, and languages and in multiple social networks, the concept of transnationalism denoting a new pattern of immigration has been critiqued and questioned by scholars who study issues related to migration (see Foner 1997; Grosofuguel and Cordero-Guzman 1998; Portes 1999; Portes, Guarnizo, and Landolt 1999). This critique has been framed around three main questions. The first is concerned with the "newness" of the transnational phenomenon. In this vein, Grosofuguel and Cordero-Guzman (1998) ask, "Is there such a huge difference between yesterday's and today's immigrants?" They contend that many contemporary scholars who have studied the historical patterns of migration in Irish, Italian, or Puerto Rican communities at the turn of the century find that the term *transnational* could easily apply to those communities as well.

Similarly, Foner noted that there may be nothing novel about the concept of transnationalism, that the concept of transnationalism

> is not new, even though it often seems as if it was invented yesterday. Contemporary immigrant New Yorkers are not the first newcomers to live with what scholars now call transnational lives. While there are new dynamics to immigrants' transnational connections and communities today, there are also significant continuities with the past. (Foner 1997, p. 355)

Foner acknowledges that transnational practices are part of the modern migration patterns. However, she believes that we need to clearly mark out the comparisons and contrasts and continuities and departures that exist in old and new patterns of migration. Grosofuguel and Cordero-Guzman found that first, "while it can be said that the speed and the frequency of the contact have changed, we are not sure that the intensity and content of the experience have" (1998, p. 359). Second, they ask whether transmigrants are "only those that circulate back and forth across borders, or does the category include those that maintain connections with their communities of origin through remittances, information, capital commodities that cross nation state boundaries, even if the senders do not themselves circulate back and forth?" (p. 360). Third, Foner (1997) is skeptical about whether or not the second generation maintains transnational connections with their parents' homeland. In this vein, Portes, Guarnizo, and Landolt (1999) proposed that the concept of transnationalism seems to be a catchall category that must be narrowed down, that we need to define the units of analysis comprising the term *transnational*. Does "transnational" refer to the individual, the communities, the institutional structures, or the nation state? Portes and colleagues emphasize that what needs to be studied is the different types of transnationalism and the conditions necessary to produce the phenomenon of transnationalism.

Vertovec gives an important critique of the concept of transnationalism by scholars in fields like anthropology, political science, and sociology. He points out that transnationalism is not a "new theoretical approach" and has become "overused" in the literature on migration (Vertovec 2001, p. 576). Many proponents of the concept of transnationalism have responded to such critiques and have incorporated some version of them into their new body of research (see Glick Schiller 1997; Glick Schiller and Fouron 2001; Smith 2000). Regardless of these ongoing debates, many of these scholars of migration—whether they adopt an assimilation or transnational model—agree that concepts such as transnationalism and diaspora are important cultural sites for studying personhood and identity. Vertovec summarizes this point of view: "Despite these shortcomings surrounding the notion of transnationalism, there has nevertheless emerged a considerable and growing body of empirical studies that contribute to expanding our understanding of relevant concepts and processes" (2001, p. 577).

Clifford contends that the new immigration of mostly non-European peoples of color who live in transnational networks ruptures linear assimilation narratives of identity. He explains that the national narrative of assimilation may be based on a shared point of origin or gathered populations but that it will not be able to assimilate those diasporas or groups with strong links and connections to their homeland. The resistance to assimilationist ideologies is particularly fierce when these new diasporas see themselves as subjects of social and institutional, structural prejudice and racism. In this regard, Clifford observed that "while there is a range of acceptance and alienation associated with ethnic and class variation, the masses of new arrivals are kept in subordinate positions by established structures of racial exclusion" (1994, p. 311). But he cautions that although we must distinguish between the experiences of old immigrants and new non-European immigrants of color, such a distinction should not be formulated too rigidly.

Clifford points out that many immigrants from Ireland and from outside western Europe were racialized, excluded, and marginalized from the larger society. Similarly, in the early twentieth century, many European Jews were subject to both explicit and inexplicit forms of anti-Semitism. Clifford explains that "generally speaking, European immigrants have, with time, come to participate as 'ethnic' whites in multicultural America. The same cannot be said, overall, of populations of color, although region or origin, shade of skin, culture and class may attenuate racist exclusion" (1994, p. 330).

In sum, transnational practices and diaspora communities have become important sites to reconstruct culture, identity, diversity, and difference. In these sites, personhood acquires hybrid, creolized, hyphenated cultural properties and is transformed into an "other" with multiple, shifting, and conflicting identities.[9] The politics of race, gender, and class are intertwined with multiple migrant identities, incompatible cultural positions, and a fluctuating sense of self. How can we understand the complex and multilayered psychological processes in the acculturation of these transnational migrants?

Postcolonial Selves and Diasporas

In order to understand the acculturation processes of transnational, first-generation professional Indians, we must locate their sense of self within the larger postcolonial contexts that have helped shape their migrant self in their new homeland (Grewal 1994). Over the last two decades, the scholarship in fields such as critical/cultural anthropology and postcolonial studies has stressed the continuous and ongoing process through which immigrants reconstitute and negotiate their identity.[10] In particular, scholarship undertaken from a postcolonial perspective has had a significant impact on both the humanities and social studies. The fields of psychology, communication, and human development are now just beginning to pay attention to postcolonial and diaspora theories (Bhatia and Ram 2001b; Hermans and Kempen 1998; Shome and Hegde 2002). Postcolonial studies[11] incorporate the study of "all the effects of European colonization in the majority of the cultures of the world" (Sagar 1996, p. 423). For instance, postcolonial scholars study social phenomena spurred by Euro-American colonization, such as "Third World" diasporas in "First World" communities; the construction of novel cultural practices under imperialism; the transportation of indentured labor and slavery; the representation of the colonized subjects by the colonist in terms of power, race, gender, and ethnicity; and the creation of nations and nationalism in relation to and in opposition to the influential, discursive practices of Europe and the United States.[12]

The idea that the construction of self and identity is not a naturally occurring phenomenon that can be objectively studied but is constituted by historical, political, and social forces is particularly and forcefully maintained by postcolonial theorists like Bhabha (1994) and Said (1979). Postcolonial studies specifically contest Eurocentric metanarratives of enlightenment, ideals of logic and linearity, and the orientalization of the other. One part of the broader focus of postcolonial projects is specifically concerned with studying how colonial and neocolonial practices and policies are intermingled with the present-day migratory experience. For example, according to Chambers, the postcolonial context of migrancy "involves a movement in which neither the points of departure nor those of arrival are immutable or certain. It calls for a dwelling in language, in histories, in identities that are constantly subject to mutation" (1994, p. 5). According to Bammer (1998), such movements of dislocation and displacement are the defining feature of the twentieth century. Much of this displacement has occurred and continues to do so in relation to imperialist and colonial legacies, "for in some sense, the Third-Worldization and hybridization in the First World merely follow upon the prior flows of population, armies, goods, and capital that in the colonial era mainly moved outward" (Lavie and Swedenburg 1996, p. 9).

As Ashcroft, Griffiths, and Tiffin discovered, European imperialism came in many forms that were unleashed over many different countries and continents and over hundreds of years through both "conscious planning and contingent occurrence" (1995, p. 1). The term *postcolonial* refers mainly to the planned and deliberate colonization of the so-called Third World nations and cultures in Asia, Africa, and the Caribbean by modern European imperialists. Some critics extend the term to include the "surviving and indigenous non-European" minority populations in the "European ex-settled colonies of Australia, New Zealand and North America" (Sagar 1996, p. 224). Furthermore, postcolonial critics explain that the prefix *post* in postcolonial does not mean that there was a neat separation between the former European colonial powers and their colonized subjects. That is, colonization did not cease when the European nations' flags came down and the colonized nations' flags went up. In fact, most postcolonial critics believe that "all postcolonial societies are still subject in one way or another to overt or subtle forms of neocolonial domination and independence has not solved the problem. . . . Postcolonialism is a continuous process of resistance and reconstruction" (Ashcroft, Griffiths, and Tiffin, 1995, p. 2).

With its emphasis on understanding the construction of self and identity in terms of colonial histories and on present-day transnational migration, postcolonial research is relevant to understanding issues related to acculturation and immigrant identities in the field of cultural psychology and human development. Furthermore, I argue that taking a postcolonial perspective to understand acculturation allows us to consider the distinct experiences of non-Western, non- European immigrants. Race has always played a key role in U.S. state-sponsored immigration, naturalization, and citizenship laws (López 1996; Mohanty 1991). Moreover, given the existence of racial prejudice in American society, non-European/nonwhite immigrants have been more likely to face exclusion and discrimination than their European counterparts. Subsequently, through personal and collective remembering, tales of discrimination, hardships, and sheer exploitation are kept alive in most non-European, nonwhite immigrant communities. Such narratives have played a large part in constructing and maintaining what are known as *diasporas.*

Diasporas consciously attempt to maintain (real and/or imagined) connections and commitments to their homeland as well as to recognize themselves and act as a collective community. In other words, people who simply live outside their ancestral homeland cannot automatically be considered members of diasporas (Tölöyan 1996). Examples of diasporic immigrants in the United States are Armenian Americans, Japanese Americans, Asian Indians, and Latino/a and Chicano/a communities. These non-European/nonwhite diasporic communities bring to the fore the sense of constantly having to negotiate between here and there, past and present, homeland and host land, self and other (Bhatia 2002a; Bhatia and Ram 2001b). Such negotiations have not been adequately recognized or understood in many of the existing acculturation models, as the following example illustrates:

Deepali is a forty-five-year-old woman with a doctoral degree in biochemistry. She lives in Old Lyme and works for a local biotechnical company. When Deepali's daughter, Karishma, was beginning elementary school, she was not invited to a single "play date" in the neighborhood. Deepali believed that her daughter's "color" deterred most white parents from inviting her daughter to their homes. She explained:

> I just wait for her to get a play date. She doesn't get a single play date. All they see is color. And the parents wouldn't talk to us . . . because they only see color. They don't know how to approach us. They are all talking to each other, but they wouldn't approach us. And for three weeks, I waited for someone to make the first move, but there was not a single move. And then I said well, "I'm a second-class citizen. Either I make it, or I don't, and for my daughter's sake, I have to do it."

Deepali called several families in the neighborhood, hoping to get a playmate for Karishma. After making more than thirty phone calls, she succeeded in getting a few parents to agree to let their children play with Karishma. According to Deepali, most of the suburban mothers knew how to talk with one another because of their shared class and racial identity. Deepali felt that her status as "Indian" migrant woman positioned her as an outsider and a foreigner in this middle-class white suburb. Her inability to get a play date for her daughter illustrates how the components of class and race shape the acculturation process of many migrants who try to carve out a space for themselves in American suburbia.

On another occasion, Deepali remarked that her own difference was accentuated by her daughter's experience at the Veterans Day parade in Old Lyme, Connecticut. Karishma was one of the few nonwhite students selected by her teachers to participate in the Veterans Day parade. Deepali told me that the essay her daughter wrote about Veterans Day was considered by her teachers to be one of the best essays ever written by a student at Karishma's school. The teachers even displayed Karishma's essay on the school's main bulletin board. Although this was a proud moment for Deepali, it was ruined by the way that Karishma was treated by the veterans at the parade. Deepali summarized the details of the event.

> [There were] several veterans sitting in that room, and they were, of course, all white. . . . Some couldn't even stand up. And I noticed Kar-

ishma was in the first row, that they weren't even looking at her. They were trying hard to focus on all the other white kids and not her . . . and I think that it is very commendable that the gym teacher chose her for a Veterans Day parade, and little issues like that will come up.

Why was Deepali so upset that the white veterans were not looking at Karishma during the ceremonies? Why was it so important to Deepali that her daughter be under the gaze of the veterans' eyes? In her view, it was easy for the veterans to look at kids who were similar to them or who looked like their own daughters and granddaughters.

Deepali felt uncomfortable with this particular episode. Although she was proud that her daughter was in the same room with the rest of her American friends on Veterans Day, she also believed that her daughter was perceived as not really belonging there. Several other Indian parents echoed this feeling of being in a third space between belonging and not belonging. Deepali's and her daughter's experience of migrant identity is intertwined with sociocultural factors like colonialism, immigration, and the racialized laws and formations of diasporic cultures. To fully understand migrant identity, we need to ask how the meanings of self and identity are transformed in the formation of diasporas across the world.

The key point for many scholars of migration is that if the concept of diaspora is to serve as a useful analytical tool to understand new forms of identity, the diasporic journey and formations must be historicized and explained through a framework that shows the differences between and similarities of groups and explains how these groups are positioned in relation to the dominant group in the society's social structures and divisions.

The question is not simply about *who travels* but *when, how* and *under what circumstances?* What socio-economic, political and cultural conditions mark the trajectories of these journeys? What regimes of power inscribe the formation of a specific diaspora? . . . If the circumstances of leaving are important, so, too are those of arrival and settling down. (Brah 1996, p. 182, italics in original)

The concept of diaspora, Clifford emphasizes, with its overreaching and all-encompassing function, often results in a slippage "between invocations of diaspora experience, diasporic discourses, and distinct historical experiences of diaspora." These three themes of the diaspora do indeed get entangled with one another in practice because "theorizing" about the diaspora, according to Clifford, is "always embedded in particular maps and histories" (1994, p. 302). Therefore, if the concept of diaspora is to serve as an analytical tool for comprehending the construction of cultural identity in the present global world, we must uncover the specific "maps and histories" that produce such identities.

I use the notion of diaspora as theorized in postcolonial studies in order to study how the postcolonial Indian immigrants living in hybrid cultures and diasporic locations are constantly negotiating their multiple and often conflicting histories and subject positions.[13] Such a reexamination or rethinking of the migratory/acculturation process takes into consideration the complexities to which many postcolonial theorists have alluded. Immigrant communities that make a shared, active attempt to resist nameless homogenization and strive to keep alive a sense of home outside the geographical boundaries of their culture are referred to as *diasporas* (Tölöyan 1996). How do we understand the acculturation experiences of the postcolonial Indian migrants of the suburban American diaspora?

Acculturation and Dialogical Self

Diasporas are transnational communities created out of the migrants' back-and-forth movement across societies; nations; the transportation of goods, labor, and commodities; and the contact between cultural rituals and the technology instantly connecting them to their home society. This transnational movement is important to shaping migrants' acculturation trajectories in the United States. When new immigrants—whether Caribbean, Chilean, Chinese, Indian, Mexican, or Vietnamese—enter the United States, they are introduced to the stories, legacies, and immigration heritage of their respective ethnic group. Kondo (1996) analyzed the memory of the incarceration of Japanese Americans and emblematic cases such as the beating death of Vincent Chin, a Chinese American engineer, by two white unemployed autoworkers as representing the contested notions of community and home as experienced and narrated by many Asian immigrants.

My ethnographic study of the Indian diasporas reveals that through personal and collective remembering, tales of discrimination and exploitation are kept alive in immigrant communities. Many of these narratives of acculturation are circulated as unofficial histories of immigrant communities and are closely bound up with the formation of an individual immigrant's identity. Increasingly, these accounts are being recorded by immigrant and diasporic writers through autobiographical narratives, memoirs, and novels (Alexander 1996; Anzaldua 1987; Maira and Srikanth 1996; Rushdie 1991). Many of these, by first-generation immigrants, underscore the embeddedness of their selfhood in the concrete, material histories and political realities of oppression, discrimination, and exploitation. One issue that often surfaces in the participants' postcolonial histories is concerned with questions of acculturation: Am I an authentic Indian, American, or both? Do I belong here or there or nowhere? Am I black, brown, or white? Why am I invisible?

In the last two decades, sociological studies of migration; postcolonial, ethnic, and cultural studies; and cultural anthropology have provided us with new theoretical frameworks examining the transnational movement and global flows of people, commodities, commerce, culture, media, and technology. These studies show how concepts such as culture, community, nation, and society are changing in the face of these mass migrations. The field of psychology, however, has not yet paid much attention to the psychological processes in the transnational movement of migrants between social fields, communities, homes, and languages.

Traditionally, much of mainstream psychology has been occupied with developing universal, linear models and theories of immigrant identity, acculturation, and adaptation. For instance, cross-cultural psychologists have studied topics like acculturation and acculturative stress (Berry 1998), socialization and enculturation (Camilleri and Malewska-Peyre 1997), and bicultural identity (LaFromboise, Coleman, and Gerton 1998). This body of cross-cultural research,[14] though commendable for bringing issues of immigrant identity to the table, has largely presented migration as a series of fixed phases and stages that do not account for the specific culturally distinct and politically entrenched experiences of new transnational immigrants.

This book takes as a point of departure Hubert Hermans's (2001) proposal that the notions of travel, diaspora, and immigration require that we come up with a dynamic, multivoiced, and *dialogical* notion of

self. Hermans, a cultural/clinical psychologist, states that universal notions of culture and self fail to explain the challenges accompanying the
acculturation process in a world where cultures are mixing and moving
and the local and global are merging and creating new "contact zones"
among different cultures. Consequently, Hermans alerts those scholars
studying the relationship between culture and human development that
the field of "developmental psychology is challenged by the increasing
necessity to study a variety of developmental trajectories on the contact
zones between cultures" (Hermans 2001, p. 28).

I used a dialogical approach to examine how professional Indians living in a Connecticut suburb negotiate their multiple ethnic and racial
identities. More specifically, the dialogical model of self allowed me to analyze how the voices of the larger majority help shape their identity. I
then used the concept of voice to analyze their contradictory movements
between assignations and assertions of racial and cultural identity.

In the last decade, a number of psychologists have adopted a dialogical
approach to understand the multiple and shifting contours of individual
identity (Hermans and Kempen 1993; Josephs 1998; Sampson 1993;
Valsiner 1998, 2000; Wertsch 1991, 1998). A dialogical model of self has
allowed us to show that negotiating one's migrant identity requires multiple negotiations with larger sets of cultural, political, and historical practices. Drawing on Bakhtin's concept of polyphony and multivoicedness,
Hermans thus constructed a dialogical conception of self.

An important dimension of the polyphonic novel is the distinction
between "logical" and "dialogical" relationships. Hermans, Kempen, and
van Loon (1992) explain this difference using Bakhtin's examples: "life is
good" and "life is good." They suggest that from an Aristotelian perspective, these two phrases are connected by a relationship of identity and are
exactly the same. But from a dialogical point of view, they may be described as a sequence in a conversation between two persons in agreement with each other. In this way, these two phrases can be seen as different utterances or speech acts. Thus, the first "life is good" is a statement,
and the second "life is good" is a confirmation (Hermans, Kempen, and
van Loon 1992, p. 27).

The polyphonic novel—with its multitude of characters, each with his
or her own voice and ideological positions that are independent yet
linked to the voices of the *other* through internal or external dialogue—is

crucial to the formulation of the dialogical self (Bakhtin 1984). Like Dostoevsky's characters, Hermans and his colleagues conceive of the self in terms of several dynamic but relatively autonomous "I" positions that are in dialogue with real, actual, and imagined others. The "I" is not static but can move from one position to another with changes in time and circumstances:

> The "I" fluctuates among different and even opposed "I" positions. The "I" has the capacity to imaginatively endow each position with a voice so that dialogical relations between positions can be established. The voices function like interacting characters in a story, involved in the process of question and answer, agreement and disagreement. The dialogical self is conceived as social; not in the sense that a self-contained individual enters into social interactions with other outside people, but in the sense that other people occupy positions in the multivoiced self. (Hermans, Kempen, and van Loon 1992, pp. 28–29)

From the point of view of the dialogical self, individual "I" positions can be in disagreement, contradiction, opposition, and agreement. The concept of voice and positions in the dialogical self can be analyzed using the metaphor of space. Hermans maintains that "voice assumes an embodied actor located in space," acting and coordinating with other actors (1996, p. 44). Similarly, a position is always located in either relation or opposition to other positions. The concept of "voice and position" can be metaphorically employed to define the dialogical self as an "imaginal space" between different positions.

The professional Indians of the local diaspora speak in plural and conflicting voices about their identity, and these multiple voices also challenge the notion of a monolithic and homogenous cultural and national identity. Their reflections on their migrancy and displacement raise important questions about how we should theorize about the self and the multiplicity of voices in the context of moving cultures, globalization, and the formation of diasporic communities.

In addition to struggling with the asymmetrical cultural positions and oppressive political discourses in the host culture, many immigrants are entangled in contradictory discourses related to home, tradition, community, nation, and loyalty. The Indian diaspora of my ethnographic study, for example, embodies such contradictory voices, positions, and locations. Two important books on South Asian identity, *The Karma of Brown Folk* by Vijay Prashad (2000) and *Passport Photos* by Amitava Kumar (2000), address the Indian migrant's predicament of living as *desis* (Hindi word for natives of South Asia) in America. Both these books emphasize that being part of the South Asian diaspora involves complex negotiations with the racial politics of the American culture as well as with the sense of "India" imported from the homeland. They illustrate that the idea and essence of India kept alive in the midst of our diasporic communities are homogenous, static, and ahistorical. Prashad observed that "*desi* 'culture' is treated as an ahistorical trait, a fetish, that must be inhabited to avoid being suspect of cultural treason" (2000, p. 124). Similarly, Kumar noted that South Asian "diasporic articulations" often leave out the idea of India or the "culture" of the native homeland as heterogeneous and diverse (2000, p. 168).

There are many reasons for keeping the notion of Indian or Pakistani culture in the diaspora as traditional, pure, ancient, and spiritual (Prashad 2001). Das Dasgupta pointed out that one reason that outdated customs persist is to reaffirm the mainstream image of the South Asian community as a "model minority" (1998, p. 5). For example, many diverse groups of Indian immigrants (battered women's societies, gays and lesbians, taxi drivers) are often not included as part of the image of "Indian culture" that community members want to brandish to the American society. Several scholars studying issues related to diasporic identity note that South Asian women are often the victims of the community's attempt to present itself as a spiritual, traditional, and homogeneous group with ancient cultural roots. According to Das Dasgupta, "The main casualty of our communities' efforts to reformulate homogenous 'authenticity' are women. . . . South-Asian women in America are given the task of perpetuating anachronistic customs and traditions" (1998, p. 5). Thus, scholars examining the construction of South Asian women in the diaspora argue that they are struggling to "know" their place in the society (Mani 1994). On one hand, they have to face racial discrimination from the larger American society and prejudice as brown minority women, but on the other hand, they have to deal with the oppression in their own communities. What these scholars are pointing out is essentially that the acculturation of many nonwhite, non-European/Western immigrants, especially women, to U.S. society is a painful, difficult, and complex process. Their acculturation process occurs at the intersection of race, gender, and nationality and represents the different personal and cultural "I" positions of the diasporic self.

Hermans and Kempen's (1998) concept of culture as mixing and moving can be used to understand why the acculturation of Third World diasporic immigrants in the First World societies involves an ongoing negotiation with the multiple voices and positions connected to issues related to race, gender, imperialism, and power (Bhatia and Ram 2001b; Bhatia and Ram 2004). The United States is a case in point, as its state-sponsored immigration, naturalization, and citizenship laws were historically based on racist ideologies and were crucial to shaping and defining the "I" positions of several Third World non-European immigrants.

This book argues that recognizing and identifying the polyphonic construction of self helps us understand that for immigrants from the diaspora, acculturation cannot be considered a static category that will or will not be achieved by first- or second-generation immigrants. Instead, the polyphony of the dialogical self suggests that acculturation is a dynamic, plural, and infinite process resulting in new cultural meanings and definitions, many of which are contradictory and are always interminable. In contrast to the universal models of acculturation in cross-cultural psychology, the dialogical view of acculturation does not insist that the conflicting voices need to be replaced by a set of voices that are integrated or harmonious. Rather, a dialogical approach to acculturation means that the asymmetrical power relations between conflicting voices and "I" positions are very much part of the diasporic self. Universal models of acculturation erase the social situatedness and culturally constructed nature of hybrid identities and fail to recognize the diversity and variability for immigrants and their children struggling to come to terms with their multiple voices and worlds.

My study is situated in what Denzin and Lincoln (1994) described as the "fifth moment" in the history of ethnography. The fifth moment in ethnography has led to such questions as: Who makes meanings? How are meanings represented? Are meanings stored in the cognitive structures? Are all meanings contained in discourse? Do meanings reside in the interpretive community? Such questions characterize the crisis of representation and legitimation, and they and others have led to a serious reexamination of the notion of method in different disciplines. Some of the traditions associated with the fifth moment are a blend of many moments, such as feminist epistemology, critical theory, cultural and media studies, and ethnic studies. The question of whether one should rely on a single method or a variety of methods in pursuing one's research goals is part of the fifth moment in ethnographic history. In addition, with the blurring of the boundaries between anthropology and humanities, there is a call for seeing observations about "other" cultures as "thick descriptions" closely linked to an ethnographer's own practices (Geertz 1973).

The fifth moment in ethnography was influenced by *Writing Culture* (Clifford and Marcus 1986) and *Women Writing Culture* (Behar and Gordon 1995), which brought to the fore questions about how issues of gender, race, privilege, accountability, and voice are tied to the ethnographic process of writing about culture. Feminist ethnographies, especially those written by women of color in the 1990s (such as *Women Writing Culture*)[15] proposed a feminist theory of anthropology that was grounded in the racial and ethnic experiences of minority women of color and the ways in which a woman's location via her culture, class, and sexuality created a more differentiated category of women in the United States. One of the implications of the critique offered by both *Writing Culture* and *Women Writing Culture* was that it created several "critical disruptions" in the field of anthropology (Holland 1997, p. 166).

These critical disruptions or interruptions forced anthropologists to move away from analyzing the cultural routines and meanings of a particular group of people "as though they were indicators of an underlying cultural logic or essence equally compelling to all those raised in its folds. Instead, contest, struggle, and power have been brought to the foreground" (Holland 1997, p. 169). In the new anthropology, culture is no longer taken to be a core, integrated whole standing apart from issues of gender, race, power, struggle, and contestation. In the new anthropology, such moves call for a complete "refiguration" of social thought. According to Rosaldo, this refiguration is a move away from seeing "the detached observer using a neutral language to explain 'raw data'" (1993, p. 37). Ortner explained that modern practice theory in anthropology has been shaped by "the specific realities of asymmetry, inequality and domination in a given time and place" (1984, pp. 148–49).

In particular, *Writing Culture*, by Clifford and Marcus, as mentioned before, offers a significantly new and radical rethinking of classical and canonical works in anthropology. This book reveals a provocative and complex vision of the key concepts related to describing and interpreting cultural codes, social practices, and the lived experiences of others as suffused with both the poetical and political elements of culture. The new ways of practicing ethnography and writing about and interpreting culture no longer require only an analysis of the historical, linguistic, and cultural practices that shape and give meaning to everyday cultural routines and events. Rather, the new critical anthropology looks at cultures "as composed of seriously contested codes and representations" in which the poetic and the political, the literary, and the social scientific genres of writing are mutually constituted (Clifford 1986, p. 2).

The picture of a Western anthropologist sitting in his tent in an exotic land observing the natives and their strange cultures and rituals with both curiosity and a detached stance has become irrelevant to much of anthropology. In contrast, my ethnography of the Indian diaspora was conducted at home in a transnational diaspora. In my research, I focused on textual analysis and used rhetoric to highlight the contested modes of identity in the Indian diaspora. My ethnography underscores "the constructed, artificial nature of cultural accounts" (Clifford 1986, p. 2). It shows that the "culture concept," as made of contested codes, concerns the ways in which different modes of interpreting culture are tied to the historical, institutional, and social contexts in which these interpretations are produced.

The new outline for anthropology attests that the analysis and interpretation of cultures are made up of "partial truths" and contested realities. Clifford writes that in the new critical anthropology, "culture is contested, temporal and emergent. Representations and explanations—both by insiders and outsiders—is implicated in this emergence (1986, p. 19). At many moments in the field I felt that I belonged to the Indian diaspora as an insider, and at other moments I felt like an outsider. Following the work of new critical ethnography, this book shows that issues of representation are concerned not only with "what" is being written about cultures but also with who gets to speak and write, under what conditions and at what junctures, and who gets to collaborate with whom. The various discourses of self in this ethnography are shaped by many interpretive moves and politics of locations.

2

■　　■　　■　　■　　■　　■　　■　　■　　■

Qualitative Inquiry and Psychology

Doing Ethnography in
Transnational Cultures

This research project uses a set of methodological tools that can be best described as ethnographic. The professional Indian migrants in this study construct meanings for their identities as they move between different cultural spaces. How do they make meanings of their postcolonial migrant selves? What categories of description do they use to frame their sense of self as privileged and marginalized middle-class minorities? How do they negotiate their status as "people of color"? How do they reconstruct the meanings of race and ethnicity assigned to them by their white middle-class neighbors in the suburbs? I use participation observation and in-depth interviewing as my principal methodological tools to study the patterns of identity construction of the Indian diaspora in suburban America.

The Interpretive Turn: Why Ethnography?

Over the last three decades, scholars and critics from varied disciplines have wrestled with questions about the nature and meaning of the term *method* in the social sciences. Each discipline has tackled the question of method differently. Some researchers have articulated the philosophical differences between quantitative and qualitative approaches and challenged the objective conception of the quantitative modes of research (Shweder 1996). Other researchers (Becker 1962; Hammersley 1992) have pointed out that the distinction between qualitative and quantitative method is of limited value because all kinds of research contain an interpretive and ethnographic element, even if it is not explicitly acknowledged. Since how the term *method* should be defined has not been agreed on, the field of social sciences has experienced, as Jessor argues, numerous eruptions of "internal crises" (1996, p. 4). He notes that this internal crisis is reflected in the conflicts between the epistemologies of the mainstream, positivistic approaches and the epistemologies of ethnographic research.

What has prompted many researchers in the social sciences either to integrate ethnographic with positivistic methods or to completely abandon the positivistic framework? Jessor argues that many researchers in the social sciences have turned to qualitative methods because they are generally discontented with the current climate of positivistic science, and he cites five main reasons for the discontent. First, many researchers perceive the current social scientific knowledge to have "limited relevance" (1996, p. 4) to society's problems. Second, many researchers are concerned with the context-stripping nature of social scientific knowledge. Jessor contends that much social science research is acontextual, devoid of any connection to the social setting in which all knowledge is embedded. Third, he believes that many social scientists are reluctant to deal with the subjectivities of human life, that questions about meaning in the social sciences often are shuffled aside to the domain of humanities. Fourth, Jessor observes that the notion of a person has disappeared from the larger body of social scientific knowledge. Instead, the preoccupation in the social sciences is not with the person but with the "relations among variables" (1996, p. 4). Fifth, much of social science research has had very little to say about the long-term development of institutions and societies. In addition, the social sciences' "seemingly ingrained preference" for large sample research has missed out on the richness of studying development in individual cases in local settings (Jessor 1996, p. 4). The so-called interpretive turn has given us a plethora of theories regarding how we read texts and attribute meaning to them. The theoretical views of the reader-response model, structuralist theory, Marxist and psychoanalytic schools, narrative and discourse theorists, and new criticism and feminist criticism all try to understand and explain the relationship between the author and the text, the reader and the text, and the structure and codes by which one understands cultural discourses (Culler 1982).

Theories of reading and stories of reading are interpreted in terms of signifiers, interpretive communities, implied reader, authorial intentions, discursive practices, the fantastic, linguistics markers, logocentrism, readerly texts, and writerly texts. Those scholars who adopt a cultural and critical perspective turn have raised important questions about method. What is knowledge? What are empirical data? What is interpretation? What counts as fact, evidence, and truth claims? These questions are at the heart of the critical/interpretive turn (Packer and Tappan 2001). Jessor observes that such interrogation about modes of inquiry has led to debates about "the shallowness or surface quality of usual findings and apprehension about the failure of research findings to cumulate or tell a story that has coherence, broad applicability and permanence" (1996, p. 4).

Proponents of the interpretive turn have similarly argued that the agent in the social sciences, especially psychology, is often defined as an unmediated, ahistorical, and experimental variable that can be studied objectively through mechanistic-causal laws. These causal explanations are offered through polarized dichotomies such as subjective-objective, stimulus-response, reflection-action, appearance-reality, emotions-thinking, and mind-body dualism. Many psychological theories that define the notion of agent and other through these binary oppositions often tend to overlook the symbolic and sense-making aspects of human action.

By contrast, researchers subscribing to an interpretive or hermeneutic paradigm contend that an agent should be viewed as someone engaged in and shaped by a series of cultural practices. Many researchers working in the interpretive tradition argue that if psychological theories have to capture the meaning-making aspect of human activity, then they must recognize that notions about the self and the world are not brute data "out there" in the world. Rather, as actors in the world, we postulate their meaning, and they in turn act as devices that make our experiences meaningful and comprehensible (Bruner 1986; Gergen 1985).

Denzin and Lincoln (1994), however, point out that now quite a few social science researchers do not work with the "brute data" approach but instead use qualitative methods to study the stipulatory, context-bound, historically grounded notion of an agent and the world. Although what now is termed *qualitative methods* was once firmly entrenched in ethnographic research, many different research traditions have now emerged under the banner of qualitative methods. For instance, many researchers have noted that qualitative methods draw on the distinct but related approaches of narrative, discourse and semiotic analysis, ethnomethodology, phenomenology, hermeneutics, feminism, deconstructionism, ethnographies, interviews, and cultural studies (Bochner 1997; Conquergood 1991; Denzin and Lincoln 1994; Guba and Lincoln 1994; Kiesinger 1998; Taylor and Bogdan 1998). Specifically, Hymes contends that the term *ethnographies of communication* explores "the communicative habits of a community in their totality, determining what counts as communicative events, and their components, and conceiving no communicative behavior as independent of the set framed by some setting or implicit question" (1990, p. 22).

Hymes and others who work with an ethnographic approach to language are concerned with which relevant features of a communicative event should be observed or studied. That is, in the random flow of events, the moment-to-moment buzzing of social activity, how does one select the event that seems most relevant, interesting, significant, or valuable to one's study? Is the sun's setting part of the communicative event, or should a boy's footsteps be included in the communication context? How does one choose a few communicative behaviors from an infinite number of socially situated actions? Most ethnographers would argue that it is the question that directs us to the phenomenon that we are interested in highlighting and explaining. Denzin and Lincoln (1994) contend that in interpretive or ethnographic research, questions about validity are products of the eras or moments in which those questions are raised. They cite "five moments" in ethnographic research that have helped contextualize the questions and rationale of my study.

Denzin and Lincoln (1994) suggest that the "first moment" (1900–1945) of ethnography is associated with the traditional period. During this period, the "lone ethnographer" asked questions essentially about how to write up "objective accounts" about cultures in which exotic, strange, and foreign people resided (see Rosaldo 1993). The works of

Malinowski (1948) and Margaret Mead (1960) are examples of this tradition. The "second moment" in ethnographic history (1945–1970) is described as the modernist phase. Modernist ethnographers, according to Denzin and Lincoln, introduced vigorous qualitative analysis in order to answer questions about such social issues as poverty, racism, and schooling. Modernist ethnographers studied social phenomena using a multi-method approach that combined open-ended and quasi-structured interviewing, participant observation, and descriptive statistics like frequencies and proportions. Their social theories use the language of both the positivist and the critical theorist. Some of the traditions associated with the modernist ethnographic approach are ethnomethodology, phenomenology, critical theory, and dramaturgical analysis.

The "third moment" (1970–1986), described by the authors as "blurred genres," began with the introduction of Clifford Geertz's (1973) seminal book *Interpretation of Cultures.* In this phase, ethnographers raised questions about meaning and representation. Denzin and Lincoln note that this new perspective focused mainly on the interpretations of the various meanings embedded in a cultural context. According to Geertz, all meanings about the "other" can be captured mainly in the "thick descriptions" of rituals and custom. Thus according to Denzin and Lincoln, Geertz concluded "that all anthropological writings were interpretations of interpretations. The central task of theory was to make sense out of local situations" (1994, p. 9). Many different genres aimed at making sense of local orders became associated with the concept of blurred genres. Some of these genres were called poststructuralism, travelogues, ritual theories of drama and culture, semiotics, and hermeneutics.

The "fourth moment" (1980–1990), termed the *crisis of representation,* completely rejects all kinds of classical norms and instead features the role of class, gender, and race in observations of social life. Researchers in the "fourth moment" ask self-reflexive questions about the ideologies, assumptions, interpretations, and background knowledge they bring to the ethnographic setting. During this period, the knower and the known and the observer and the observed no longer are separated. Some of the traditions associated with the fourth moment are postcolonial theories of class, nationality, gender, and culture and postmodern theories like critical and feminist epistemologies. Of special interest to us is the fact that the fourth moment is punctuated by a double crisis. Denzin and Lincoln explain:

> The linguistic turn makes possible two key assumptions of qualitative research. The first is that qualitative researchers can directly capture lived experience. Such experience, it is now argued, is created in the social text written by the researcher. This is the representational crisis. The second assumption makes the traditional criteria for evaluating and interpreting qualitative research problematic. This is the legitimation crisis. It involves serious rethinking of terms such as validity, generalizability, and reliability. (1994, p. 11)

This double crisis of representation and legitimation marks the fifth moment in history of ethnography. The double crisis reminds us that we can never make any claims about capturing the lived experiences of the people we study because so much of what is said about the "other" is constructed mainly through the researcher's writing. With this idea in mind, Altheide and Johnson (1994) proposed that ethnographers no longer interpret what they observe. Rather, the ethnographer's observations should be regarded as narrative tales created out of good storytelling (Van Maanen 1988). The ethnographer writes texts and audiences make sense of them in accordance with the "interpretive community" in which they have been socialized (Altheide and Johnson 1994, p. 488).

The crisis of legitimation stems from the creation and acceptance of diverse, multimethod approaches that have led to a sort of epistemological openness that almost any form of knowledge claim can pass off as falling under the banner of qualitative research. Denzin and Lincoln maintain that ethnographic research offers so many paradigms that there is an "embarrassment of choices" in the field of qualitative research (1994, p. 11). There is no longer a central authority or a canonical text to which one can refer to sort out the messiness that has plagued qualitative research. Altheide and Johnson believe that some ethnographic researchers have engaged in a kind of "hyperreflexiveness" that has almost taken the field to a dead end:

> The confusion in coming to grips with "reflexivity" has ironically led to a radical antifunctionalist position. This stance claims that knowledge, even

the knowledge process is without grounding, without authority, and therefore, many things "go." That is, knowledge is no longer the criterion, because all "knowledge claims" are based on various assumptions. Research is
no longer coupled with knowledge, but has been given multiple choices
(such as liberation, emancipation, programmatic politics, expressive art).
(Altheide and Johnson 1994, p. 487)

The double crisis of legitimation and representation has entered many
disciplines, with no clear-cut answers to this tension and contradiction.
On one hand, mainstream social scientists believe that claims about validity can be settled only through the laws of empirical science. In such a
view, quantitative or numerical data accurately represent objective reality.
This perspective also includes the widely held view that a valid representation of the world can be captured only through careful hypothesis testing
of variables, the theory of falsification, hard data, reliable methods, and
accuracy of findings. On the other hand, Altheide and Johnson (1994)
argue that a growing body of researchers believe that we must either
abandon the term *validity* or should radically revise it. Proponents of this
view believe that all claims to knowledge are culturally grounded and tied
to personal locations, history, and the context shared by the researcher
and the researched.

Although psychologists have been slow to incorporate ethnographic
frameworks as a mode of inquiry, a few have broken the "empiricist"
mold and adopted middle-of-the-road ethnographic frameworks (see
Jessor, Colby, and Shweder 1996). To analyze human interaction, such
ethnographic frameworks rely on a mixture of methods such as narrative analysis, interviews, case studies, participant observation, coding, descriptive statistics, and graphs. If we were to adopt Denzin and Lincoln's
"five moments" of ethnographic research, we would characterize this
study of the Indian diaspora as belonging to the "fifth moment." Research using ethnographic and mainstream quantitative methods directly
or indirectly questions the meaning of terms like *reliability* and/or *validity*. In this vein, Rogoff, Mistry, Göncü, and Mosier propose that in
conventional psychological research, reliability and/or validity can be
achieved by training observers to arrive at a "criterion of agreement"
on how to label a specific behavior. Moreover, just because a number of

trained observers unanimously agree to give a behavior the same label, this does not mean that the label is true or objective. Rather, they suggest that

> if another person were similarly trained (enculturated), he or she would likely call that behavior by the same label. Hence, objectivity is no more than shared subjectivity, in conventional approaches just as in all others. All accounts are interpretations; they vary only in the basis on which they were made. (Rogoff et al. 1993, p. 31)

We can hear echoes of Denzin and Lincoln's fifth moment of ethnographic research in this quotation: the critical, interpretive, and hermeneutic moment. The comments by Rogoff and colleagues about objectivity are congruent with Denzin and Lincoln's double crisis of representation and legitimation. They all believe that we need multiple methods and multiple criteria to evaluate what counts as "valid" knowledge and are asking for nothing less than a complete reappraisal of the meaning of such terms *validity, reliability,* and *objectivity.* One of the major contributions of this fifth moment is its body of feminist and experimental anthropology demonstrating that the activity of writing about culture is closely connected with the textual strategies, language, rhetoric plots, dramas, and narratives that people use to capture the cultural meanings and practices being investigated.

In summary, we learn from the new critical ethnography that the meaning of culture is derived from contested social codes, power relationships, and one's politics of location; the concept of culture is made up of conflicting representations of gender, race, class, and sexuality; concepts of self-reflexivity, accountability, and voice are integral to the relationship between the researcher and the researched; and descriptions of culture are connected to the act of writing itself. I examined the particular issues related to validity in research that integrate both ethnographic and conventional methods of research study in order to provide a context for my study. My methodological framework thus follows the interpretive ethnographers' tradition of doing research, and my rationale, questions, and methodology come out of the fifth moment of ethnographic research.

Doing Homework in the Field: Ethnography in a Transnational Setting

An important development of this fifth moment is an examination of what it means to be doing fieldwork in the face of traveling cultures, global migration, displacement of people, and movements of labor and goods. The traditional conception of doing fieldwork in some distant, exotic place has been reconceptualized to include multiple transnational sites and research locations. Doing ethnography in this global world has been described as "anthropology on the move" or "multisited" (Marcus 1998) and "anthropology at home" (Caputo 2000). The distinctions among doing anthropology at home and abroad, "here and there," and in "our own" and "other societies" have been scrutinized (Amit 2000; Gupta and Ferguson 1997; Marcus 1995; Okley 1996). What does it mean to do fieldwork at home in one's community? Where does the field begin and end? Is the field contained in home, and vice versa? What does it mean to take field notes at home?

Fieldwork I: Cultural Practices

Following Goodall (2000) and de Certeau (1984), I observed and recorded three kinds of cultural practices in the Indian community: (1) routines (everyday life: work, social outings, family dinners), (2) rituals (sacred and important activities: temple ceremonies and *pujas* or prayers), and (3) rites of passage (practices that significantly alter one's sense of self: birthday parties, marriages, and anniversaries). Field notes on these various practices provide insights into how Indian immigrants keep the notion of "home" and "Indian tradition" alive in the United States. While I was in the field, I took notes on my participants' actions and discourse: their language, phrases, talk, and conversation. When I could not take field notes, I relied on my mnemonic—visual, kinetic, or auditory memory—to recreate in writing the scenes of these interactions (Emerson, Fretz, and Shaw 1995; Goodall 2000; Van Maanen 1988).

Arrival in the Field

I arrived in New London, Connecticut, in August 1999. Then in December 1999 I came up with the idea of my research project, immediately after my coauthor, Anjali Ram, and I had finished writing the article "Rethinking Acculturation," which was later published in the journal *Human Development* (Bhatia and Ram 2001b). In the article, we used the notion of "diaspora" to show that traditional approaches to culture in cross-cultural psychology are confining and obstruct more fluid, dynamic, and socially situated conceptions of culture. More specifically, we proposed rethinking and reformulating the process of acculturation in the context of non-Western, "Third World" migration to "First World" countries like Australia, Canada, France, Germany, the United States, and the United Kingdom. This article raised several questions about the acculturation processes of non-European post-1965 immigrants in United States. Is there such a thing as a univocal, monolithic, American, English, Arabic, or Indian culture? How is the diasporic identity shaped by, and linked to, the cultural and political issues of race, gender, colonization, and power present in the host land and the homeland? We showed that postcolonial research, with its emphasis on understanding the construction of self and identity in terms of colonial histories, and present-day transnational migration are relevant to understanding issues related to acculturation and immigrant identities in the field of human development.

In January 2000, I became interested in exploring the acculturation processes of the professional middle-class Indian migrants living in suburban America. I wondered how first- and second-generation Indian Americans negotiate, reinvent, and reconstruct their cultural identity as they move among different cultural spaces. How do they negotiate their identities as successful, professional "brown" people at work and in their suburban lives? What is their relationship to India?

With these general questions in mind, I began to locate the "Indian community" in the suburbs of southeastern Connecticut. My first contact with a local Indian family was through the chair of my department, Peggy Sheridan. One day in February 2000 Peggy knocked on my door, "Here is Vishal. I have been talking to him about you." Vishal and Peggy were friends and had known each other's families for a long time. When I arrived at the Department of Human Development at Connecticut College and was beginning to conceptualize the details of my study on the Indian diaspora, Peggy mentioned Vishal as being an "important person" in the Indian community.

Vishal and I instantly connected with each other. He was warm, soft-spoken, and very enthusiastic about his involvement with the Indian community. We shared our brief migrant autobiographies, giving each other encapsulated snapshots of our journey from India to the United States. Those summaries revealed where we came from: our family background, class position, educational status, and our struggles en route to America. Vishal told me that his daughter went to Connecticut College and that he had a strong relationship with the college and the Indian community. He said, "There are quite a number of Indian families around. We should introduce you to the community." He owned a small, management consulting company and had been living in the area for thirty-two years. Vishal was one of the founding members of the Indian temple in Middletown, Connecticut, and was well connected with the social network of the Indian diaspora. In sum, Vishal turned out to be my "gatekeeper" to the Indian community.

My meeting with Vishal turned out to be significant for both personal and professional reasons. Vishal sent me numerous invitations by fax, e-mail, and phone to attend musical events, dinners, temple *pujas*, and political events. My wife and I attended the IAPC (Indian American Political Caucus) political event, where money was being raised from the Indian community for the reelection of Democrat Sam Gejdenson to the House of Representatives. At that event I made contact with Ashok, the director of global operations at the ABC Computer Corporation. Ashok and his wife, Archana, invited us for dinner at their house in Plainville. Most of the Indian migrants living in the area worked for ABC, and Ashok summarized the socio-demographic profile of the Indian diaspora. Archana talked about the different religious groups in the Indian diaspora and complained to me that "many of these Indians stick to themselves and don't mingle with other ethnic communities." By the end of the evening, I had some idea about the social-class divisions and various groups in the area. I also learned that one "core" group of about fifteen Indian families interacted regularly with one another. This group therefore formed a collective Indian diaspora in the suburb of East Lyme.

First Contact with the Diaspora

My first contact with this core group was in October 2000 when Vishal invited my wife and me to attend the Diwali dinner and celebration in the community. Diwali, which means "festival of lights," is a Hindu religious festival and one of India's most widely celebrated events over several days in October and November. The festival symbolizes the victory of good over evil and is marked by wearing new clothes, distributing sweets to family and friends, and lighting firecrackers. A modified version of the Diwali festival is usually celebrated in all Indian Hindu diaspora communities across the United States. The Diwali festival here was held in mid-November and was the biggest cultural event organized by the "core group" of the Indian diaspora. The Diwali dinner, at a local church, was a perfect opportunity to meet other Indians and be a part of the community and form a social network of friends outside the college. Vishal had faxed a note to the hosts of the Diwali dinner that my wife and I would be attending. The following excerpt is from my field notes about the Diwali celebration:

Scene 1

Anjali and I enter the room. We are greeted by two teenaged girls dressed in colorful *chanya cholis* (traditional blouse and skirt). They wish us "Happy Diwali" and serve us *jilebis* (type of sweet) on a banana leaf. This large rectangular room, located behind the main church, was decorated with lights. There were about thirty round tables covered with blue tablecloths, around which many Indian families were sitting. Some families were engaged in animated conversation, and others were sitting silently around the table. A couple of young men and women had pulled their chairs away from the round table and were observing the general flow of activity. About ten older men and women were sitting at the round tables with their families. Many of these elderly guests were the parents and grandparents of the migrant families and were visiting from India. The women were busy setting up the dinner and getting ready to participate in several dance events. Three men from the catering service, dressed in white shirts and black trousers, were setting up five tables on one side of the room and pouring food from large cauldrons into stainless steel serving containers. In the center of the room was a large makeshift *shamiana* (podium) with a carpeted floor. A *tabla* (percussion instrument), harmonuim, and a microphone were on the floor. Next to the shamiana was an altar for the various Hindu gods and goddesses. Young boys dressed in *kurta* pajamas (traditional clothing worn by males) were chasing one another. A group of girls dressed in chunya choli and *salwar khameez* (traditional clothing worn by Indian women) were practicing their dance steps. The guests seated at the table were conversing in Gujarati, Marathi, Hindi, and English.

When we entered the room, Anjali and I were not sure about the seating arrangements and were looking around for a table. Kanchan and Kiran, the hosts of the dinner, approached us. I told them, "We are Vishal's guests." Kiran replied, "Yes, we got the fax from him." Kanchan asked, "Are you new to the area?" I replied, "I joined Connecticut College about a year ago." Kanchan told me that her daughter, Gita, was ready to go to college, and we had a brief conversation about liberal arts colleges. Kanchan remarked, "Gita wants to study engineering like her dad and is interested in going to a big university." As we mingled with other families, Rohan and his wife, Asha, came up to us. Rohan remarked, "Almost all the Indians here work for the local computer company. It's nice to know some non-ABC people." Rohan was curious about the courses I taught at the college. He said, "My daughter, Sheetal, is getting ready to go to college next year. She is interested in psychology and wants to go to a liberal arts college." I replied, "If you need any help with her application, let me know," and Rohan and I talked about the benefits of studying at a liberal arts college. As though we were his guests, Rohan introduced Anjali and me to several other Indian families. Within a couple of hours after my arrival at the church, I had met about ten families. I met Ashok, Arun, Shailesh, Kishore, Abhishek, Poonam, Arun, Hema, Naina, Rekha, Raju, Ashok, Rani, and Prashant. In short, I had met the "core group" of the Indian diaspora. Raju said that he played squash with a professor at Connecticut College, and Abhishek knew some of my colleagues in the chemistry department and noted that the president of the college "lives down the road from our house."

Scene 2

The entertainment segment of evening began. I sat with Prashant, Shailesh, and Arun. Raghu was playing the tabla, and his wife, Simran, was singing a Punjabi song, "Long Da Vacha." They entertained the audiences with some more Punjabi songs. Then Vinay took the harmonium and sang old "Mukesh songs." There were about seventy-five Indians in the hall, all sitting around the various round tables. Vinay continued to play in the background, and then Victor (whose real name is Vikram) took over the microphone and announced abruptly, "Now we are going to play a game." Vinay continued to play the harmonium. A small basket, containing small sheets of paper, or "chits," with various activities written on them, was passed around the table. Each person picked up a chit and had to perform the activity written on it. The first chit had a famous dialogue from a Hindi film, *Deewaar,* and the person who picked it up was asked to recite the dialogue. The basket was passed around a few more tables. Some of the chits contained questions like "What makes one successful?" and others about the "culture" of India. "Why do we celebrate Diwali?" "What is Ramayana?" Although Victor continued to talk to the audience, no one seemed interested in playing the game, some participants being reluctant to perform in public. Victor then moved on to the "comedic" segment of the evening. Ramesh, who owned a gas station in one of the local neighborhoods, took center stage and began reciting long "jokes."

Anjali and I were sitting at a table where everyone was speaking Marathi. Because I am from Pune, where Marathi is the regional language, I could understand at least the gist of their conversation. But Anjali and I felt left out and awkward about sitting at this table, as Shailesh and Karan talked about the politics at their work throughout the evening. Indeed, most of the people in the hall had migrated to the United States in the 1960s and 1970s, and it soon became clear that there were two generations of migrants in the room. The entertainment segment ended with Indian classical dance performances.

Sam Gejdenson, a Democratic Congressman from Connecticut, walked in with his aides. In the next election, he would be in a competitive race for his seat with the Republican contender, Rob Simmons. Gejdenson repeated the "We are all immigrants" speech that he had given at the IAPC event I had attended. He praised the successes of the professional Indians and their numerous contributions to the American society. He brought up the Kashmir issue and told the audience that he had fought hard to see that America understood India's position on Kashmir. Gejdenson was given a standing ovation, and then he left the room with his aides. It was about 9.30 P.M., and Poonam and Abhishek moved toward the altar to do puja of the deities. Everyone in the hall got up to sing the Hindu prayer "*Om jai jgadish.*" After the *puja,* everyone stood in line for food.

Because there were three or four different lines to the food tables, people were not sure which one to stand in. Anjali and I joined Rohan in one of the longest lines. I got my plate of food and sat with a family who were discussing the benefits of yoga and meditation. We spent the next several hours at the table talking about spirituality in India.

My membership in the Indian diaspora began with that Diwali dinner in November 2000. This entry into the community offered me several opportunities to form friendships and relationships with numerous members of the Indian community. My participation in the Diwali dinner also became a defining moment of my study, for I realized that as soon as I was greeted by the two teenagers at the entrance to the church, I was locating myself in a community that would also be the "field" for my ethnographic research for the coming year. In the next eleven months, from October 2000 to September 2001, my field became my home and my home became my field.

Participant Observation in the Field/Home

After the Diwali dinner, Rohan and Asha invited my wife and me for dinner at their home to meet some of their close family friends in the suburb of East Lyme. I was introduced to new Indian families whom I had not met at the Diwali dinner and developed a closer relationship with those whom I already had met. During the next eleven months, I attended many dinners with a core of seven families. My wife and I met for these weekend dinners with the families of Vishal and Neeta, Abhishek and Poonam, Rohan and Asha, Raju and Naina, Vivek and Kajol, Prashant and Rekha, and Kishore and Kanchan. These evening dinners with families in the Indian community had a familiar pattern. We all would arrive at the hosts' home around 7 P.M. The men and women automatically sat in different groups, although there were no cultural taboos preventing them from sitting together. The women usually would cook together and talk in the kitchen or around the kitchen table. Both men and women talked about work, Hindi films, or politics in America or India. Popular film or classical Indian music always seemed to be playing in the background. The children played in the basement or one of the bedrooms, and the older children were given the task of supervising the younger ones. On many occasions, the college-aged second generation joined the adults.

The dinner was organized buffet style, and by about 9:00 P.M. we all would sit in the family room on the carpet, sofa, and chairs. These dinners were informal, and mostly English was spoken throughout the dinner. These "desi only" social get-togethers were intimate, friendly, and relaxing, a time for the members of the Indian diaspora to carve out a physical and mental space for themselves in which they could feel comfortable about expressing their "Indian culture" or "Indianness." At only a few evening parties was the discussion mostly about the politics of religion in India or race issues at work in the United States. Rohan and Asha's family were the "social hub" of the Indian diaspora in East Lyme. They were friendly, warm, and outgoing and believed in creating a sense of Indian community. We regularly met the core families at Rohan and Asha's house as well as those families new to the area.

Although our meetings in the Indian diaspora were mostly confined to suburban homes, there were other forms of socializing in the collective life of this migrant community. I invited all seven or eight families to my house for dinner, in groups of three or four. We followed the same "desi dinner routine" that I just described. I was developing a strong social network with about ten local Indian families. My wife and I and Rohan's family went to restaurants for dinner and movies. The Mittals also had two grand community events at their home, to which they invited about one hundred people. They were daylong events with lunch, snacks, music, games, and an evening of *gazzals* and *shayari*. We went to their homes on several occasions and met other Indians who worked at the ABC Computer Company. Rohan and Asha had their annual potluck picnic at the Harkness Park where we played cricket. In between, I participated in numerous cultural events, such as performances of Indian classical music and children's birthday parties. I knew I had acquired an "insider status" in the community when Rekha and Asha asked me to be a member of their exclusive potluck dinner club that met monthly at one of its members' homes. This club was a close group of about fifteen, who were mainly responsible for organizing the social and cultural life of the Indian diaspora.

Throughout my eleven months of immersion in the Indian diaspora, I did not know when I was in the field or out of it. Although my friends in the community were also participants in my study, most of my time was spent building intimate and trusting relationships with my participants. I was deeply immersed in the field as both a community member and an ethnographer, roles that constantly overlapped. I took field notes on most of the events I had participated in and observed, trying to capture the textures and impressions—the smell, noise, color, and movements—of the field. I focused on the people's social interactions and made mental notes of the conversations I had with several members of the group. Although many events in the Indian community had a familiar routine, these "same events" held different meanings for the participants. In particular, I was concerned with those cultural patterns that provided insights into the dynamics of identity construction in the Indian diaspora.

Following the advice of ethnographers (Emerson, Fretz, and Shaw 1995; Goodall 2000; Van Maanen 1988), I organized my field notes around key questions: How do the participants see and experience their world in the diaspora? How do they make sense of these evening dinners and other cultural rituals? What do they find meaningful in their social interactions and processes? Balancing the dual roles of being a community member and an ethnographer requires, as Goodall (2000) states, learning how to write notes about the field, learning about one's self as a fieldworker, and understanding how an ethnographer's identity can be "strategically deployed" to capture the unfolding nuances of the local culture. As a member of the community I was studying, I was focused on writing about the "big picture" of the Indian diaspora in which their everyday lived experiences made sense. In accordance with Goodall's (2000) work on the new ethnography, I was hanging out with my participants in their life space, talking to them, sharing and learning about their life in the suburbs, making notes, and engaging in self-reflection and analysis of my participation in the diaspora. Most of my fieldwork consisted of engaging with my participants in verbal exchanges—exchanging information, teasing, joking, debating, arguing, negotiating, and having dialogues. I also spent a great deal of time participating in the "everyday practices" of my community, observing and engaging in the cultural practices of going to the temple, watching Hindi movies, having dinner, indulging in nostalgic moments about home, recollecting memories of life in India, and talking about life as a migrant in America.

My personal identity as Hindu Indian and my professional identity as a professor at a liberal arts college gave me a natural and automatic access to this middle-class Indian community. My participants never interrogated or questioned my social class and religious identity. Rather, I could relate to most of them through our similar childhood experiences in India—playing cricket, watching Hindi movies, and being part of a vast network of aunts, uncles, and relatives. There were many instances in the field, however, when I felt like a complete outsider in the Indian diaspora. That is, the ways in which I understand my identity through the vectors of class, race, and community created many moments of disconnection and distance between the members of the diaspora and me. My fieldwork consisted of both moments of connection and disconnection, intimacy and distance, and silence and dialogue with my participants. There was no one real, genuine Indian diaspora in southern Connecticut, and thus nobody could claim to be a real native or an insider. Every member of the Indian diaspora felt like an outsider when moving from his or her own small group to other groups. Several scholars have questioned this "insider-outsider" status in ethnography, or an ethnographer positioning oneself as native doing ethnography in one's native, homogenous community (Chow 1994; Narayan 1993; Raj 2003; Shukla 2003).

The Indian diaspora of my ethnographic study was made up almost exclusively of engineers, doctors, computers scientists, programmers, management consultants, architects, biologists, geneticists, biochemists, psychologists, psychiatrists, and social workers. Missing from this picture were the other Indians living in the same geographical space: cabdrivers, working-class migrants, cooks, mechanics, business merchants, motel employees, gas-station workers, illegal Indian migrants, and Muslims, Christians, and other South Asians. This other group of Indians lived segregated lives and formed their own diasporas—creating a cultural and community life for their members. These small diasporas within the larger diaspora were mostly formed on the basis of class, language, religion, and community. The social-class stratification in the Indian diaspora replicated the class structure that existed in both India and America. The lives of the members from different religious and social class groups rarely intersected, and many of these individuals had nothing in common with one another except their being from India. However, it was not my "Indianness" alone that allowed me to be a part of the middle-class Indian diaspora of my study. My social position as a professor was seen as part of a natural fit with their professional world, and my identity as a nonscientist, non-ABC employee also was appealing to the members of the larger diaspora. In short, my wife, Anjali, who also is a professor, and I were seen as part of their model minority status. After a year of establishing rapport, trust, membership, and friendship with a group of about ten Indian families and getting to know some additional thirty families, I was ready to begin the second stage of the study: interviewing the members of "my own" community.

Fieldwork II: The Interviews

With the interconnectedness in the world and the fluid movements between cultures, the distinction between home and field has become blurred for transnational immigrants and researchers. Fieldwork and homework entails back-and-forth relationships between the home and the field, border crossings, multisited research, and plural sites of belonging (Amit 2000; Gupta and Ferguson 1992; Kearney 1995; Marcus 1995; Marcus and Fischer 1986; Okley 1996). I used in-depth interviewing to examine how diasporic families reinterpret the physical and emotional terrain of self, "other," and home as they move back and forth among multiple cultural locations. Several scholars have written about conducting various types of in-depth, qualitative interviews (Johnson 2001; Rubin and Rubin 1995) and introspective and collaborative interviews in one's own community and with a family member (Goodall 2000; Kiesinger 1998; Trujillo 1998). What does an in-depth interview with a participant entail? According to Johnson,

> A researcher who uses in-depth interviewing commonly seeks "deep" information and knowledge—usually deeper information and knowledge than is sought in surveys, informal interviewing, or focus groups, for example. This information usually concerns very personal matters, such as an individual's self, lived experiences, values and decisions, occupational ideology, cultural knowledge, or perspective. (2001, p. 104)

An important methodological question that should be asked here is, What does it mean to do "deep" interviews? Johnson clarified the various meanings of "deep" in the context of an interview. First, members of a culture hold "deep understandings" about their life space, their everyday cultural activities, routines, events, and places. The interviewer therefore tries to achieve the same level of understanding as the participant's about his or her cultural activities. Second, in-depth interviews aim to understand the folk theories and the mythic, causal, or scientific explanations and perceptions that a culture invokes in order to understand their ways of life. The interviewer essentially "aims to explore the contextual boundaries of that experience or perception, to uncover what is usually hidden from ordinary view or reflection or to penetrate to a more reflective understanding about the nature of that experience" (Johnson 2001, p. 106). Third, in this type of interview methodology, a deep understanding can tell us how our sense of selves and identity are tied to the particular language that we use to understand and frame meanings about culture. Fourth, deep interviewing also captures individual members' various and conflicting representations of their individual and collective life space. Deep understanding tries to go beyond the homogenous conception of cultural meanings to a more nuanced, agentive, heterogeneous, and contested view of the participant's life.

During my interviews with the participants, I asked open-ended questions in order to understand how my participants moved among various cultural and racial positions and how they dealt with their sense of being accepted and marginalized by American society. These semistructured interview questions (in Hindi and English) were designed to understand how they negotiated their sense of simultaneously being in two cultures. Each of these qualitative interview questions centered on topics such as race, gender, work, moral codes, community, and social status (Rubin and Rubin 1995). Each participant was given oral sentence completion tasks. For example, some of the questions that I asked were

> I came to America because _____; as an Indian immigrant living in America I feel different because _____; a few important turning points in my in life in America are _____; as an Indian, nonwhite, living and working in America I experience _____; being a successful Indian in America means _____; I cultivate a sense of "Indianness" _____ and I cultivate a sense of "Americanness" _____

Throughout the interview, at different points, I asked follow-up questions to clarify, explain, and provide more detailed information in order to bring out both the general and subtle aspects of the participants' responses. Most of the interviews lasted for between sixty and ninety minutes and took the form of a conversation or discussion. Rather than asking about "what it means to reproduce Indian culture in the diaspora," my questions were geared toward understanding how the participants viewed their sense of difference in their new homeland. What meanings did they attribute to their racial and ethnic identity? How did they reconstruct and reframe the meaning of self and personhood assigned to them by the larger majority? What terms did they use to articulate that difference?

These issues of difference are closely connected to issues of "Indian culture," "Indianness," or how Indianness is imagined. I was not particularly interested in understanding how concepts of Indian culture were used to invoke "nostalgia" or shore up an essential, stable sense of "Indianness." Instead, I was interested in how "nostalgia for home" in the Indian diaspora was strategically used to rearticulate a sense of identity, community, and difference. I share this particular focus of my study with Raj's work on Hindu Punjabis in Britain, whose ethnography explores how "nostalgia for culture makes Indian versus British a meaningful way to think about diversity . . . how people are thinking through culture, difference, ethnicity, identity, and community" (2003, p. 7). I was interested in exploring how the Indian diaspora comes to terms with being different, not just as passive victims of racism and prejudice, but also as active agents in this transnational world. How did they understand their dual status as privileged and marginalized others in the American multicultural society? What choices did they make regarding their understanding of their ethnic and racial identity? What kind of language did they choose to assert their identity? My questions were not focused just on how the larger society constructed their otherness or marked them as the other but instead on how the middle-class Indian diaspora framed their meaning of difference. What categories of identity did they use to understand their new status in their new world "as people of color"? What did it mean to be in a culture in which their identity was positioned as the other? What kind of inside/outside spaces did they create to deal with the fragmented sense of being both privileged and marginalized?

Ethnography and the Public and Private Culture

I distinctly remember one moment in my ethnographic study when I asked Prashant, a first-generation Indian immigrant living in the United States, to complete the following open-ended statement: "I cultivate a sense of Indianness by . . . ." In reply to my question, Prashant paused, looked up at me, and asked, "Inside the house or outside or both?" Slightly taken aback, I said, " Yeah, actually both. You can start with the house first." Prashant remarked that he and his wife tried to create an "Indian atmosphere" at home. In fact, several of the participants I interviewed used the phrase "Indian atmosphere," and it generally referred to what Prashant described as "a collection of some Indian things to make it feel, you know, Indian. So Indian paintings, Indian idols (we have all the gods up there) and Indian music, Indian books, Indian TV."

Prashant's answer demonstrates how concepts like culture and identity are radically changed when they are reinvented and recreated in new spaces. He tries to create an authentic Indian atmosphere in the "inside" realm of his raised ranch home that sits in a quiet suburb, surrounded by homes owned by mostly white middle-class families. He carves up the concept of culture and places them in the public and private spaces. The inside, home space symbolizes all that is truly private and Indian, and the vast, outside space is seen as belonging to others. The inside space is strategically recreated and reimagined to give the inhabitants an "authentic" feel of the Indian atmosphere, by means of smells, scents, values, rituals, customs, language, gods, and goddesses.

This approach to writing, describing, and framing the concept of culture and cultural representation in the field of cultural anthropology has significantly changed in the last two decades. A number of works deal with the methodological rethinking of key concepts such as culture, self, and ethnography in cultural anthropology (Behar and Gordon 1995; Clifford and Marcus 1986; Rosaldo 1993). James Clifford and George Marcus (1986) proposed a major reevaluation and overhauling of how culture and cultural texts are interpreted and written up in anthropology. In particular, their book *Writing Culture* offered a new analysis and rethinking of the canonical concepts in anthropology such as fieldwork, ethnography, and cultural interpretation. Although Clifford and Marcus deliberately excluded feminist voices in anthropology, works made up for this absence and focused on how issues of gender, race, privilege, accountability, and voice are tied to the ethnographic process of writing about culture. Amit writes that

> there is surely no other form of scholarly inquiry in which relationships of intimacy and familiarity between researcher and subject are envisioned as a fundamental medium of investigation rather than as an extraneous by-product or even an impediment. This onus toward comradeship, however incompletely and sporadically achieved, provides a vantage point imbued at once with significant analytical advantages as well as poignant dilemmas and ethics of social location. (2000, p. 2)

What were the problems with studying my own community?

After the first phase of fieldwork, when I scheduled interviews with my first set of participants, they questioned the methodological assumptions of my research project and were reluctant to be part of it. During an annual picnic at a local park in July 2001, I approached Subash, who works as a mechanical engineer at a local nuclear plant, with the intention of setting up an interview with him and his wife, Kiran. He asked, "What is your methodology?" I explained to him that I would be using qualitative/ethnographic methods to frame the questions, rationale, and analysis of the study, to which he replied, "Your study is unscientific." Subash, then, was not just reluctant to give me an interview but also dismissed my project as "not having a clear hypothesis." Although I had sensed hostility, I was not sure why he was so resistant. This was my only second interview, and I was dismayed and disappointed. Although Subash was not part of the core group of people with whom I had created a close relationship, I had met him on several occasions in the community. I knew that Subash and his wife, Kiran, were influential members of the community, so I was afraid that my one year in the field would be wasted if I encountered similar resistance from other members of the diaspora.

A week later, Rekha, the first participant in this study, called me.

> I understand Subash and Kiran did not want to do their interviews for the project. I hope they did not tell you that my experience of interviewing with you was negative. All I told them was that "the questions were hard"

and one had to think deeply to answer them. I think the reason they did not want to be interviewed was because Subash and Kiran were not comfortable with disclosing the details of their lives to both of you.

Rekha's explanation came as an immense relief. I thought that perhaps Subash did not trust me and did not want to talk about the details of his life as a migrant. He therefore had used the methodology issue as a way to refuse the interview because, I believe, he did not want to be seen by the core group as someone who was afraid, intimidated, or shy about being interviewed. I was caught in a web of relationships with regard to this incident in the field. Rekha had found the interview challenging and told me that "it made her think about her life in America." She also wanted to make sure that Subash or Kiran had not told me directly "that they did not want to do the interviews because it was a negative experience for Rekha."

Subash's reluctance to be interviewed was an important methodological moment. As an ethnographer, I wanted to honor his voice, but I also acknowledged his power to refuse and reject the methodological premises of my study. Moreover, I was afraid that Subash would use his power and influence in the community to persuade the core members of the Indian diaspora to refuse to be interviewed. My dilemma of working in the community and negotiating my relationships as an ethnographer and a friend with various members of the community resonated with the ongoing debates in feminist ethnography.

The classic essay by Judith Stacey, "Can There Be a Feminist Ethnography?" explores whether feminist ethnography can carry out a "genuine" feminist interpretation of cultural texts and selves that are located in these practices. She challenges the intellectual alliance between the intersecting domains of feminism and ethnography as a method by questioning the goals of both ethnography and feminism. Stacey writes that feminist scholars, disenchanted by the mechanistic and detached way of coming to terms with their participants, advocate an "integrative, transdisciplinary approach to knowledge, one that would ground theory concretely in everyday women's lives" (1991, p. 111). She tells us that when she was first introduced to ethnography, she felt that its emphasis on interpersonal relationships, giving voice to others, and highlighting the role of empathy and connection made it a viable methodological tool for a feminist ethnography. But after spending about two years of doing fieldwork, she confronted an uneasy engagement and an inherent contradiction between feminist ideas and ethnography as a methodical tool. She offered two reasons that she believes there can be no feminist ethnography.

First, "precisely, because ethnographic research depends upon human relationships, engagement and attachment it places research subjects at a grave risk for manipulation" (Stacey 1991, p. 113). Stacey is concerned with the asymmetrical power relationships between the ethnographer and his or her informants and reminds us that the possibility always exists for the ethnographer to deceive, exploit, and manipulate the informants. Such a method goes against the grain of feminist principles, which are concerned primarily with constructing knowledge about women's lives that is based on connection and relationships. The second contradiction, according to Stacey, is the "dissonance" between feminist principles and the ethnographic method, "between fieldwork practice and ethnographic product. In the last instance, an ethnography is a written document structured primarily by a researcher's purposes" (1991, p. 114).

Other feminist ethnographers, such as Visweswaran (1994) and Abu-Lughod (1991), appreciate and are sympathetic to Stacey's rejection of the feminist ethnography but argue that if it is textually innovative and centered on women's lived experiences, it is possible. Visweswaran (1994) reminds us that the idea that the possibility of betrayal, manipulation, and treachery is present in any relationship between an ethnographer and his or her participants.

Although Subash's and Kiran's reluctance to participate in my project cannot be construed as betrayal or treachery, I felt that Subash had tried to influence other members of the diaspora by telling them that my project was "unscientific" and not worthy of their participation—which I learned from several families whom I had interviewed. Some of these families had close friendships with Subash and Kiran, but they also used this opportunity to present an image of themselves as different from Subash and Kiran. One member of the diaspora suggested, "Why would someone refuse to do an interview? This should be such a fun task. I am looking forward to it."

Visweswaran contends that the idea of betrayal as integral to the relationship between the researcher and the researched should be the starting point for a feminist ethnography rather than a signal of the "impossibility of a feminist ethnography" (1994, p. 40). She writes that much of feminist writing about women's subjectivities "take the problematic of voicing as the starting point" (p. 31). Instead, Visweswaran argues that feminist anthropology should work on women's issues with the assumption that women are willing to talk. We need to determine, she notes, "what strictures are placed on their speech, what avenues of creativity they have appropriated, what degree of freedom they possess" (p. 30).

For Visweswaran, feminist ethnography should learn from women's speech as well as from their *silences*. She believes that feminist ethnography should be read through the metaphor of allegory because it emphasizes contrasts and differences. According to Clifford,

> a recognition of allegory emphasizes the fact that realistic portraits, to the extent they are "convincing" or "rich," are extended metaphors, patterns of association that point to coherent (theoretical, esthetic, moral) additional meanings. . . . Allegory draws attention to a narrative character of cultural representations and to stories that are built into the representation process itself. (1986, p. 100)

As an example of the allegorical nature of ethnography, Visweswaran (1994) observed that her own feminist ethnography is punctuated with interruptions, uneven descriptions, and moments when she undermines her own ethnographic authority.

Visweswaran's ethnography (1994) examines a few South Indian women's stories about their participation as nationalists in the Indian independence movement against the British. She approached these women —Uma and Janaki—assuming that their own sense of identity was bound up with their narrative of nationalism. But these women strategically resisted the narrative of being nationalists and occasionally hid secrets from each other and her. She describes her ethnography of these women as made up of betrayals, failures, and resistances but points out that these junctures or moments of failure revealed to her that her own location as a Western feminist, the unequal power relationship between herself and the subjects, and the larger issues of history, memory, and colonial contexts made her rethink the goals of her ethnography and cultural reading of others.

The Interview

What are the implications of Visweswaran's comments for my ethnography? The moments of failure and resistance in my ethnography can be read as moments of revelation during which the complexities and conflicts in the relationships between the participants and me became transparent. There were some definite moments of failure, resistance in the field, when I was unable to engage the participants and gain their trust. But most of the core members of the Indian diaspora were willing to participate in this project because they wanted to support my research project and they felt that I was studying issues about them. I had developed a close relationship with them, and interviewing for this project was within the boundaries of our relationship. Some of the participants agreed to be interviewed because my project was about "Indian culture," and in addition, they would be paid $50 for their time. Almost all the interviews were conducted at the participants' homes.

Most of the interviews took place over a cup of tea or coffee, and my participants generously extended their "Indian hospitality" to me. My wife was pregnant when I conducted these interviews, and a number of families gave me a container of food to bring to her. They also offered me tips on how my wife could reduce her morning sickness and nausea and gave me a list of foods that would ensure a healthy pregnancy. One Gujarati woman made *dhokla* (a type of sour snack) immediately after the interview because she said that "pregnant women like to eat it." Rohan and his wife, Asha, cooked about four meals for us and brought them to our home. Rohan also often called to find out how my interviews were progressing and gave me names of people whom I did not know and who might be interested in being interviewed.

I usually spent three to four hours on an interview and usually ended having dinner or lunch with the family of the participant. On many occasions, I arrived around noon and left after dinner at around 8:00 P.M. Our conversations were about life in America, work, marriage, children, and movies, and the participants wanted to know about the project, suggested new questions, asked me to alter some questions, and recommended other topics that I should study. At the end of each interview, I asked the participants whether they wanted to add any questions or wanted to make comments about the interview. Most of them thought they had covered everything that seemed important. But very often, the most interesting segments of the interview came after the tape recorder had been switched off. We would be eating dinner, and the participant would comment on his or her own responses in the interview. These times were especially important because it was then that the participants often offered insights into their life experiences in America that they were hesitant to have recorded on tape.

Accordingly, Visweswaran's research forces us to question how we characterize the relationship between the researcher and the researched ethnography. We learn from her ethnography that all "identities are multiple, contradictory, partial and strategic" (1994, p. 50). That is, the participant's or the subject's narrative is made up of contradictory social and political elements. Thus anyone concerned with the role of agency in cultural psychology should read these narratives as being constituted by and expressive of the larger ideologies but not yet marked by an individual sense of agency.

Doing ethnography in the field implies looking at knowledge as relational; that is, where who said what to whom is equally important to understanding how cultural knowledge is produced. From this perspective, power is crucial to structuring the relationships between those who write about culture and those whose lives make up a culture. Cultural knowledge is produced at the overlapping points of the relationship between the participants and the researcher's relationships with them. Thus, ethnographic knowledge about cultures is produced at the intersection of several relationships in the field: relationships marked by silences, subversions, resistance, and betrayals between the researcher and the subject. As Visweswaran claims about her ethnography,

> Here truth is refracted through a series of unequal relationships of power: that between me and Uma, me and Janaki; between Uma and Janaki, Janaki and Tangam. Janaki's reluctance to speak is framed by Tangam's betrayal of her and her own betrayal of Uma. Interpretation was now seriated through a chain of relationships. (1994, p. 51)

My Representation and Analysis of
Interviews and Field Notes

While doing my fieldwork and interviews, I felt accountable to my participants, as there were many moments when I felt this project was also about my own community and myself. Sometimes I was plagued with doubts. How should I portray these participants? Am I getting the right responses? Am I being too harsh? Am I too friendly and too gentle with them? Am I spending too much or too little time in the field? Am I portraying them too negatively? Why are they denying their "brownness"? In other words, I was concerned with my representation of my participants' culture, identities, and voices. Likewise, feminist anthropologists writing about culture have been concerned about their accountability to their participants and their audience. The problem for both the "halfies" (those with multiple cultural identities and selfhood) and feminists are their concerns about speaking to multiple audiences and communities and being accountable to those different communities (Abu-Lughod 1991). The notion of accountability with which feminist anthropologists have been wrestling has implications for cultural psychology as well. Because cultural psychologists belong to one or more communities and do research on their own or other communities in their own country or abroad, they also must be accountable to their participants. Abu-Lughod (1991) noted that unlike other anthropologists, feminist anthropologists are writing not just for one audience but are accountable to both feminists and anthropologists.

Abu-Lughod argues that when halfies and feminist ethnographers represent the "other," they are essentially describing and "representing themselves, they speak with a complex awareness of and investment in reception." Both the halfies and feminist anthropologists force cultural psychology "to confront squarely the politics and ethics of representations." She writes that contrary to other anthropologists' work in Western societies, feminists and halfies are aware that their self-other relationships are shaped by power. Women anthropologists, foreigners, and others with a hybrid and multiracial heritage who live and work in the West are likely to experience sexism, racism, ethnic discrimination, and other forms of "othering" as a result of living and working in the West. Thus, Abu-Lughod observes that because both feminists and halfies inhabit split subjectivities, they "travel uneasily between speaking 'for' and speaking 'from.'" This uneasy transition between positions of speaking "for" and speaking "from" is at the crux of much theorizing about culture and self in feminist anthropology and is expressed through heterogeneous genres of writing (1991, p. 142).

Ethnography and Anthropological
Readings of Culture

The new anthropology incorporates the writing genres offered by other disciplines such as cultural criticism, semiotics, practice-based theories, and literature. For example, Clifford (1986) contends that cultural descriptions of customs or the everyday patterns of a community are appealing not just because they are well written or conform to a particular genre of writing. Rather, he asserts, there is a certain "literariness" to all these accounts. The literary devices of metaphor, narrative, plot, drama, and character shape the writing of cultural events "from the first jotted 'observations' to the completed book, to the ways the configurations 'make sense' in determined acts of reading" (Clifford 1986, p. 4).

The books *Writing Culture* (Clifford and Marcus 1986) and *Women Writing Culture* (Behar and Gordon 1995) emphasize that literary convention permeates the entire process of cultural representation. We know well from different strands of narrative research in cultural psychology that ethnographic accounts are constructed and tell particular stories (see Bruner 1986, 1990). But feminist ethnography goes a step further and "calls attentions to its own textuality, how different narrative strategies may be authorized at specific moments in history by complex negotiations of community, identity, and accountability. Fiction, as we know, is political" (Visweswaran 1994, p. 15).

For example, Visweswaran's (1994) writing employs a variety of narrative strategies to question the canon in anthropology. In her writing, she represents herself as a hyphenated ethnographer speaking from multiple locations and practices. Her writing, as she observes, aims to understand identities as located in cultures that are not essential but conjectural. This conjecturalist approach to ethnographic writing about identity emphasizes the conditional and the contingent. The conjecturalist approach to feminist writing is used to "describe moments, social formations, subject positions, and practice which arise out of an unfolding axis of colonization/decolonization, interwoven with the unfolding of other axes, in uneven, unequal relations with one another" (Visweswaran 1994, p. 12). Such an approach to framing questions about culture and human development in cultural psychology pushes the subject into the very act of writing, thinking, and reading about cultures.

Feminists anthropologists have theorized about writing in anthropology that shows one's vulnerability. For example, a number of writers in the *Women Writing Culture* project move away from a depersonalized, objective genre of writing and instead resort to a kind of creative writing that includes stories, autobiography, memoirs, poetry, fiction, and their own emotions. These representations of oneself, others, and cultural realities through the new genre of life history, autoethnography, and personal narratives add a personal and intimate dimension to ethnographic descriptions of cultures. One of the goals of *Women Writing Culture* was to show how the field of feminist anthropology experiments with creative textual strategies and techniques. The book's dialogical, multivoiced perspective is revealed in the "biographical, historical and literary essay, fictions, autobiography, theater, poetry, life stories, travelogues[, and] social criticism" (Behar and Gordon 1995, p. xii).

The editors acknowledge that the book was drafted as a feminist response to *Writing Culture* but that in the end, it goes beyond its original agenda. The writing in this volume is marked by theoretical overtures, poetry, and prose and demonstrates how the subject and content of the anthropology have been shaped by the form and flow of their writing. Behar writes that feminists' use of a variety of research is "always about a new way of looking at all categories, not just at 'woman'" (1995, p. 6). The reluctance to see creative writing as separate from critical writing is an important move in feminist anthropology and reminds cultural psychologists of the power of describing the cultural activities and the linguistic, social, and historical practices through multiple modes of writing.

The concept of self-reflexivity is central in this ethnography and also has shaped my interpretation and analyses of identity formation in the Indian diaspora. The ethnographic approach has allowed me to make meaningful links between culture and identity, especially how race and class are already constituted in the participants' various social and cultural locations. Clifford tells us that the dominant metaphor in classical anthropology assumes an outsider looking in, observing, gazing, and constructing knowledge about the other. From the standpoint of self-reflexivity, what becomes evident to anyone working with the concept of culture is that "every version of an 'other' where ever found, is also the construction of a 'self' . . . Cultural *poesis*—and politics—is the constant reconstitution of selves and other through specific exclusions, conventions, and discursive practices" (Clifford 1986, p. 23). The shifting cultural meanings of identity construction in the Indian diaspora emerged from self-reflexive "partial truths" (Clifford 1986, p. 7) and "positioned truths" (Abu-Lughod 1991, p. 142). Fieldwork, participant observation, and the interview data gave me the lens through which I formed "partial" representations of my participants.

3

■　■　■　■　■　■　■　■　■

Des-Pardes in the American Suburbia

*Narratives from the Suburban
Indian Diaspora*

In the last decade, there has been a growing interest in researching and studying the concept of diaspora.[1] This outpouring of scholarship
has led to a proliferation of terms—such as *borderlands, travel, hybrid,*
and *hyphenated identities*—to explain the rapid back-and-forth movement
of people across nations. The ever expanding literature on transnationalism and diaspora has created an "unruly crowd of descriptive/interpre-
tive terms" that attempt to describe the processes of travel, displacement,
and migration (Clifford 1994, p. 302). Indeed, terms related to diaspora
have become a new "mantra" in many disciplines and are being used to
address issues of transnational migration and the cultural, economic, and
political formations accompanying this back-and-forth movement (Anthias 1998a).

For example, Kivisto (2001) provides a critical analysis of contemporary theories of diaspora and transnational migration by grouping them
according to perspectives from various fields like cultural anthropology,
sociology, and political theory. Other scholars, such as Anthias (1998a,
2001), analyze the theories of transnationalism and diasporic identities
from the perspectives of fields like sociology and cultural studies, and

Kearney draws on the perspectives offered by "non-Western transnational feminists on global theories and local feminists identities" (1995, p. 560). In addition, scholars who combine the fields of communication and post-colonial studies have examined how colonial and neocolonial practices and policies intermingle with the current transnational migratory experience of the diaspora and globalization practices (Hegde 1998; Shome 1996; Shome and Hegde 2002).

In this chapter, I use the concept of diaspora as an interpretive and heuristic device for analyzing concepts of identity, self, community, and belonging in the Indian migrant community. I begin by differentiating the term *diaspora as a typology* from *diaspora as a condition*. This distinction was formulated by the sociologist Floya Anthias (1998a) and is a useful way of delineating the term's various complexities and nuances in different disciplines. I use the personal stories and narratives of the post-1965 Indian diaspora to show that the waves of highly skilled immigrants benefited from certain migration laws and the racial inequalities between the majority and domestic minority groups. A brief glimpse into the immigration history of Indian immigrants before and after 1965 helps clarify the shifting web of meanings associated with class, ethnic, and racial identity in the middle-class Indian diaspora. The ways in which the Indian migrants understand themselves and give meaning to their lives abroad is intricately connected to this history.

Finally, this chapter tries to capture the "lived experiences" of the participants of the Indian diaspora by describing the circumstances of their immigration to the United States. These brief stories clarify the social-class backgrounds of the first generation of Indian professionals to migrate to America. The stories not only explain their reasons for immigrating but also tell us how their lives unfolded in their first months and years in America. These stories of arrival are closely connected to the participants' class positions, family history, and educational experiences in India.

Kachig Tölöyan (1996), editor of the journal *Diaspora*, traced the genealogy of the term *diaspora* and explained its implications for any study of cultural differences. He observes that whereas once the term was used to refer to the migrations of Jewish populations, it now refers to a broad range of dislocations of several groups of people. The term *diaspora* has been increasingly used in both scholarly discourse and the larger lay community. Tölöyan attributes the expanding usage of this term partly to the acceleration of immigration to the industrialized world; to many immigrant groups' lack of assimilation; to their institutional links with the homeland; to their work to create and maintain their own religious institutions, language schools, community centers, newspapers, and radio stations; and to the American university itself, where many diasporan elites have converged to forge theoretical sites to address immigrant identity and transnationalism.

Tölöyan (1996) argues that given the increase in travel, media, and communication technology, more and more immigrants can be considered to be living in diasporas. Similarly, Appadurai writes that mass migrations, both voluntary and forced, are not new in human history. However, he contends, "when it is juxtaposed with mass mediated images, scripts, and sensations, we have a new order of instability in the production of modern subjectivities. . . . These create diasporic public spheres, phenomena that confound theories that depend on the continued salience of the nation-state" (1996, p. 40).

The configuration of the concept of homeland in the imagination of the diasporic community helps distinguish it from the concept of homeland for refugees, tourists, and immigrants. A useful way to talk about diaspora is to examine it as a typology, a descriptive term, or a "condition" produced through and embedded in particular historical, sociocultural, economic, and political experiences of movement, dislocation, and displacement (Anthias 1998a; Brah 1996; Vertovec 1999).

Diaspora as a Typology

The classical notion of diaspora as a typology implies a forced scattering and traumatic dispersal of people, as stated in the book of Deuteronomy. *Babylonian exile,* especially, are code words in Jewish history and folklore associated with the experience of alienation, exile, oppression, and rootlessness. Cohen reminds us that although the word *Babylon* "connotes captivity and oppression, a rereading of the Babylonian period of exile" epitomizes the creation of a civilization that becomes transformed as a locus of art, learning and culture (1997, p. 4).

Scholars mapping an objective or classical definition of diaspora often work from a list of features or qualities that have become the criteria for defining the boundaries of the concept of diaspora. For example, according to Safran (1991), members of a diasporic community (1) share a history of being dispersed from a common point of origin or homeland, (2) construct memories of the homeland and express a deep longing for the eventual return to their homeland, (3) often experience discrimination and marginality in their new location, and (4) maintain a sense of collective consciousness and solidarity with one another.

The "expatriate minority community" is transformed into a diaspora because the dispersed members make a collective effort to build a shared identity based primarily on their memories, identification, and desire to return to that homeland. The Jewish diaspora exemplifies all these classical features of a diaspora, which have been increasingly used to understand the formation of the Greek, Armenian, and African diaspora in different parts of the world. Clifford contends that Safran's objectivist criteria for identifying groups as diasporas are based on an "ideal type" that mainly fits the Jewish diaspora and that not all diasporas or stories of displacement and violent dispersal are based on a "teleology of return" (Clifford 1994, p. 306).

Clifford (1994) also points to South Asian and African diasporas in the United States and Britain and argues that these dispersed communities are not necessarily seeking an eventual return to their homeland but are mainly interested in maintaining and creating the culture they left behind.[2]

Cohen (1997) agrees with Clifford's (1994) recommendations and suggests that W. Safran's (1991) description of a diaspora may be too limited to accommodate the contemporary migration of the various transnational ethnic groups who have multiple dwellings, homes, and identities. Cohen is open to incorporating the experiences and patterns of transnational immigrants, but he believes that a descriptive typology of diaspora is important to narrowing the domain of diaspora. He thus builds on and modifies Safran's typology of diaspora to contain nine features: (1) being traumatically moved from one's homeland to more than two foreign regions; (2) being uprooted from one's homeland for economic opportunities; (3) retaining a collective memory of the homeland; (4) idealizing the homeland; (5) wanting to return eventually to the homeland; (6) having an ethnic consciousness and feeling of solidarity; (7) feeling marginalized and alienated in the host society; (8) feeling a sense of community with fellow ethnics settled in other foreign locations; and (9) believing in the promise of a rich, imaginative, and inventive life in the host country.

After discussing these features of a diaspora, Cohen (1997) formulates five typologies of diaspora: victim, labor, trade, imperial, and cultural, and he uses Jews, Africans, and Armenians as examples of victim diasporas. Indians represent the labor diaspora; the British exemplify the imperial diaspora; the Chinese and Lebanese are examples of trading diasporas; and Caribbean people signify the cultural diaspora. But Cohen does believe that diasporas cannot be segmented into strict boundaries and acknowledges that these typologies overlap, as some can be both a labor and a cultural diaspora.

According to Anthias (1998a), several conceptual problems with this typological or descriptive approach make it difficult to understand the term *diaspora*. First, she points out that Cohen's typology is based on an inductive form of thinking, stating that "in allocating a group to one of the types, there is a reliance, essentially and foremost on the origins or the intentionality of dispersal" (1998a, p. 563). Furthermore, Anthias notes that some of the types are based on the group's occupation and that others are based on the experience of violent displacement. Still others are based on colonization or invasion. This analysis of types of diasporas based on occupation or various other modes of dispersal does not explain, however, the "accommodation patterns [or] their forms of identity" in their foreign locations (Anthias 1998a, p. 563). Second, Anthias writes that lurking beneath the typological approaches, as reflected in Cohen's and Safran's work, is the idea that the diaspora is formed through some sort of a primordial attachment with home and that such a bonding of the members produces a homogenous community with no divisions and differences.

What the descriptive framework of diaspora does not explain is the fact that various members of the diaspora may have different collective representations of the diasporic community and may use different cultural symbols to organize the cultural practices of their homeland. In turn, the performance of diverse cultural rituals and routines may give rise to a sense of ethnic identity that incorporates notions of race, class, and gender in radically different ways. What the typological approaches do not mention, Anthias (1998a) asserts, is the way in which the different diaspora groups are socially positioned to one another within and between groups and also in relation to the larger society of their homeland.

In contrast to the typological approaches to diaspora, some scholars (Brah 1996; Chow 1993; Clifford 1994; Gilroy 1987; Hall 1990, 1991a) argue that the notion of diaspora based on links to common origins and physical geography or a symbolic map of the homeland may be as important as a diasporic identity based on a shared condition of displacement and experiences of exclusion, alienation, and resistance in the new homeland.[3]

Diaspora as a Condition

Anthias (1998a) explains that the diasporic condition is not created only as a result of movement and displacement but is also intricately interwoven with the cultural shifts in both the modern and the postmodern worlds. She explains that the diasporic condition

> is put into play through the experience of being *from* one place and of another, and it is identified with the idea of particular sentiments towards the homeland, whilst being formed by those of the place of settlement. This place is one where one is constructed in and through *difference*, and yet is one that produces differential forms of cultural accommodation or syncretism: in some version of hybridity. To treat diaspora as a condition is to pose a problem in terms of the specificities pertaining to the process of territorial and cultural shifts. (Anthias 1998a, pp. 555–566, italics in original)

For many scholars across several disciplines, the concept of diaspora has come to represent a *condition* rather than the properties of a group. Brah (1996) maintains that although the concept of the diaspora invokes images of journeys, not all journeys can be described as diasporas.

Diasporas are not the same as traveling or being a sojourner. Instead, diasporic journeys are about traveling elsewhere and putting down roots. They are about arriving at a new location, settling down, and having a memory and a longing for "elsewhere" or another place. A brief survey of the history of diasporic journeys undertaken by different groups points to both shared and different diasporic moments and trajectories. In some instances, we notice that diasporic communities are established through the colonial experience, as in the formation of multicultural diasporas of people who were once a part of the European colonies and are now working in the various cosmopolitan cites of Europe, like the South Asian diaspora in Britain and the Surinamese community in the Netherlands.

Diasporas also have been formed as a result of slavery and indentured labor, as exemplified by the African and Asian diaspora in the Caribbean and Asian communities. Of course, diasporas associated with persecution and dispersal are widely known, especially in the history of the Jewish and Armenian diasporas. More recent diasporas have been formed as a result of ethnic and political strife, with refugees and groups like the Sri Lankan, Somali, and Bosnian Muslims as examples. New diasporas have been formed from the large-scale movement of both high-tech professionals and unskilled, low-wage labor in the wake of economic globalization (Brah 1996). The Turks in Germany, South Asians in Britain and the United States, and Mexicans and Chinese in the United States have created diasporas resulting from such economic and cultural shifts occurring around the world. Furthermore, as we probe deeper into the cultural formations of the post-1965, mostly non-European immigrant communities, we notice the emergence of a transnational sphere or a transnational moment distinguishing old, ethnic immigrant communities from the new diasporas.

The Indian diaspora in the United States began to emerge as a collective group around the turn of the twentieth century. After 1965, the first wave of professional Indian migrants began to create several diasporic communities in the metropolitan cities of the United States. In the next section we locate the maps and histories that have created the diasporic condition of the Indian migrants in the United States. Because of the many detailed stories and histories regarding the India diaspora in the United States, my objective is to sketch those maps that can augment the "lived experiences" of the middle-class Indian diaspora.

Des(Home)-*Pardes*(Abroad): The Indian Diaspora in the United States

The Indian diaspora in the United States was formed from many arrivals and departures, some of which were imaginary and some based on the material and physical existence of India. The heterogeneous and diverse cultural elements of the Indian diaspora make it difficult to define the concept of Indianness, India, or Indian culture. Indianness, or Indian culture in the diaspora, is obviously connected to the physical map of the Indian homeland, although no single fixed point in that vast geographical location can be used to define it.

Vishal, a sixty-year-old CEO of a management consultant company and one of the participants of my study, reinforced this point. "I so often wonder what is really Indianness? It's very hard for me to really identify what, what makes me an Indian." Despite Vishal's amorphous definitions of Indianness, some participants did define what it means to be Indian. Although they found it hard to define "Indianness," they were able to agree on some common presuppositions concerning India, such as a family's sense of togetherness, hard work, self-sacrificing mentality, and reverence for parents, religious practices, and ancient cultural heritage. They also saw Indianness in individual personality traits and cultural customs, such as eating and marriage rituals, sexual taboos, celebrations of gods and goddesses, and religious festivals.

Overall, the concept of India and Indianness acquires its meanings against the backdrop of both India and America. For instance, Dilip, another participant in my study, stated, "I should say, Indian people are more, kind of, religious minded, compared to what Americans are, I should say, and more family and social oriented, you know?" Similarly, Ashok told me that in America, "you don't have that nurturing environment, and, obviously, a lot of the relationships out here are more professional, and that has a expectation of, 'I'll do this instead, and in return you do this for me.'" In order to understand the formation of self and personhood in the Indian middle-class diaspora, we must situate these new professional, elite immigrant experiences against the history of Indian migration in America.

The Punjabi Diaspora

At the beginning of the twentieth century, one of the first groups of Indian migrants to settle in North America arrived on the Pacific Coast to work on the railroads and in the lumber mills of Bellingham, Washington, near Vancouver. These first Indian workers in North America were Punjabi Sikhs, mostly young farmers and soldiers who had fought in the

British army but did not want to stay in the service. Jensen (1988) writes that these Sikh migrants who worked in Bellingham's lumber mills were paid $2 a day, and over time, they began to be recognized as reliable, hardworking, and efficient. Soon the Punjabi Sikh workers began to replace the white Euro-American workers who, in turn, became increasingly resentful of the migrants and registered their protests with the owners of the mill companies. Furthermore, the white Euro-American workers threatened and/or physically attacked some of the Punjabi workers and even chased them out of the mills. Tuly Singh Johl was one of the original Sikh migrants who worked in the Bellingham mill. He recalled that the mill owner told the Punjabi workers that they should immediately leave because he "feared that his mill would be burned by angry white workers" (Jensen 1988, p. 30). Subsequently, Tuly Singh Johl and many other Sikh workers from these mills moved to Chico, California, and began working there on the railroads.

The first group of Punjabi immigrants came to California's Imperial Valley from Canada down the Pacific coast from British Columbia also to work on the railroads and in the lumbering and agriculture industries. Agriculture was quickly becoming a big business in California, so most of the Sikh migrants left the railroads to work as farmers. Farming wages were competitive, and many of the Sikh migrants were skillful farmers owing to their familiarity with farming in Punjab (Jensen 1988).

The Sikh migration from British Columbia to California also led to an increase in the immigration of Sikh farmers directly from Punjab to California. The young Sikh men who worked in California's cotton plantations and orchards were mostly in their early twenties and came from the Hoshiarpur and Jullundur districts of Punjab. Their reason for migrating to the United States while the British governed India was, as Leonard observed, "primary population pressure, subdivision of land, and rural debt" (1992, p. 29). Initially, many of the Punjabi Sikhs worked in the rural and agricultural areas of California. But then, when faced with racial discrimination, several Punjabi men moved to California's more remote areas and towns. In some of the cities, Punjabi boarding houses were located near Chinatown, and in other places, they shared their accommodations with Chinese, Japanese, and Mexican laborers.

Leonard writes that because Punjabi migrants were not welcomed in California, "they moved in groups, with a 'boss man' who spoke English and contracted for jobs on behalf of the group." The first set of Punjabi migrants found work in the orchards, vineyards, and sugar-beet fields around Marysville, Newcastle, and Vacaville in California. Then they started "working in vineyards in Fresno and citrus groves in Tulare, finally following the annual sequence of harvests, they picked cantaloupes in Imperial valley" (Leonard 1992, p. 32). In addition to these regular jobs, the men also chopped wood, cut and boxed asparagus, picked grapes in the vineyards, and dug potatoes and stones.

The Punjabi men earned between $1.25 and $1.50 a day while working in the agriculture areas of Sacramento and the San Joaquin Valley and soon distinguished themselves as laborers with a good work ethic. Their workday usually began at 4.30 A.M. and ended at 7.30 P.M. (Jensen 1988; Leonard 1992). Through hard work and thrift and with a tight community network, the Sikh farmers rapidly moved from being laborers to leasing land from the local banks. In a few years, the Punjabi diasporas in the agricultural areas of Sacramento, the San Joaquin Valley, and the Imperial Valley began to grow, and the Sikh migrants began to form small residential communities in many parts of California.

By 1912 many of the farmers began to pool their assets and money to lease large acres of agricultural land. They conducted their agriculture business as a collective unit and divided their costs and profits among themselves. The Sikh migrants' business meetings with the bankers usually were carried out through a spokesperson, and they soon earned reputations as excellent negotiators. Some of the Sikh farmers also earned the title of the "Rice Kings of Colusa County" (Jensen 1988, p. 39).

Even though the Punjabi migrants were successful, the prejudice and racial abuse from Americans did not cease. The *Holtville Tribune* in 1910 printed an article on why the Hindus should be barred from settling in California. Indeed, both the people and the press often referred to the Sikh migrants as the "Hindu undesirables," "menace to the whole valley," and "ragheads" (Leonard 1992, pp. 45–49). But when the Punjabi men started to be recognized as good farmers, the attitudes of banks and government officials, and people in general, changed.

Jensen writes that even though the Punjabi farmers gained economic acceptance in society, they usually were segregated from both the mainstream Anglo society and other ethnic communities living on the margins. Thus the Sikh men circulated among themselves and stayed away from the Japanese and Chinese communities. The Japanese, Jensen (1988) notes, insulted the Sikhs by calling them "English slaves," but the Punjabi Sikhs were more readily accepted in the Mexican American and African American communities. A few Punjabis worked in the cities by passing as Mexicans or blacks, because they believed that the Anglos were likely to be more prejudiced against Punjabi Sikhs. Over time, the incidents of overt racism, harassment, and prejudice against the Sikhs waned, and these strange-looking foreign men with "rags" and "towels on their heads" were less "despised" and even began to be perceived as "dependable" neighbors (Leonard 1992, p. 59).

The Alien Land Law of California, passed in 1913, prevented all foreigners and noncitizens from owning or leasing land, although in a very few cases, the Punjabi farmers were able to buy land by marrying Mexican women. Most Sikh farmers were able to circumvent the law by forming business partnerships with Anglo lawyers and judges in California and Arizona, by "working out verbal understandings with Anglo farmers, bankers, lawyers, who held land in their own names for Punjabi farmers. The director of the Holtville Bank did this, 'earning for his bank the name Hindu Bank'" (Leonard 1992, p. 52).

Because most of the states had miscegenation laws, Sikh men were barred from marrying white women. So increasingly, the Punjabi men married Mexican women, who had been uprooted by the Mexican revolution and were working in Southern California's cotton plantations. The number of Punjabi-Mexican marriages grew rapidly and expanded into a complex network of relationships. Ninety-three percent of the wives of Punjabi men in the Imperial Valley were Hispanic. Leonard (1992) writes that most of these marriages involved some courtship, and women had some choice of whom they would marry. Later, as the Punjabi-Mexican diaspora expanded, the Mexican women helped arrange marriages for their friends with eligible Punjabi men. The marriages between Punjabi men and Mexican women were characterized by love, convenience, loyalty, familial ties, and religious, linguistic, and cultural differences.

In 1917, Congress passed the Barred Zone Act, which prevented all Asians (except Filipinos) from entering the United States. Subsequently, the Indian migration to the United States almost completely halted. According to Rangaswamy,

By 1930s, Indians in the United States were mostly Pacific coast farmers, numbering roughly 3,000. There were about another 1,000 skilled workers, merchants and traders in the United States. Others in the Indian immigrant category included about five hundred students scattered throughout the United States, and 25 to 30 swamis or holy men. (2000, p. 43)

A small but dedicated group of Indian students in California instigated nationalist activities against the British Raj, and some of these university students and farmers on the West Coast formed a party called Ghadar (meaning "rebellion" or "revolution") to dethrone the imperial power of the British.

The Ghadar Party at Berkeley

The Ghadar Party was inspired by the 1857 Sepoy Rebellion against the British.[4] The purpose of the party and the newspaper, also entitled *Ghadar*, was announced as follows:

> Today in a foreign country, but in the language of our own country, we start a war against the British Raj. What is our name? *Ghadar*. What is our work? *Ghadar*. Where will *Ghadar* break out? In India. The time will come when rifles and blood will take place of pen and ink. (Prashad 2000, p. 127)

Several courageous Punjabi migrants helped keep the Ghadar Party alive and functioning. Baba Sohan Singh was an important member of the party, and when he arrived in Seattle from Punjab, the immigration officer questioned him about the polygamy and polyandry that were practiced in some parts of Punjab. Because Sohan Singh did not directly deny knowing about these cultural practices, the officer asked how he could deny believing in such marital practices if they existed in his village. To this, Sohan Singh remarked, "Everyone has the right to reject a particular tradition or custom which he does not like" (Prashad 2000, p. 127). Prashad considers Sohan Singh's statement as testimony to the bravery and the radical culture of the Ghadar Party.

Similarly, other important members of the party, such as Bud Dhillon and Kartar Dhillon, shared Sohan Singh's fierce nationalism and radical anti-British feeling. In November 1913 another loyal member and organizer of the Ghadar Party, Har Dayal, placed an advertisement in the first issue of *Ghadar* that read, "Wanted Brave soldiers to stir up *Ghadar* in India, pay-Death, Praise-martyrdom, Pension-Liberty, Field of Battle-India" (Jensen 1988, p. 183). Har Dayal used these militant anti-British slogans to mobilize the members of the Ghadar Party and to make people aware of their political rights and the oppressive rule of the British Empire.

In 1914, some important members of the Ghadar Party about to travel from San Francisco to Calcutta to start a rebellion in Punjab were arrested for "violating the American neutrality law." Soon thereafter the Ghadar Party lost both its popularity and its influence (Helweg and Helweg 1990, p. 50). The Ghadarites were not the only Indian migrants who battled with the local and federal governments about their revolutionary beliefs; a few other Indian migrants also were waging a battle in American courts, but this battle was slightly different.

Some Indian migrants fought in the American courts to qualify as Caucasians so they could be granted U.S. citizenship. Rangaswamy (2000) writes that based on the cases of *The United States v. Balsara* (1910) and *A. Kumar Mazumdar* (1913), the U.S. Supreme Court decided that Indians could be American citizens because they were now categorized as Caucasians and therefore white. Based on this ruling, nearly one hundred Indians were granted citizenship between 1913 and 1923. Later, however, that citizenship was taken away because of a new U.S. Supreme Court ruling. Rangaswamy explains:

> Then in a dramatic reversal in the *Bhagat Singh Thind* case, Justice George Sutherland ruled that being Caucasian was not enough to be white. Following this ruling the U.S. government revoked the citizenship of some fifty Indians. Aware that many Indians were unwelcome in the United States, some 3000 India left for India between 1920 and 1940. (2000, p. 44)

The year 1946 is an important milestone in the history of Indian migration because in that year Congress passed the Luce-Celler Bill. This bill qualified Indians to become U.S. citizens, and as a result of these new rights, they could own property and land and bring family members to the states.

It is interesting that the Punjabi-Mexican community "chose" to give their own ethnic meaning to their group. Although outsiders saw them as Hindu Mexicans, they saw themselves as Hindus rather than Mexicans. This reinterpretation of their ethnicity as Hindu exemplifies Mary Waters's (1990) point that although outsiders or the state may assign a certain ethnicity to a group of people, many migrants decide to select certain parts of their ancestry over others and thus choose their "ethnic options." We also should recognize the working-class backgrounds of the first Indian immigrants to the United States. The journey of the Punjabi diaspora shows us that they were inserted into the racist, multicultural discourses that existed at the turn of the twentieth century. Indeed, these Punjabi men were some of the first Indians to be collectively discriminated against and racialized as a group. As a result, they faced enormous physical hardships and mental anguish and lived mostly on the margins of society.

The collective determination of the diasporic members allowed them to eke out a space for themselves where they could assert their cultural identities, reimagine their home, and reconstitute their identities as Punjabi Mexicans. These Punjabi Sikhs in the United States were labeled "foreigners," "coolies," "English slaves," "Hindu untouchables," and "ragheads," a new minority identity that was radically different from that as rural farmers of Punjab, India. Many of these Sikh migrants were not, by any means, wealthy or even middle class, but before their migration, they had never been subjected to this kind of alienating "otherness" in their homeland. The Punjabi Sikh migrants were now living in a society in which their beards, turbans, *kirpans,* brown skin, language, religion, and customs were seen as strange, exotic, backward, and primitive. The story of the Punjabi Sikh diaspora, like the stories of many other diasporas, reminds us that when referring to an immigrant's acculturation, we must be attentive to issues of race, gender, and religion, and we must also understand the immigrant's status both before and after migration to the host country.

The acculturation process in the United States has a different developmental trajectory if, say, the migrant were part of a powerful center or majority in his or her local milieu before migration and found himself or herself to be a part of a minority living on the margins after migration. As Frankenberg and Mani (1993) allege, race and gender are crucial signifiers of our locations and positions either in the center or on the margins. We use these signifiers to identify ourselves and our selfhood, and others as well use them to identify us. They describe several personal incidents to demonstrate that modes of othering and racialization are inseparable from the everyday experiences of a non-European/nonwhite immigrant in the United States.

In general, gender is rarely paid much attention when theorizing about the acculturation process. Cultural groups are often regarded in homogeneous terms, and the particular experiences of women are ignored. If considered, gender usually is given the status of a variable that is uniformly present in all cultures. Buijs (1993) observed that in studies of migrancy until the mid-1970s, women were invisible. Even contemporary scholars have made few attempts to examine the particular experiences and responses of immigrant women as they deal with dislocation and displacement. Instead, most of the literature in psychology that deals with immigration is centered on men, and the guiding assumption generally has been that women's experiences are either identical to men's or simply not important enough to warrant inclusion. Espín (1999) complained that gendered migrant experiences were understudied, and her most recent work is an attempt to redress this problem. By focusing on the lived experiences of immigrant women, she provides very localized, detailed, and illuminating analyses of how immigrant women negotiate with their gender and sexual identity.

Thinking about gender in relation to migration forces us to abandon our universal models of acculturation. Similarly, we need to recognize that both old and new immigrants, whether they are labeled as Asian Americans, Europeans, Caribbeans, Latino/as, or Chicano/as, are socially and historically positioned to one another and to the dominant groups in the United States. When we adhere to universal models of acculturation, we undervalue the asymmetrical relations of power and the inequities and injustices faced by certain immigrant groups as a result of their nationality, race, or gender. The history of the Punjabi migrants shows us that being labeled an "other" or racialized is part of many non-European immigrants' acculturation experience and closely connected to the migrants' evolving conceptions of selfhood. These experiences are revealed in both everyday, routine intercultural encounters and a government's or a state's history of laws regarding nationality, citizenship, and immigration.

Migration Laws, Race, and "Third World" Diasporas

The United States' immigration and citizenship policies over the last two hundred years fostered "racial regimes" intended to keep "slaves," "indentured laborers," and non-European "foreigners" as aliens and outsiders (Mohanty 1991, pp. 23–25). Furthermore, Mohanty suggests that the history of immigration and naturalization in the United States parallels the racialization leading to the annihilation of Native Americans, the history of slavery, and the civil rights movement. When comparing the history of the immigration of European people with the history of the immigration of "people of color" to the United States, Mohanty found patterns in the immigration and citizenship laws for both the European and non-European groups that were based on racial heritage and the "economic exigencies of " the state (1991, p. 24).

Mohanty observes that in the nineteenth century, White, Negro, and Indian were the three racial categories used in the labor market. Only after the "1848 treaty of Guadalupe Hidalgo" were Mexicans given the status of free laborers who could take a variety of jobs anywhere in the country (Mohanty 1991, p. 24). And it was only in 1854 that the U.S. Supreme Court decided that the Chinese, who mainly worked as cheap labor in exploitative conditions on the West Coast, could be included under the category of "Indian."[5] The U.S. immigration laws also influenced the day-to-day lives of the immigrant workers. Their effects could be seen in the configurations of immigrant families (in some cases, women and children could not migrate) and, in the end, set firm boundaries between outsiders and insiders, First World immigrants and Third World immigrants, and natives and foreigners. Such outside-inside relationships among different immigrants were maintained through a series of U.S.-sponsored exclusionary acts.

The Chinese Exclusion Act was passed in 1882 in response to the perception that Chinese immigrants were culturally unassimilable (Sharpe 1995), and in 1907 a "gentleman's agreement" limited Japanese immigration. In 1917 Asian Indian immigrants were restricted. In 1924 the Oriental Exclusion Act suspended labor immigration from mainland Asia, and in 1934 the Tydings-McDuffie Act restricted Filipino immigration to the United States (Mohanty 1991). Between 1924 and 1943 citizenship through naturalization was denied to all Asians. The main reason for these exclusion acts was to contain the flow of non-European immigrants and to allow "in" only enough to meet the demands of the fluctuating labor markets in the United States. Later, in the 1960s when the U.S. labor markets needed highly qualified and skillful workers, immigration laws allowed a few technically well-trained and highly educated professionals. Sharpe notes that policymakers did not anticipate that the new laws would dramatically shift immigration demographics, making the "new immigrants" primarily Asians, Central Americans, Mexicans, and Caribbeans. Rather, they viewed these reforms as a "social redress of Catholics and Jews from southern and eastern Europe" who were affected by the 1965 Immigration and Nationality Act (Sharpe 1995, p. 188). Thus historically, the U.S. state-sponsored immigration, naturalization, and citizenship laws were based on racist ideologies that helped shape and define the acculturation experiences of many Third World non-European immigrants. Furthermore, this stereotyping and racializing was directly connected to the economic conditions in the United States.

With the passage of the Immigration and Nationality Act of 1965, most of the new Indian migrants arriving in America were highly talented professional or technical workers, and within a relatively short time, they became known for their hard work, merit, and ability to adapt to the changing work environment in the United States. Helweg and Helweg were among the first scholars to write a comprehensive book on the life of successful Indian professionals in the United States. The new Indian migrants in

> America, in a short time, obtained prominent or dominant positions in many areas of the culture. . . . They have made inroads into medical, engineering, scientific, and other professional fields.. . . Indians are evident or dominant in particular area of business enterprise.. . . In fact, they operate 28 percent (15,000) of the nations' 53,629 motels and hotels. (1990, p. 156)

The success story of the post-1965 migrants of the Indian diaspora made them model minorities in the United States, and the language of the model minority discourse became the criterion by which Indian immigrants began to measure their rapid success in America.

▪

The next section describes the lived experiences of professional elite migrants living in a Connecticut suburb. These stories also reveal the extent to which America and "American culture" were already part of the lives of these migrants before they arrived in America. These stories point to the specific personal, familial, and cultural conditions under which Indian migrants began traveling to their future diasporas.

Narratives from an Indian Diaspora in Suburban Connecticut

Most of the men and women of the post-1965 Indian migration came from middle-class families and had resided in small towns and cities. The salaries of the parents of these migrants were modest, but they invested heavily in the education of their children. Even though some of the family members of these migrants were wealthy, almost all of them were able to come to the United States only because they were given tuition waivers, full scholarships, teaching stipends, and other fellowships by American universities. Once these professional migrants had enrolled in American universities, they began to rely on their advanced education, educational competence, professional networks, strong work ethic, and savings to build their economic and cultural capital. The members of the post-1965 migration "came without access to or holding large amounts of capital (in dollars), thereby ensuring their place in the middle class was to be secured entirely by current income (and the moderate saving from that income)" (Prashad 2000, p. 101).

Most of my conversations with the participants would begin with the following open-ended statement: "I came to America because . . ." They would then fill in the blank with a word or a sentence, and I would follow up with a question or comment and ask them probing questions about their statement. Next is an excerpt from my conversation with Rohan:

> *I*: The first one, I came to America because . . .
> *R*: Because my father said so . . . (laughter)

I had a general sense of why some of the participants had come to the United States, but the open-ended statement forced the men and women of this diaspora to describe not only why they came to America but also their cultural and familial circumstances before coming to the United States. This information about professional Indian migrants is important because it reveals their level of preparedness and readiness for working and living in American culture. The remainder of my interview with Rohan sheds light on his personal circumstances in Delhi and also how those circumstances laid the groundwork for a successful life in America.

"Will You Teach Me How to Make Rice?"
Coming to America

Rohan, forty-nine years old, comes from Delhi, where he had just finished his bachelor of science degree at Delhi University in the early 1970s when his father told him that he should go to the United States to go to graduate school. Rohan recalled that his father got him the college and university application forms but he never filled them out. He also remembered in vivid detail the obstacles he faced when he finally made up his mind to study in an American university. Although he did get a loan to come to the United States, his admission to a large university on the East Coast still was not final. The Parsee Trust in Delhi, which gave Rohan his scholarship, was concerned about his admission status. In other words, he had received a scholarship to study in the United States but had not yet been admitted to an American university. Rohan explained:

> They said, "Everybody is going to the U.S. in the fall, when are you going?" I said, "I guess in January." I had just mailed the application the day before the interview for the scholarship, so I had money but no admission. Then I got admission, but my GRE got messed up.

Later, Rohan told me that on the day he was going to take his TOEFL exams, his train did not show up on time. He had his GRE scores, his scholarship money, and a tentative "yes" from the university on the East Coast, but he did not have his TOEFL scores. The university made it clear to Rohan that it would not send him a final admission letter until he had taken his TOEFL exams.

Not knowing how to proceed, Rohan went to the American consulate in Delhi, and at the end of a ten-minute interview with an officer at the consulate, he was told, "I think you can go to the U.S. to study." The officer who interviewed Rohan was convinced of his proficiency in English. He was ready to make his trip to the United States. As Rohan was walking out of the consulate, he realized that he had exactly fourteen days to prepare for what was going to be one of the most significant journeys of his life. He was both anxious and excited about the possibility of studying abroad as well as overwhelmed by the prospect of leaving his homeland with barely two weeks to prepare:

> You have to get your visa. You have to get your foreign exchange stuff. You have to get a ticket, and you have to get your stuff together. I had never flown, I had never been outside India, and I'd never seen snow. In one twenty-four-hour period, all of that happened, and all of a sudden, I was sitting on a plane, heading for the U.S., and when I got here . . . New York was coming out of a big snowstorm.

The story that Rohan told about coming to America was very similar to the immigration stories of several of the other members of the community. Although they varied in content, characters, and place, all the stories had the same goal: to tell the migrant's humble, middle-class beginnings and the struggles they underwent in India in order to come to the United States.

The post-1965 professional migrants in my study were mainly professionals with limited incomes, and most of them had never before traveled abroad. This was the first major international travel experience for many Indians of the postindependence generation, and the memories of leaving home, their friends, and their family were still vivid. Rohan continued: "I never really cooked back home, but finally when I was leaving, I asked my mom, 'Will you teach me how to make rice?' She started crying. I said, 'Don't worry, I'll figure it out.' That's what happened. The first couple of times the rice was burned or not cooked." Unlike the first wave of Punjabi working-class and labor migrants, these Indian migrant students were going straight into the safety of the university culture, which gave them some protection and insulation from the harsh realities of being a foreigner in American culture.

Rohan recalled his first trip to his academic department when he arrived at his university. "By the time I walked from the bus stop to the department, my teeth were frozen. I tried to speak to the secretary and I could not speak. . . . She brought a warm cup of tea or coffee or something and helped me thaw, and then I went to work."[6]

The post-1965 generation was part of a tradition in India in which parents pressure their children to excel in school. These migrants had been well taught to appreciate education and, more specifically, the power of science. They had graduated from "English-speaking schools" that placed a very high degree of importance on math and science education. Accordingly, these professional, middle-class, post-1965 Indian immigrants had a rather smooth and unproblematic entry into the American culture, as their exceptional talents and abilities protected them from the hardships that many working-class, low-skilled migrants face in the United States. Rohan wrote to his family about what it felt like to sit in the morning on a cold toilet seat, to ride in fast cars, and to smell the exhaust from cars speeding on the highway.

I commiserated with Rohan and told him about my experiences as a new graduate student at my university. For the first couple of semesters, I remember walking around feeling very out of place in my new cultural surroundings. On many days, the nostalgia and longing for home—food, friends, and crowds—seemed overpowering. But Rohan disagreed. "I was never depressed about it. It was more subconscious pressure that there is really no going back. You have to accomplish the goal that you set out for." Indeed, many of the first-generation immigrants in my study reported that they focused on the goal of succeeding in America and the idea of not being able to return home.

"Yeah, I Had a Scholarship There": The PhD Generation

The transition from a modest lifestyle in India to that in an American university gave the Indian students time and space to understand how the American educational system functioned. During their time in the university, they acquired the basic skills and understanding of the social and cultural codes making up the diversity of American culture. Consider, for example, my conversation with Prashant, a forty-nine-year-old senior computer programmer, who works for a computer corporation. I asked him about his first months and years in the United States. Prashant said he went to a state university in the Midwest. When I asked him how he got there, Prashant replied in matter-of-fact tone, "Yeah. I had a scholarship there. That's where I did my PhD."

Although Prashant had been in the United States for more than twenty years, I asked him to describe his first experiences in America. He said that America had been a new experience for him and not very different from the America experienced now by many new Indian graduate students. He elaborated, "Number one, you're trying to make sure the school part is taken care of. Number two, you're trying to figure out what America is all about, you know? What the system is . . ." For most Indian graduate students, taking care of academics and schoolwork comes rather easily. They are fluent in English, and within a few semesters, most of the Indian students impress their advisers and professors. Rather, in the first few years, their main concern is doing well and proving to their professors and peers that they deserve their scholarship. As they are becoming acquainted with the American educational system, they also are trying to understand the nuances and complexities of American culture. Understanding the American way of life is not always easy, and some of these students had to learn American cultural codes through trial and error.

Prashant's first cultural encounter with America occurred as soon as he stepped off the plane. After arriving at the airport, he went immediately to a cafeteria and asked the server behind the counter to give him a Coke from the soft-drink machine.

> So I went and I stood in the line. I asked for a Coke. [The server] was a big, tall, black guy. He picked up a cup, filled it fully with crushed ice, and then started adding the soda to it. I thought he was pulling a fast one on me. I said, "I didn't want the ice, you know, take it out." So he looked at me strangely, and he was wondering, you know, "Why can't he fill his own soda, and, on top of that when I give it to him, he is asking me to take out the ice."

In India during the 1970s and 1980s, soft drinks like Coca-Cola, Limca, Fanta, Thumbs Up, and Campa Cola were expensive, and only upper-class and rich people could afford to have soft drinks often. Consequently, in India, family members commonly extended soft drinks by adding ice to them, usually so they could be shared by a number of people. When Prashant saw the server adding crushed ice to his Coke, he thought he was diluting the soft drink with water. In addition, Prashant did not realize that the soft-drink machine was self-serve and that the server was doing him a favor by serving him.

Almost everyone I interviewed for this study had at least one story that highlighted their unfamiliarity with American culture. Some of these stories were funny, others were embarrassing, and some were humiliating.

Because the professional Indians of the southern Connecticut diaspora had academic talent and were skilled researchers, scientists, and medical doctors, they were on a trajectory to enormous success. Indeed, their academic success in the first few years of their life in America had given them a taste of the endless possibilities that life could offer once they graduated. With this in mind, Prashant said that although he felt like a foreigner in this country, he relished his days as a graduate student in America. "The first two years in America—what experiences you get— probably stays with you. I think it's more long-lasting than you know." Prashant looks back fondly on his graduate days and told me, "I guess I was fortunate I didn't have any huge struggles with either the money part or the school part." Many of my participants had little difficulty with either their finances or their academic work in graduate school, which allowed them to turn the "American dream" into a reality.

Vilayti Babu or America: Return as Role Models

Many of my participants in this study grew up in family networks with some knowledge of about the West, particularly England or America. Although the life and culture of England had taken a firm hold in the imagination of the *babus* and brown *sahibs*,[7] in "1962 the British Parliament placed restrictions on Commonwealth immigration," and consequently America was opening its gates to skilled migrants while Britain was restricting its migration policy. (Helweg and Helweg 1990, p. 60). The idea that America was the new "land of opportunity" where educated people could live in luxury had permeated the imagination of many middle-class Indian families. Many of participants in my study had either a family member or a friend who had been to America or England and had qualified for "America return" or "*Vilyati babu.*" *Vilayati babu,* or "America return," family members either studied at U.S. graduate schools or visited the United States and then, after returning home, shared some remarkable stories about the riches, luxuries, and big cars in the United States.

Stories circulated about a poor cousin or a working-class person from the neighborhood whose journey to the United States had made him rich, and there were plenty of stories about students who went to the United States to become doctors and engineers and "made it big," buying big houses and cars. These successful immigrants would send home pictures from the United States of their big houses with manicured green lawns, many bedrooms, two cars, and all the other amenities. They also sent pictures from their vacations to Niagara Falls, Disneyland, or Paris, reminders to everyone in the family that the migrants in the United States owned a piece of the American dream. When these "American" relatives or friends returned to India on their annual visits, they often painted a rosy picture of their successful lives in America, their work ethic, the clean streets, the huge highways, their cars, and the general culture of abundance. This idea of America was deeply etched in the lives of these participants, and their journey from life in the Indian streets to the universities and multinational companies in the United States seemed destined.

In its many forms, America was part of the lives of these participants even before they had arrived at their universities. For example, Ashok, a forty-eight-year-old man, was the vice president of a computer company's global marketing division. He came to the United States in 1975 to do doctoral work in chemical engineering at a large midwestern university, and he also received an MBA from a well-reputed midwestern university. At the time of the interview, he had spent twenty-six years in America. Our conversation began at his home, and when I asked him why he had come to America, he immediately replied, "Doctoral studies." I followed up with another question, "After you were in the U.S., did you ever think about going back to India?" Ashok replied: "No, because I went to a university in India where half the faculty members were Americans. My university was a joint program that was basically set up with U.S. aid and . . . all the professors who taught me as an undergraduate in India taught me again in the U.S." For Ashok, there was no other option but to come to America, since most of his professors who had taught him in India were

Americans. He also was certain that once he left for America, he would not go back to India. Indeed, his response indicates that he had already made up his mind to stay in the United States even before he left India, while he was still a student at IIT, Madras. He had had a taste of the America education system in India and knew that he was destined to come to the United States. The most fascinating part of Ashok's interview emerged when he told me that although he had grown up in Mumbai, he was almost "like a second-generation Indian, being in America."

Ashok's father visited the United States in the late 1940s and returned to India in the early 1950s. His father had grown up during the independence movement and had an intensely patriotic attachment to India. In fact, a number of participants were strongly shaped by the culture of the British Raj and the postcolonial recreation of the vision of India. Vishal, who earned his MBA in the United States in 1969, said he was deeply influenced by his father's rebellion against the British government. He told me that his father was one of the first Indian students from his region to graduate from "the British-run college system, and then he refused to work for the British as an independence movement kind of thing. He left some wonderful jobs and really struggled through all of that, being an independent engineer and contractor."

Vishal's father's decision not to work for the British government had impressed him as a great act of defiance, but he was also proud that his father was one of the first Indian students from his area to graduate from the British educational system. His father's success was conveyed to his family through stories about the value of succeeding in a British-run college system. But at the same time, his father also revealed his animosity toward British rule: "I very strictly did not want to have to go out— leave aside America and England, or anything to do with the West. That was that! I will not do it, so I had no interest in coming out." Because Vishal's father opposed British rule and was a staunch nationalist, he had always felt ambivalent about the West. Then, in the early 1960s, Vishal had an opportunity to go to Dubai as a business consultant for an Indian American company. While he was there, he also did some work for an American company, and the American workers were impressed with Vishal's work ethic and his sophisticated technical skills.

Vishal's first contact with America was thus through working with Americans. He found them respectful and learned that they valued freedom and creativity, all of which changed his view of Americans and "Westerners." He recalled, "It is not that I liked all the Westerners. . . . But there was a suddenly a bit of an awe about these white-skinned Westerners—very free." Vishal was impressed by the Americans' work culture, their advanced knowledge systems, and the enormous amount of creative freedom they had. Subsequently, Vishal was admitted to an MBA program at a university in California, and he arrived in the United States with his wife, Neeta, in 1967. But he had made his first contact with America, or the West, long before he had arrived in America, and so he had acquired linguistic, cultural, and educational skills that translated into enormous success.

Abhishek's migration to the United States and his success in the technological field are typical of post-1965 migrants. Abhishek came to the United States in 1969 to do postdoctoral work in mechanical engineering at a large midwestern university, and within a year he had his green card. While he was finishing his postdoctoral work, he applied for his green card expecting that he would never get it. He explained, "So as a lark, I just filled it out—I had absolutely no expectations I would even get it. So, I filled it in, and the professor wrote a very good recommendation, and the ball just started rolling."

While Abhishek's application was being processed, he began to look for a position in the telecommunication and technology industry. A large multinational computer company called him for an interview, and when he returned to Indiana after the interview, the computer corporation called to offer him the job. During my conversation with Abhishek, he recalled an interesting episode that occurred during an interview with the company's research and development scientists.

> Everything worked out well. It was nice. I met people, I'd just, by the way, also written a book while I was in India . . . and all the guys at the interview were actually people whom I had cited as authors, and they became the author index of my book! So it was, I was quite—but I think it worked both ways because they said, "Oh, he's written a book."

The fact that Abhishek actually met most of the people he had cited in his book on the fundamentals of mechanical engineering was pivotal because it created a sense of familiarity between the Indian scientist, who had written an academic book in English thousand of miles away in the city of Pune, and the scientists who were interviewing him at ABC Computer Corporation. Not only did Abhishek and his interviewers at the computer corporation speak the same language of science; they also were able to establish a personal connection through similar academic frameworks and paradigms. Abhishek's interview brought out both the postcolonial element of the Indian education system and his socialization into expert academic knowledge that was immensely valued in American universities and corporations.

"I Was Brought up on English": The Self in Postcolonial Culture

Abhishek's fluency in the English language is not an exception. Most professional, urban Indian immigrants have attended "English medium" or "convent schools" and are fluent speakers and writers of English. In fact, many of India's urban, middle-, and upper-class populations can read, write, and think in English, and their fluency in the language gives them a certain edge, or "linguistic capital," when they arrive in the United States.[8] The enormous success enjoyed by Abhishek and other first-generation Indian migrants can also be attributed to the ways in which being fluent in the English language connects them to the remnants of the "English" or "Western culture" in India. In several postcolonial sites, the remnants of colonial Englishness have permeated the lives and culture of many millions of middle-class Indians, and, this Englishness continues to be a dominant force in metropolitan homes in India. Abhishek's links to these colonial legacies are a good example of the postcolonial self made up of fragments of both *angrezi* (English) and *desi* (Indian) history.

Abhishek's father was a professor of English and later joined the IAS (Indian Administrative Service), which was created by the British to govern India's vast network of people from the villages to the cities, to collect taxes, and to enforce the laws of the land. The British government also appointed "cadre officers" to powerful positions in India's central, state, and local governments. Even today, these IAS positions are coveted because they represent job security, power, prestige, and status in

Indian society. During the British rule, most of India's IAS officers were recruited by the Imperial British government for positions such as general mangers, commissioners, tax collectors, and deputy collectors. After the British Raj ended, many of these positions went to upper-class and upper-caste Indians and to those who were seen as important, learned people who could speak English and were familiar with the colonial ways of life. The exchange between Anjali—my cointerviewer who conducted a few interviews with me—and Abhishek provides an interesting glimpse of Abhishek's postcolonial identity in India.

Abhishek told Anjali that at his house, speaking English was considered quite important. He went to an English convent school for his primary education and then attended St. Stephens in Delhi for his college education, with English the language of instruction in both places. He thus was exposed to the English language early in life. Although his father also taught his mother English, he would not allow her to go to college. As Abhishek remarked, "He trained her, and he forced her to learn English, although he did not let her do higher studies which would have been great for her, and she always regrets it, but she did pick up English." He continued, "So English was spoken in my house, and we were put in schools that were English based. So the result was that I was brought up on, on English, did a lot of reading in English, such as the *Famous Five*.[9] You wouldn't know anything about [them]."

A notable postcolonial moment came when Abhishek told Anjali that he grew up reading the *Famous Five* and then assumed that she knew nothing about these characters. But Anjali jumped into the conversation enthusiastically. "*Famous Five*! Yes, Enid Blyton." She named the author of the *Famous Five*, and Abhishek responded, "That's right." It is worth looking at the conversation in some detail in order to see that the "*angrezi basha*" (English language) was also the point around which Anjali and Abhishek found a common identity.

> *I*: Because I totally—of course I know—yeah! Of course! You tell me any of those books I will know! I have—
> *A*: (laughing) We have history now!
> *I*: Oh, I have some of these books at home, you know, right.
> *A*: I probably have one paperback somewhere down there.

I: Yeah, oh, I used to read that avidly. I used to wait for *Famous Five*, and there were many others.

A: Then, the ones—I guess the boys' type called The Biggles—[10]

I: *Biggles*!

A: You read that?

I: *Yes, yes, yes yes*! I used to read everything. . . .

A: So that's what I was brought up on.

I: Same here.

A: And then I picked up *Tarzan of the Apes* somewhere, so all those. . . . And there was another one . . . just trying to rethink back into the past. There's the guy who they modeled 007 on him, and this fellow was a detective—anyhow. . . . Leslie Chartris was the author and, umm, then they modeled this . . .

I: James Bond?

A: James Bond was modeled on—since then I've learned there was an English television program on that fellow Leslie Chartris . . . *The Saint*!

I: *The Saint*!

What this conversation reveals is the importance of the English language and remnants of the colonial British culture to both Abhishek's and Anjali's postcolonial identity. Enid Blyton and P. G. Wodehouse are two quintessentially British authors who have many fans in English-speaking Indian families. Reading books, especially those written by P. G. Wodehouse, is considered a great literary pastime in middle-class India. Abhishek's comment, "So *this* was what I was brought up with," points to the influence of English and Englishness on his identity. Abhishek found commonality with Anjali ("We now have a history") through the English books that they read in their childhood.

This cultural meaning in the narrative-interview was clearly co-constructed by both the interviewer and the interviewee. Anjali provided the names of the author that Abhishek was trying to recall, and he was surprised that her generation of English-speaking Indians had "also read that stuff." Anjali followed up by saying that she knew a whole generation of Indians who had had a colonial education and thus had a great appreciation of English music and literature. As she told Abhishek, "My father was very much like that as well, so I can really understand and relate to what you're saying . . . which is one of the reasons, actually, I speak English better than I speak any other Indian language." Anjali may speak English better than any other language, but this may not be true for all Indians in the local diaspora, although English was indeed the vehicle for conversation among the different members of the community.

For many generations of professional Indians, "America" or "American culture" was experienced through the postcolonial hybridity of urban Indianness and leftover colonial Englishness. The generation of Indians who immigrated to the United States after 1965 had the right formula for success in their new homeland. Their English education and close connection to postcolonial culture, their great appreciation of learning, the prestige of IIT and other Indian universities, and their families' professional networks ensured their positions as professionals in the workplace.

I described the middle-class backgrounds of the professional migrants in my study not only because they contrast with the story of the Punjabi migration of the agricultural lands of California but also because I am interested in the conditions under which the professional Indian migrants began their diasporic journeys. The seeds of the Indian diaspora were sown in India, but the maps, routes, and histories of the Indian diaspora in suburban America lie in the towns, streets, and *gullies* (narrow lanes) of Indian cities and towns.

My purpose in sketching the various autobiographical elements of Indian migrants is to demonstrate the cultural and discursive continuities in the migrants' lives before and after they created a space for themselves in the Indian diaspora in the United States. This is not to say that their success in America was entirely due to the continuity of the educational knowledge systems and intellectual discourses of postcolonial urban India and the American university. Instead, these Indian migrants were hardworking, intelligent students who gained entry into these universities on the basis of their own intelligence. But their class position and cultural and symbolic capital gathered through family networks propelled them into one of the most professional, elite segments of U.S. society.

Many of the women participants in my study had almost the same middle-class histories as those of the professional men. These women were also from social backgrounds that allowed them privileged access to "convent schools," "English medium schools," and a postcolonial culture that taught them how to negotiate the boundaries of Indian traditions with the "forward" culture of America. But the trajectory of these middle-class, Indian professional women in the United States differed from that of Indian professional men. Although the women gave many reasons for coming to America, several were following their husbands as wives of professional Indian, middle-class men settling in America. Once they were on American soil, most of these women became dutiful Indian wives and simultaneously struggled to carve out a professional career for themselves.

"I Followed Him": Married to the Middle-Class Desi Man

Kajol, who worked at a computer corporation, had finished her PhD in computer science from an Ivy League university on the East Coast and had established a career of her own. Anjali began the interview with her by asking why Kajol had come to America. She responded, "I met Vivek when he came to India and we got married and then I followed him. You know, all my colleagues in my classes were all applying for graduate school in the U.S., and I never ever tried doing anything. . . . I knew I was going to come here because of Vivek, but it was, I guess, it was more like, OK we are gonna get married, and I am coming here." While Kajol was studying for her undergraduate degree in science in India, her friends were applying for admission to graduate programs in the United States. At that point, Kajol had not given much thought to studying in the United States. Instead, she came because of her marriage to Vivek, who at that time was a doctoral student in biochemistry at the same Ivy League university on the East Coast to which Kajol was admitted.

When the women's families in India were looking for prospective husbands, it was important that they had professional backgrounds in science or medicine. Those men who were studying in doctoral programs or were already in the American workforce as engineers and doctors were considered slightly more attractive prospects than other professional men in India.[11] But the women did not marry these men because marriage would guarantee them a ticket to the United States. Rather, for a traditional Indian family, it was easier for the parents to send their daughter abroad as a wife than as a single woman.

"I Wouldn't Want to Do It Again": Negotiating
Family and Careers

By arranging a marriage with a man who was studying or working abroad, a woman could fulfill her role as a wife and then start her own career in America. The Indian men in my study were married to women who were well educated and had successful careers in America as doctors, scientists, teachers, certified public accountants, and real estate agents. When Rekha was asked to fill in the open-ended statement "I came to America because . . . ," she answered, "Well, because I married a guy who was living here, basically, and he had told me that after you come to the United States, we'll see how you like it and then make a decision where we want to move." When she married Prashant, Rekha already had a bachelor's degree in science from an Indian university. Then, when her two children entered preschool (ages three and six), Rekha decided to get an MBA from a prestigious university in Massachusetts. She drove from her suburban home in Connecticut to the Massachusetts campus every day for her evening classes and returned home at night to put her kids to bed.

Rekha remembered doing her course assignments and homework between 3:00 and 7:00 A.M. She explained, "I just decided to use the time when kids were asleep. So I would study from 3:00 to 7:00 A.M. or 8:00 A.M. until kids got up, and then sometimes I will take a nap with them in the afternoon. . . . Oh it was . . . I wouldn't want to do it again."

After her MBA degree, Rekha got a BSW in social work so she could work part time in the local branch of Connecticut's Department of Child and Family Services. This allowed her to care for her children and have a professional career as well. Although Rekha's career does not use her MBA, she feels successful because she can attend to her husband's needs and provide a nurturing academic, social, and recreational environment for her children. Rekha's decision to take a position in social work instead of pursuing a career in corporate America helped her husband, Prashant. His work life and career were not interrupted while she juggled the tasks of a social worker and mother.

These women were further challenged because they were trying to figure out the American system while also trying to build friendships with other Indian families in the Indian diaspora. Asha, a forty-seven-year-old woman, who works as a certified public accountant and lives in one of the suburbs of southeastern Connecticut, said that she came to America

> because I got married to a guy who was here originally, and figured that, "Oh, I don't know, I suppose this is where, supposedly, the opportunities lay, and that's what one's impression was." And so I came because of that, too. When I was thinking about getting married, my impression was that all the good guys were here and if you wanted somebody good, you had to come here.

Asha's comment that all the "good men" who were eligible for marriage lived in the United States was expressed by many other Indian women as well. Indeed, marriage to an NRI (nonresident Indian) was seen as a stepping-stone for their own careers.

Before she married Rohan, Asha already had a master's degree in English literature from a British university. After her arrival in the United States, she received a degree in communications from a well-known university on the East Coast. When her two children were ready for school, she decided to become an accountant, and after some years of preparation, she got her CPA (certified public accountant) degree and was licensed to work as a senior accountant in the state of Connecticut. Asha maintained that she never had any difficulty adapting to the American culture because she had gone to an American international school in England and had had contact with Americans before coming to the United States.` It is important to note here that these women of the Indian diaspora had a sound educational base from which they could launch their professional careers.

Poonam, a fifty-five-year-old Indian woman, came to the United States in the 1970s with a PhD in botany from an Indian university. After her marriage, she decided to give up her scientific career. "I felt my children were growing up. I had that responsibility. I was married to my colleague and, um, adjusting into husband and wife role—an Indian husband and Indian wife role—and seeing what was going on outside." Her husband worked as an engineer and then in top-level management for a computer company. During the 1970s, corporations discouraged husbands and wives from working in the same place. So Poonam tried getting a teaching job and applied to local colleges and universities, but because she was offered only part-time jobs, she eventually decided to be a full-time mom.

"There Was Also a Sort of Guilt": Being the "Traditional" Indian Mother

Poonam remarked that the early 1970s were a challenging time for her, as she had to give up a "flourishing career" and focus on her marriage, home, and children. She explained, "I was myself trying to understand, trying to hang on to the Indian traditions. There was also a sort of guilt." In her attempt to focus on her kids and home, she stopped pursuing a career in research and science and instead set up a business that sold international books. Poonam recalls, "In the 1980s, I had taken a career path of business, and that was—and fortunately the business that I acquired was—is selling an international product—so I could very much identify with it. Customers identified with me. They trusted me more." The book business was a success, and it became the vehicle through which Poonam could define her identity as a talented, independent professional. Her business also allowed her the flexibility to be a caring mother to her two children.

Many of the women in my study eventually established their careers as teachers, doctors, software engineers, business consultants, counselors, and business owners while simultaneously struggling to take care of household chores and be an engaged parent to their children. These women had to find ways to be both good mothers and successful, professional working women, two roles that often were at odds with each other.

Neeta worked as a medical resident in the 1970s in the United States, and her story is a reminder of the numerous challenges these women faced in the workplace. She had a medical degree from Bangalore University in India and then got a master's degree in public health (MPH) from a university in California. Subsequently, Neeta moved to Connecticut when her husband, Vishal, started his own management consulting firm. Neeta began applying to local hospitals and universities to complete her residency in order to get her medical degree from a U.S. medical school.

During one of her interviews, the chairperson of Neeta's search committee asked her how she would manage her duties as a resident if she became pregnant and decided to have children.

> He asked me, "What happens if you have children?" So I said, "Well, this is a normal physiology of a human being, whether you're married or not married." At that time marriage was very important. So society said. Once you're married, you would like to complete the cycle of the human cycle, which means having children and raising the family, and that is to be expected. And he said, "You know how are you going to manage that if you have children." And I said, "Well, I don't think my children or my husband has come for the interview."

Subsequently, Neeta interviewed at another prestigious medical school for her residency training, and the admission committee told her that she would be expected to do more research. Although this prestigious hospital offered Neeta the residency, she turned it down. Instead, Neeta went to another hospital where she felt she would have fewer research expectations and might be able to balance her duties as a doctor and still be able to take care of her children.

In contrast to the men's stories, the women's arrival stories carried the extra burden of being a traditional wife, mother, and professional career woman. The numerous difficulties that many of these women experienced when they had just arrived in America should not be underestimated. Many of their early months were spent as lonely and alienated foreign migrants. In some instances, they had to put their professional careers on hold until their children had grown up, and in other instances they continued, as Neeta did, to struggle to balance their careers with motherhood.

Other women, like Ragini and Hema, gave up their careers for full-time caregiving. But many women's stories of their first few years in America also show a different kind of struggle. These women were not just struggling with their roles as wives and mothers, but they had also internalized expectations of being good "Indian mothers and wives." The expectation, of both self and others, of being a traditional Indian mother and wife was an aspiration and a burden that these women found confusing. These women of the local diaspora were raising their children without the collective wisdom of their mothers, aunts, and other family members. They had seen their mothers carry the burden of being a "good Indian wife" and a mother, and seen how some of these oppressive traditions had prevented them from working outside their home.

Most of the mothers of the first-generation women in my study had given up their professional lives for the well-being of their children and families. On one hand, the women of the diaspora looked at America as a place where they would be able to break the grip of tradition and realize their potential as free, professional women. On the other hand, the model of the traditional Indian mother also seemed appealing, and many women wanted to be the kind of mother that their mothers had been. Assuming the role of an Indian mother was also a way to distinguish themselves from other "American women" in order to create their own cultural identity in the diaspora. Poonam, who had given up her career as a scientist in order to be a full-time mother, had to live with this loss once she made the transition from being a wife to a mother. She elaborated, "I was different in the sense that I was trying to grab on to this American, so to say, American culture. At the same time, I was struggling with the traditions and of course you know . . ."

Poonam came to the United States as a young twenty-six-year-old woman, and once she became a mother, she missed not having her own mother around to give her advice on issues related to child rearing. Every time a contentious issue arose in her marriage or problems came up in the upbringing of her children, she would think of her mother in India. Poonam recalled, "I would think, you know, how did my mother deal with it? How will it fit here? So not knowing the formula of how things will happen . . . how will I deal with my children? I always used to have these doubts." The struggle of making it as a professional woman in the American workplace and negotiating their role as a traditional Indian mother and wife was the hardest challenge these women faced in their early years in America.

Many of the women in this study constructed their image as a woman in relation to both their mother's experiences in India and the model of the "liberated American woman." They saw families breaking up with divorce, which was also regarded as an "un-Indian" thing to do. For most of the women of the local diaspora, the role of the self-sacrificing, "traditional Indian" woman was quite appealing in the context of American culture. Rekha explained:

To me, success means success for the whole family. It's not just husband or just wife or just one kid. . . . I would call myself successful if my kids get a good education. They go to good schools, and they have good spouses and have a good family. That's when I will call myself successful.

In this instance, Rekha's sense of self is clearly tied to the well-being of her children and family. She deeply believes that she gave up her career in corporate America for the stability of her family, which fits well with her ideas of an ideal Indian woman. These women were also seen as the receptacles through which Indian culture would be transmitted to their children.

Several scholars studying issues related to diasporic identity have found that South Asian women are often the victims of the community's attempt to present itself as a spiritual, traditional, and homogeneous group with ancient cultural roots. According to Das Dasgupta, "The main casualty of our communities' efforts to reformulate homogenous 'authenticity' are women. . . . South Asian women in America are given the task of perpetuating anachronistic customs and traditions" (1998, p. 5). Thus, scholars examining the construction of South Asian women in the diaspora argue that second-generation South Asian Americans particularly are struggling to "know" their place in the society (Mani 1994). On the one hand, they have to face racial discrimination and prejudice from the larger American society as "brown" minority women, and on the other hand, they have to deal with the oppression within their own communities.

What these scholars are pointing out is essentially that the acculturation of many nonwhite, non-European/non-Western, immigrants, especially women, to U.S. society is painful, difficult, and complex. Their acculturation, as I have documented, follows a different trajectory from that of the Indian professional men of the post-1965 generation in the United States. However, most of the men and women of the local Indian diaspora were earning good salaries as skilled teachers, professors, counselors, doctors, real estate agents, engineers, and computer scientists. Their good wages, class position, and professional networking culture eventually led them to create a diasporic space for themselves in suburban America.

The Indians in the diaspora are "people of color" and part of the non-European wave of migration that began in the 1960s. The next chapter shows how these professional migrants understand and frame their sense of otherness in the new world. What kinds of racial and cultural meanings of otherness are assigned to these professional Indians in their daily life? How do these professional, elite, transnational migrants understand their racial designation as nonwhite people or "people of color"? How do members of the Indian professional diaspora collectively represent their sense of identity? How does their status as "elite" professionals affect their understanding of being both privileged and marginalized minorities?

4

■　■　■　■　■　■　■　■　■

Saris, Chutney Sandwiches, and "Thick Accents"

Constructing Difference

While conducting my ethnographic fieldwork in the Indian diaspora, I asked Rani, who lived in a suburb of Connecticut, to recall an episode that made her feel "unwelcome" or "unwanted" as an Indian immigrant in the United States. Rani mentioned one question that her friends and neighbors often ask her: "So, when are you planning to go back home?" This question usually follows "'Where are you from, and blah, blah?' 'What is this *bindi* for?' and all that, but then they will say, 'When are you going back?' . . . and then they will say, 'But when are you going back?' And I'll say, 'I don't know.' So I would just feel very defensive."

For Rani, the question "When are you going back?" symbolizes being unaccepted. It is also a constant reminder that she will never be able to shed her migrant identity. Many participants in my study feel this sense of difference or "otherness" when they are repeatedly asked, "When are you going back home?" The implication is that they do not belong "here" and that their home is elsewhere. Many Indian students who come here as graduate students are asked when they will return to their homeland, and at that point in their lives, the question seems legitimate. Many professional Indians who come to the United States for graduate school—

whether in sociology, engineering, medicine, or computer science—initially do think about returning home and giving something back to their country.

For Rani and many other Indian immigrants like her who have made a home in the United States, these questions are constant reminders that they are outsiders living in a foreign country. How should we understand their cultural and racial identity? In reformulating her discussion about South Asian racial formation, Koshy (1998) proposed exploring South Asians' negotiations—the tensions and ambiguities—when the majority groups assign certain identities to them. She suggested that we examine the concept of identity that immigrants bring with them and use as their assertions or as expressions of their identity. Clearly, the Indian participants living in the diaspora are viewed as being different, but the ethnographic data reveal that these participants are extremely ambivalent about their racial and cultural differences. How can we understand this contradiction?

In this chapter, we discuss the ambivalences of and contradictions between the self-identities that Indian Americans carry with them to the United States and the ways in which their identities are positioned by the larger U.S. society, that is, how they articulate the racial otherness assigned to them by the majority culture. In particular, we look at how professional, middle-class Indians living in suburban America conceptualize the ways in which the professional Indian diaspora has been inserted into the racial dynamics of American society.

I offer three ways in which otherness is constructed in the Indian diaspora: generic otherness, marked otherness, and disruptive otherness. *Generic otherness* refers to the "voices" appropriated by the participants and points to an undifferentiated and general notion of cultural difference. That is, a general identifying mark about a person's identity creates an environment of otherness. The second type, *marked otherness,* centers on specific identifying markers, such as accent, language, and mannerisms that mark a person as different. The third type of otherness, *disruptive otherness,* creates deep feelings of alienation and marginality in the participants. These feelings of inadequacy and pain are the direct result of acts of racism, ethnic bias, and gender discrimination.

I use a dialogical approach to examine how members of the local diaspora reproduce their racial assignations. A dialogical approach focuses on the multiplicity of subject positions and themes and thereby emphasizes the alternating and often paradoxical "voices" lying beneath these assignations. The model of a dialogical self also is useful to understanding how the self appropriates these powerful, dominant, and competing "I" positions.

My principal sources are the work of Mikhail Bakhtin and other contemporary scholars—such as Hermans and Kempen (1993, 1998), Wertsch (1991, 1998), and Valsiner (2000, 2002)—which I use to analyze the assignations reported by the participants. These labels or assignations are given to them mainly by their white American neighbors, friends, and coworkers; it is they who most often regard their Indian neighbors as different. Other groups, such as African Americans, Chinese, Japanese, and working-class Indian immigrants, also contribute to how professional Indian immigrants locate and frame their foreignness and sense of difference, but these voices often play a muted or secondary role in their construction of self. First-generation immigrants do not just passively absorb this labeling as "other" but give it new interpretations and cultural meanings.

I examine the different ways in which the participants strategically appropriate the voices of the dominant others, reconstruct them, and give them local meanings in their sociocultural context. The model of dialogical self enables us to show how the Indian participants move between the otherness that is constructed for and assigned to them and the ways in which the self strategically reinterprets those constructions. I first consider the salient characteristics of the dialogical model of self.

Voices of the Dialogical Self

In the last decade, many scholars and researchers in psychology and related disciplines explored the development of self as dialogical (Bhatia 2002a; Day and Tappan 1996; Fogel 1993; Gergen 1994; Hermans 1996; Hermans and Kempen 1993; Josephs 1998; Sampson 1993; Valsiner 1998, 2000; Wertsch 1991). Inspired by the writings of the Russian literary theorist Mikhail Bakhtin, I use the concept of a relational self embedded in a network of conversations and dialogues with others to explain the stories of self-identity that emerge from the Indian diaspora.

That is, the concept of a "dialogical self" explores the emergence of self through history, culture, and social interaction.

Bakhtin constructed his concept of a dialogical self by analyzing literature—especially novels written by the Russian novelist Dostoyevsky. Bakhtin believed that dialogical relationships are much more that just replies to utterances or statements. Instead, dialogue is universal: it is part of conversation and speech and mediates all our social interactions and interpersonal relationships. Dialogue provides the means by which a person's self is created or revealed: It is the ground on which the self is constructed. That is, a person creates and transforms the properties of his or her self by engaging in dialogue with others.

In an often-quoted text, Bakhtin writes that the word belongs at least partially to someone else:

> It becomes "one's own" only when the speaker populates it with his own intention, his own accent, when he appropriates the word, adapting to his own semantic and expressive intention. Prior to this moment of appropriation, the word does not exist in a neutral and impersonal language (it is not, after all, out of a dictionary that the speaker gets his word!) . . . but rather it exists in other people's mouths, in other people's contexts, serving other people's intention. It is from there that one must take the word and make it one's own. (Bakhtin 1981, p. 293)

When as the addressor and the addressee, the self and the other come into contact with each other's voices, the self becomes *multivoiced.* When Bakhtin uses the term *voice,* he does not mean "auditory signals" but, rather, the "speaking personality" or the "speaking consciousness" (Wertsch 1991, p. 12). How do we appropriate someone else's voice?

Rogoff (1990) argues that we should move away from the concept of internalizing the collaborative activity and instead emphasize the different ways that individuals learn from participating in shared social activities. This sharing can be conceptualized as appropriation that is intrinsically tied to the process of participation. We must move away from using the concept of internalization because it invokes the image of something being transported from the outside to the inside. According to Wertsch (1998), the concept of appropriation implies that the act of uttering a word also means reconstructing the word in one's own voice and one's own language.[1] The concept of appropriation also suggests that individuals actively resist and select certain voices assigned by the members of the dominant culture. How can we explain the theory of the dialogical self in the context of the Indian diaspora?

The concept of "dialogicality" is activated when one or more utterances of the "speaking subject" come into contact and give meaning to the voice of the other (Wertsch 1991). The utterance is an important element of dialogicality because of its focus on "addressivity," which in turn is a concept that requires at least two voices, those of the author and the addressee, the self and the other (Wertsch 1991, p. 52). As an addressee, the other comes in many forms, and a person can dialogically engage with the addressee through face-to-face, verbal communication as a participant or an interlocutor in an ongoing conversation. As the other, an addressee can be a professional, specialist, foreigner, native, outsider, opponent, boss, employer, institution, or "unconcretized" imaginal other (Bakhtin 1986, p. 95).

The real challenge of studying dialogicality is to spell out how voices come into contact with one another and change their meanings. Josephs offers a definition of voice that I have found useful when analyzing the Indian participants' narratives:[2]

> The obvious characteristic of a voice is its potential to speak, to tell a story. The story is not just any story, but a motivated story, which is rooted in emotions. A voice can talk to other voices, agree or disagree with other voices' stories. A voice can also be ignored or silenced by other voices, but also by "real" others! A voice can "take over the floor" and become the monological figure on a ground of—temporarily invisible, backgrounded other voices. But a voice can also support another previously suppressed voice to come to the fore. Last but not least, a voice can change qualitatively due to its interaction with another voice. (2002, p. 162)

The concept of a dialogical self can be construed in terms of a number of dynamic but relatively autonomous "I" positions or voices that are in dialogue with real, actual, and imagined others. The "I" is not static but can move from one position to another with changes in time and circumstances (Hermans and Kempen 1993).

From the perspective of the dialogical self, any individual or "I," depending on sociocultural constraints, can take a position of ridicule, agreement, disagreement, understanding, opposition, or contradiction toward another "I" position. In order to understand the development of the dialogical self, we need to ask the Bakhtinian question "Who is doing the talking?" (Wertsch 1991, p. 81). Bakhtin argues that depending on the sociocultural setting, some voices are privileged over others because they are considered more appropriate and effective. The concept of dialogical understanding does not mean that all the voices communicating with oneself or others are always in harmonious accord. Rather, the dynamic movement among voices entails negotiation, disagreement, power, play, negation, conflict, domination, privileging, and hierarchy (Hermans and Kempen 1993).

In dialogical terms, we can think of the immigrant self as involving a back-and-forth movement between different voices or the perspectives associated with these voices (e.g., "Life here in the United States is impersonal"; "I have two cars and a house"; "Back home I never felt alienated"; "I face racism here"; "Back home there are too many political and economic problems"; "I can give my children a good life over here"; "I don't belong here"). Hermans, Kempen, and van Loon call this polyphony of voices a movement between a "multiplicity of *I* positions" (1992, p. 28). A dialogical model of self shows that one's migrant identity involves multiple negotiations with larger sets of cultural, political, and historical practices, and it encourages us to examine the contradictions, complexities, and interminable shifts of immigrant identity construction (Bhatia 2002a; Bhatia and Ram 2001a, 2001b; Bhatia and Ram 2004).

The scholarship on the dialogical self has important implications in a world in which migrants, refugees, exiles, and expatriates are redrawing its cartography. We cannot speak of a static, core, unchanging self when there is so much dynamic movement, shifting, and mixing around of its cultural boundaries. The challenge for the theory of a dialogical self is explaining how individuals coordinate and appropriate the voices of the dominant other during transnational immigration, cultural dislocation, and the hybridization of identity. How is the voice of the "other" given new meaning? The following analysis focuses on the ways in which the members of the Indian diaspora make sense of the voice of "otherness" assigned to them by the dominant group in U.S. culture.

Assignations of Generic Otherness

The external voices of the Indian participants' friends and neighbors typically focus on the display of cultural differences such as saris or the *bindi* or through skin color and nonverbal behavior. Cultural differences in this type of otherness are highlighted in general terms by commenting about a particular cultural artifact. General statements like "The other day I went to an Indian restaurant . . ." or "Do you know this other Indian person in town?" assign ethnicity and a sense of difference. Priya, a professor and a specialist in infectious diseases who teaches at a local university, talked about how these assigned meanings about her general cultural Indianness make her feel very uncomfortable. She observed that when her colleagues ask her about India, she often detects a patronizing and condescending attitude. She commented, "They'll ask all kinds of polite questions about India and me and my life here and stuff like that. But I find that very irritating. I'm very polite to them, but I don't enjoy it at all." In this dialogical construction of otherness, difference is accentuated by being labeled as exotic or just different. Priya clarified her position by stating that people often either ignore her or go out of their way to accommodate her. The general ascription of otherness is exemplified by Priya's statement that her colleagues are just paying attention to her difference. Here Priya's "Indianness" is made salient without any particular elaboration or description of that difference. In fact, Priya tries to avoid being seen as exotic by wearing a black Western dress and a scarf.

Priya uses the scarf and the dress to neutralize and shift attention away from her embodied difference, which is on display at work parties that are typically attended by upper- and middle-class white professionals. I asked Priya whether she was immediately placed in this category of "the other" at various parties because of her so-called Indian looks. She replied that she hated the terms *exotic* and *ethnic* because they only called attention to her difference as an Indian woman and often subordinated her identity as a successful doctor.

"Why Don't You Go Back to India?": Marking the Generic Other

Rani, another professional Indian woman, was immensely proud of coming to the United States in the 1970s as a "pioneer Indian woman." But during the more than three decades that she has lived in the United States, Rani has been continually asked by her friends and coworkers when is she planning to return home. During the interview, she emphasized several times that she did not come here as "someone's wife" but instead came on her own. The question of her returning to India undermines her achievement as an Indian woman who has been successful without the direct support of a husband or her parents.

As a new graduate student in the United States, Rani faced tremendous hardships, but eventually she succeeded in getting a PhD in psychology from a large midwestern state university. She was visibly agitated when she spoke about this issue:

> I did not come here as a wife, or somebody's wife or somebody's daughter. I came here as a pioneering Indian woman to study. And, um, people were, in the beginning, very inquisitive, and I became very uncomfortable. Why do I have to go back? I have stood up to my parents. . . . I wanted to come here, and I did not tell them that I plan to stay here.

The collective voices that labeled Rani as an eternal other assumed different cultural meanings in another interview. Shalini, a forty-eight-year-old woman, works as a sales clerk in an electronics store that sells discounted items like digital cameras, televisions, and computers. Shalini told me that when she was new at the store, she was bombarded with questions about her foreign identity from her coworkers. She said, "Sometimes this goes on: 'Why you are here? Why you don't go to India?'" I told Shalini that I have encountered this question several times, and rather than saying you are from India, you can say you are from Old Lyme or Massachusetts. Shalini immediately reminded me that such a statement would only invite more questions to try to situate her as a foreigner. Shalini recalled all the questions: "'What is your nationality? . . . Yeah, they say, Are you going stay here? Do you have any plans to go back to India? Why are you here? How did you end up here?' That kind of thing." Shalini feels that in this kind of dialogical exchange, she detects a certain "attitude." I probed further to find out why she thinks Americans ask these questions or what attitude is reflected in these interrogations about belonging and foreignness. Shalini observed, "They say . . . this is their own country. And we are the foreigners."

Shalini's comments reveal how her coworkers try to locate her in a bounded category of otherness based on us-versus-them, outsider-insider, and minority-majority divisions. Although Shalini has been in the United States for more than twenty years, she still is identified as a foreigner. In Shalini's view, these questions are not friendly queries that are asked as a means of developing a friendship. Along with many other Indians, she recognizes that many people ask such questions out of curiosity and not with the intention of labeling. These Americans are trying to be friendly and are genuinely interested in their Indian colleagues. But Shalini feels that the "where are you from?" questions usually are meant to place her in the social context of a foreigner. The statement "You are not from here" leads to the question "Why did you come here?"

Shalini is labeled as a foreigner because she looks different, speaks with an accent, and wears Indian clothes: a clear example of the concept of generic otherness. This difference is played out by invoking the binary signs that go back and forth between difference and familiarity. Binary signs are made up of dichotomies like boy-girl and black-white. The tension between Americans versus Indians, East versus West, and brown versus white is manifested itself in opposite, polarized, dichotomous voices.

The phenomenon of generalized otherness works in two ways. The Indian participants characterize Americans in certain ways, ascribe voices to them, and judge their ways of life and cultural practices. It is important to remember that power differentials inform the ways that Indians ascribe meaning and position to Americans, and vice versa. As a nonwhite Indian, Shalini experiences feelings of otherness, marginality, and exclusion in the large white, majority culture. But this does not mean that Shalini or other Indians in this study are not in positions of relative privilege. Indeed, their class positions and status as highly qualified professionals do not always put them in a marginal situation. Marginality is a shifting concept, because the center-periphery relationship is made up of overlapping circles in which one can be close to the center but still far away from it. At her workplace, Shalini finds herself at the further end of the power circle. Many of the Indian participants in my study feel that majority white Americans do not always have to contend with this particular type of assignation or otherness in their everyday cultural representation of themselves. Their talk, speech patterns, and ways of seeing and being in the world are considered to be normative.

Edward Said's autobiography *Out of Place* (1999) includes many such illustrations of the dialogicality of generalized otherness. Said was a Palestinian/Egyptian/Christian/Arab American postcolonial theorist who lived as a non-Western immigrant in the United States for more than four decades. His memoir describes his acculturation struggles between his different hyphenated selves and the conflicting voices of "Edward" and "Said." Said's autobiography spells out the contradictions, tensions, and cultural specificities in the experiences of a diasporic immigrant living with multiple cultures and histories that seem incompatible with one another.

At several points in the book Said elaborates on how his name became the most "contested" aspect of his identity. Although he became an American citizen, he believed that not being European and possessing a name like Edward Said caused external positions and voices to be assigned to him by people who did not know him. That is, people made innumerable assumptions about his identity. He constantly thought about responses to those outside voices, questions, and "challenges" that made him feel not only *out of place* but often gave him the feeling of being the "other," a foreigner:

> "What are you?"; "But Said is an Arab name"; "You are an American?"; "You are American without an American name"; . . . "You don't look American!"; "How come you were born in Jerusalem and you live *here*?"; "You're an Arab after all, but what kind are you? A Protestant?" (1999, pp. 5–6)

Said made many attempts to answer those questions but could never formulate a "satisfactory" or "memorable" answer. His experiences, like those of many non-Western immigrants, of being "othered" or "racialized" accentuates the pain of dislocation and displacement. Although Said's family lived in Egypt as part of a minority, they were well off, comfortable, and part of the upper class. But after migrating to the United States, he found that his name and identity as "Edward Said" placed him in a marginal position as an outsider or "other." Said's story of dislocation shows that for some immigrants, displacement or exile brings with it a loss of status and privilege.

Throughout his book, Said describes his struggles with being away from home, displaced and dislocated. At one point he notes in despair,

"To me, nothing more painful and paradoxically sought after character-
izes my life than the many displacements from countries, cities, abodes,
languages, environments that have kept me in motion all these years"
(1999, p. 217). His name, Edward Said, and his numerous unsettling departures perpetually reminded him that he was in exile, away from home
and out of place. His name and what it stood for became the site for the
fluctuating movement between contradictory voices and "I" positions.
This fluctuating narrative becomes complex and polyphonous when he
tells us how, after years of living away from home, he learned to give each
of his different selves or voices a different story. During such moments of
self-narrativization, the stories and the voices behind them would sometimes reconcile, but even when they did not, the dialogue between the
different selves was somehow maintained. Although the cultural and personal location in which Said's life unfolds is different from that of the
Indian participants in this study, they share the same experience of being
labeled as others because of their names and cultural identities.[3]

The various voices that construct otherness do not emerge solely
from the dialogical interchange between people. These voices, as Josephs
notes, also are connected to the material world or cultural materials
such as nose rings, saris, and *bindis*. The visibility of these cultural objects
"opens the floor for communication," or questions about these cultural
materials, and even the furniture in a room, may bring a host of different
voices into a dialogue (2002, p. 164).

Ladies Sangeet and the Gods and Goddesses

Josephs's notion that voices are uniquely personal and connected to material practices is illustrated by Prashant's comments about the differences
between Americans and Indians. Prashant told me that when he invites
Americans to his house, he knows that he is automatically opening the
door for others to make him feel like either an other or a foreigner. The
"Indian atmosphere" or "Indian feel" in his home prompts his American
guests to talk about India.

> It's different. You do different things you know. The activities are different;
> norms are different. Between, like, Indian families you'll prepare the house
> a certain way if you're inviting American families. You'll, you know, set up

the table differently. . . . And it's just, you know a lot of it is just common sense, but it also happens automatically.

Prashant's remarks are intriguing. He says that forks, spoons, and even the furniture are laid out differently for American and Indian guests. His American friends are curious about the artifacts in his house, and he takes pride in telling them the mythical stories and meanings of his statues of gods and goddesses. In my ethnographic study, I rarely saw Indians and Americans coming together for dinners or other functions, and there are several reasons that they often are segregated in the Indian diaspora. Issues of cultural familiarity and conversations often differ depending on whether Indians or Americans are invited. Several Indian women remarked to me that the organization of cultural artifacts and the management of rituals around food are often easier and more efficient when only Indians are invited.

Rekha talked about this experience openly. "No, I have more Indian friends because . . . it boils down to food. . . . It's very easy to cook Indian food and get together. . . . But other than that, on a regular basis, I don't hang out with that many American people." Rekha acknowledges that she has American friends but doesn't spend much time with them. Her experience is not uncommon in the local Indian diaspora. Many middle-class professionals live in culturally fragmented worlds and are comfortable using different voices and strategies to negotiate these worlds. Although generic otherness is ascribed to many Indians, in turn Indian professionals use it strategically and ascribe certain properties of otherness to their American friends. The Indians of the local diaspora often describe Americans as "hardworking," "civic minded," "professional," "too independent," "self-centered," and "materialistic."

Several men and women in my study assigned certain cultural characteristics to Americans based on their own experiences as minorities or the only nonwhite people in a group of white Americans. Consider Poonam, who gave some concrete reasons for keeping the two communities—Indians and Americans—separate at one of the major events of her daughter's wedding:

Yeah, I felt that, also I made a point not to invite Americans to this. . . . Because I have noticed, I observed when you mix them, those people are at a disadvantage, because we get together, start speaking [another] language, we have *gana bajana* [singing and dancing], *khana peena* [eating and drinking], these people get ignored, and that's not fair. Even in Meghna's wedding, the "ladies *sangeet*" that was there, I made sure that no Americans would be here, so they wouldn't be at a disadvantage.

The Hindi phrases *gana bajana* and *khana peena* refer to the different cultural practices of eating, drinking, and socially interacting with guests and family members during North Indian wedding rituals. Poonam felt it was unfair to include her American friends in these Indian cultural rituals because they would not understand them or feel that they fit or belonged there. She deliberately did not invite many of her American friends to the "ladies *sangeet*" that was organized for her daughter's marriage. Ladies *sangeet* is a North Indian wedding ritual in which all the women (and, in some cases, men) from the bride's family get together the night before the wedding to sing wedding songs and Hindi film songs, to which the women, both young and old, dance. Some of the songs also make fun of the bridegroom and his family, and they often are accompanied by a percussion instrument like a *tabla* or a *dholak*.

I was puzzled by Poonam's comments and asked her whether she felt that her American friends might not invite her to work-related parties because they likewise believed that she might feel awkward or out of place. I also asked her whether she felt the same way as Americans do when they come to Indian events when she attended these corporate events held for the elite, upper-level management of her husband's company. She replied, "I feel like I am an outsider—people make a special effort to include you and talk about things which really . . ." Her reason for not including her American friends in the various events she hosts is partly derived from her experiences of feeling like a misfit and an outsider at the all-white corporate parties that she has attended. Her act of assigning otherness to her American friends is constructed in parallel with her friends' assigning labels of difference and otherness to her.

The labels of difference constructed by Poonam's and Prashant's friends and coworkers are dialogically connected to the cultural meanings that Poonam and Prashant ascribe to their American friends. These assigned meanings are organized around a range of material products such as garments, clothing, *bindis* and tables, furniture, and gods and goddesses. Such assignations of otherness are evident when parents speak to their children about choosing their future mates. Shalini repeatedly tells her teenaged children, "No matter black or . . . anybody, make a friend. But once you think about your partner, think about what you're going to . . . don't think about your boy or girl as a partner for you, but think about it from your family's perspective, too." Here Shalini is talking about the importance of her children marrying someone of Indian origin. She believes that although one can have friends or spend time with Americans, when it comes to marriage, her children must consider only someone of Indian origin.

If my children marry Americans, Shalini warned, then they have to think about how we, as parents, will fit in to the American family culture. She imagines a scenario in which she is sitting with her daughter-in-law's American family with nothing but awkward silence and discomfort surrounding them. Shalini tells me that she has imagined this scenario several times. She is afraid that if one of her children married into an American family, they would have "no culture" to connect with and talk about. As Shalini explained, "Your parents go to your friend's house. What are we gonna talk about with them, because we don't know any culture. . . . We don't know any." She believes that they will have no common subjects to talk about and no shared culture around which they can come together as family members. Shalini sees herself as a foreigner and realizes that she will never be fully accepted in American society. Many of her American coworkers and friends view her Indian accent, color, and mannerisms negatively, and her subsequent feelings of otherness are now closely tied to her sense of self.

A brief analysis of these excerpts and comments suggests that these voices regarding self are rooted in emotions that are given life through the personal meanings associated with them (Josephs 2002). From Josephs, we learn that voices in the dialogical self are emotionally grounded and connected to the larger cultural story. In turn, the larger cultural story through which these voices assume meaning is the story of being an immigrant in an American suburban diaspora. These voices are uniquely personal but are connected to the voices of others.

The stories of generic otherness reported here are essentially a reflection of the Indian participants' acculturation struggles when moving among different cultural positions. When we ask the Bakhtinian question,

"Who is doing the talking in these narratives?" we find a host of different voices filled with contradictory dialogical themes.

These voices from the diaspora construct a story of "otherness" and cultural difference. The Indian participants' foreignness is constructed by accentuating their exotic cultural features, such as *bindis,* saris, and "Indian" cultural mannerisms. They regarded invasive general questions about nationality, origins, and belonging as tools to underscore their foreignness or status as outsiders. These evaluations by the other are given voice through the stories of Indian migrants' lives as a doctor, a sales clerk, and a businesswoman. Although we never directly hear the voices of the participants' white American friends, neighbors, and coworkers, those voices nonetheless play a pivotal role in how Indians construct meanings about themselves.

We see the various ways in which the voices of the other are "ventriloquated" through their personal histories. In telling these stories, the voices are allowed "to speak through the other" (Valsiner 2000, p. 9). Furthermore, in the storytelling process, one voice infuses the other and uses it as a medium to express its own voice or its "I" position. For example, it is common to hear people say, "It's not your voice but your mother's voice that's speaking." Such a statement would be an explicit and straightforward example of *ventriloquation.* Other forms (indirect or inexplicit) of ventriloquation "may range from interindividual enforcement of a voice in an asymmetric power relationship . . . to a person's interpsychological use of a folk-saying in one's own autodialogue" (Valsiner 2000, p. 9). The process of ventriloquation occurs as one moves between the field of ownness—the personal stories—and the field of otherness. This movement becomes more complex as we hear the narratives and stories of Indian participants as they speak about their marked otherness and differences.

Assignations of Marked Otherness

My participants' assignations did not remain general descriptions but were reconstructed or revoiced with new cultural meanings. Their stories of difference are therefore more nuanced than my analysis of generic otherness in the previous section. The ways in which others assign positions of difference to the Indian migrants and how they reprocess these positions thus need to be elaborated.

One of the most important features of the dialogical self is the role of the other. Although this other is not the direct co-narrator of these stories of cultural differences, it is an important part of the personal narratives of the Indian men and women experiencing cultural differences in the diaspora. Most of the stories of marked otherness came out when I asked the participants to finish the following sentence: "As an Indian immigrant living in the United States, I feel different because . . ." I was interested in the specific cultural markers that the Indian participants used to understand their sense of otherness in the United States. What features of their self were highlighted in their discourse about foreignness? What markers of difference are attributed to the middle-class Indians of the diaspora? Among the features distinguishing Indians from their white neighbors, which cultural identifiers do the participants see as marked? What meanings do professional Indians read into their marked sense of otherness? What characteristics do others assign to them, and how do they use them to frame their sense of self in the diaspora?

"India, to Them, Means Mahatma Gandhi or Maharishi Yogi": Creating Marked Otherness

The dialogicality of marked otherness was illustrated in several ways in my interviews with the first-generation Indian immigrants. These stories went beyond a general description of markers like the *bindi, pagdi,* sari, or the *kurta pajama.* Instead, these so-called cultural markers were given elaborate meanings, and their role in the narrative of otherness was amplified. Consider these statements by Rohan: "Well, the culture is different. It's very different. I mean, being a vegetarian is not normal out here. It's accepted now, but it's not. Not drinking alcohol, it's the same thing. . . . People here ask me, 'How does he do it?'" Even though Rohan's American friends and coworkers at the computer company where he works as a chip designer tell him that they understand his vegetarianism, they cannot understand how he makes do without alcohol. On another occasion, Rohan felt different when an American girl put her arm next to his and said, "You know, I'm still not as brown as you are. I want to be as brown as you are. What are you doing?" For Rohan, this statement was about more than skin color. It was about the ways in which skin color is intertwined with cultural practices and normative ideas about who looks "normal" and who looks different. The white girl's effort to become as brown as Rohan overlooks the racialized aspects of skin tone and color. That is, although a person's color or ethnicity sometimes carries negative cultural ascriptions, Rohan's friend did not take this into account.

Venkat remembered an incident in a grocery store when a woman walked up to him and told him, "Son, this is salted butter and this is unsalted butter." Venkat believed that she pointed out the salted and unsalted butter because she assumed that he could not read. On another occasion, a woman asked Venkat which tribe he came from. He remembered the incident clearly. "We don't have tribes in India, but I asked her what tribe she belonged to. She got all pissed at me. She was yelling and screaming." In dialogical terms, on both occasions, Venkat was given a name, a voice, and an "I" position. In his view, this woman assumed that ethnic people could not speak English. These kinds of associations or dialogical constructions of meaning regarding marked otherness take place in several different cultural and religious scenarios and contexts.

In the late 1970s Rani was going through terrible personal turmoil and was looking for friends who could help her through this difficult time. But her friends believed that Rani was going through this rough patch in her life because of her lack of faith in Christianity and her faith in paganism. She recalled feeling betrayed because her friends assumed that if she converted to Christianity, her life would be fine.

The assignations made by Rani's friends reflect the kind of meaning construction that makes a simple stereotypical association between two entities. In this case, Hinduism equaled paganism, and thus Rani's friends saw it as the cause of all her problems. In some cases, however, this kind of association also works the other way and acts as a positive stereotype. For example, Rani observed that even though she felt betrayed by her friends, she found acceptance from the "hippies" in the early 1970s. When I asked her why, she replied, "Because they thought I was more accepting. Because India, to them, means, you know, Mahatma Gandhi or Maharishi Yogi and all that."

This kind of assignation goes beyond the general assignations discussed in the previous section. Here, otherness is constructed by connecting, or making meaning of, two cultural features; call them x and y. The complex details or contexts shaping the voices of x and y are furnished by the ventriloquator. The construction of meaning can be for something as broad as religion but also can be applied to particular cultural markers such as the sari or the *pagadi* (turban).

Raju, a forty-three-year-old Sikh and a well-known professor of biology, remarked that when people see his turban, his most obvious cultural marker, they immediately believe that he must be religious.[4] "People look at me, and their first notion is that I'm very religious. And they expect, you know, me to behave or react or say certain things, and it is completely on the contrary." That is, he is expected to have certain beliefs and ideas about the world, and when they find him to be a "regular guy," an open-minded person, they are more receptive to establishing a friendship with him. Raju felt that his turban initially created a wedge between him and others, and most of the time he feels that people consider him as "very religious or a religious fanatic." I was interested in finding out from Raju whether his *pagadi* prevented him from participating in certain activities, such as going to the store or walking in certain areas of the city. I was curious to know how he used the voices of others to "regulate" and monitor his own behavior.

At first, Raju did not recall any time that he felt his *pagadi* prevented him from participating in a certain activity. Then with some prodding from me, he remembered a time in graduate school when he did not participate in a triathlon held during spring break because he imagined himself coming out of the swimming pool with his long hair and everyone staring at him.

> When I was in grad school, um, you know, a bunch of my friends had decided to do a triathlon, and, at that time, I was kind of hesitant because I have long hair, you know? "How is he going to swim and then come out?" And then you know . . . although I knew I could've done it because, you know, I've learned how to deal with that, then after a split second I changed my mind.

In this example, we see how an Indian immigrant imagines the audience and spectators to stare at him—his brown skin and long wet hair. The voices of the others that Raju imagined are part of his own self and help structure and mediate his activities. Although he is aware of the "I" positions that are assigned to him because of his turban and his religious faith, he also constructs his own "I" positions and gives them personal themes. This movement between the "I" positions assigned by others and the "I" positions constructed by the assignee is repeated in other examples of marked otherness. Despite having learned how to deal with people staring at his turban, Raju still decided not to take part in the triathlon because he was not sure how his friends would see his long wet hair and brown body. How should we interpret this fluctuating movement between how the majority assigns positions of difference to the Indian participants from the local diaspora and how they, in turn, use these positions to reconstruct their own sense of self? What is reflected in the double-voiced construction of cultural differences? How is this marked otherness ventriloquated in these stories, and how is it tied to the dialogical self?

The "I" positions of marked otherness are co-constructed by the person assigning the differences and the person receiving their assigned meanings. This type of otherness and difference is co-constructed because the theme of otherness is supplied by the person doing the assigning and the assignee reinterprets the theme, label, or mark through his or her own personal autobiography, lived experiences, and cultural location. As Hermans and his colleagues noted, an individual speaker's utterance is not just an isolated, decontextualized voice. Instead, individual voices are influenced by the culture of institutions, groups, and communities. Such privileging of other's voices or their social language is repeatedly found in the preceding narratives. The themes of "multivoicedness," "polyphony," and fluctuations among multiple "I" positions resonate throughout the narratives that I have termed *dialogicalities of marked otherness.*

Many of the participants in this study are constantly thinking of responses to those outside voices that make them feel different. The immigrants also feel that these voices marking them as different are intended to make them feel awkward, marginalized, and unwanted. These assigned or positioned meanings of race and ethnicity are wide-ranging, and the local sociocultural circumstances in which they find meaning are unique. An important component of the dialogical self is that it contains the dialogical relationship between both the utterance of the speaker and that of the imagined other. The transformation of a particular character's inner thought into an utterance enables dialogical relations between one's own utterance and the utterance of imagined others. The preceding stories of the Indian participants show the unique role of the imagined and the real other, in which the voices of the immigrants mixed with the utterances of the others are simultaneously present in their selves.

Hermans reminds us that dynamic movement between different "I" positions offers opportunities for the dialogical self to show "individual differences." Therefore, he emphasizes that in any dialogical self, some positions may be temporary and others more permanent (1996, p. 44). Some positions are supported and others are condemned by institutions, traditions, and various collective groups. Many positions assume an imaginary character and frequently enter our imagined and "real" selves even when we have no direct contact with them. Finally, some positions fluctuate between positive and negative; some are enjoyable, affirming, and validating, and others are irritating, intimidating, and threatening. The narratives containing the properties of marked otherness, with their dynamically shifting "I" meanings, capture the different kinds of dialogical negotiations that one must undertake in the wake of departure, dislocation, and movement from being on a familiar territory to being a stranger and a foreigner in a distant location.

"Oh, Maybe It's Because of Your Indian Pronunciation": Erasing Diversity

A unique aspect of the dialogical construction of self-other relationships in the Indian diaspora is that the Indian community's visibility as the other is heightened by the members' "Indian" accent. Not surprisingly, many participants in this ethnography mentioned that their sense of otherness in this country was sharpened by their accent, intonation, and pronunciation of certain words. Apart from their visible ethnicity—their skin, hair color, and nonverbal behavior—their so-called thick Indian accents conveyed a specific meaning of difference that underscored their foreignness and sense of otherness in the United States.

My interview with Deepali illustrates this point. Her encounter with her Indian accent was at her daughter's school, and I asked Deepali to talk about those occasions in the United States when she had felt different.

> As an Indian immigrant living in America, I feel different because of my pronunciations and my color. These two things, because color obviously you stand out immediately, and then the minute you open your mouth, those two things, but other than that, there is really no reason . . .

I asked Deepali to expand on her statement about "pronunciations." She began with what she described as a "funny" episode.

Deepali's daughter, Karishma, went to an excellent public school—Orange High School—in the upper-class suburb of Old Lyme. Many parents who send their children there routinely volunteer at the school for various activities. But Deepali did not think it was important for her to volunteer in Karishma's school activities and could not understand why so many parents did. One day, because of her daughter's insistence, Deepali finally decided to volunteer at the school but was unsure how her skills could be used. She consulted one of her friends, who told Deepali that she should volunteer to read in the school because Karishma excelled at reading. When the word got around that Deepali had volunteered to read in one of Karishma's classes, another "Indian mother" called her up and told her that she had offered to read in the school but was turned down.

> And so one mother called me up, an Indian mother, and she said she offered to the librarian to read, and they wouldn't let her. So I said, "Oh, maybe it's because of your Indian pronunciation. Don't you think?" And she's like, "But Deepali, I want to read." I said, "Then go and say you want to read." And so she called back, and she said I insisted and they said OK. I said, "All right, now, let me insist." So I called up Karishma's class, and I said, "So what about reading? Can I help in reading?" . . . I expected the same no, and they are, like . . . "Karishma is the best reader. Of course you must come in and read." So I went there, and I started, and I was like, uh, "I was hoping they would say no" [laughing]. But since they said yes, I was stuck. So I was signed up for, like, every other week. I had to go and read.

Initially, Deepali's friend was denied the opportunity to read because she was regarded as having a thick accent and her child was not the "best" reader in the class. Although the school officials did not state this explicitly, Deepali was sure that her friend was discouraged because of her "Indian pronunciations." Although Deepali also speaks with an Indian accent, why was she asked to read in Karishma's class?

The answer is that Deepali has a "convent" school accent, which is slightly more anglicized and has a British intonation pattern, and the teachers also assumed that she must be a good reader because her daughter was an excellent reader.[5] This example shows that cultural differences are tied to issues of power and help mediate the self-other relationship in the dialogical self. A particular type of accent, speech, and tonal quality are not by themselves either desirable or undesirable, appealing or unappealing. Instead, a particular type of accent becomes marked or romantic or harsh or thick because of the cultural interpretation of such accents. Language, utterance, accent, and voice are saturated with ideologies, which are at work throughout the cultural practices of everyday life.

The participants understood that their voices, "I" positions, moods, and histories associated with their Indian accent were heavily marked as unclear, thick, and often unintelligible. Deepali was allowed to volunteer as a reader at Karishma's school because her reading ability was seen as contributing to her daughter's success as a reader, and the librarian tolerated her Indian accent because she saw it as contributing to her daughter's success. The question to ask here is whether Deepali would have been asked to volunteer if her daughter had not been such an academic success. Deepali's friend had to call the school several times and insist on reading, and eventually she was given permission to read. The "Indian pronunciation" in this context was compared with the normative American accent. The Indian pronunciation does not carry the automatic marker of being normal, clipped, or romantic but has a marginal, asymmetrical relationship to the normative accent.

One of the recurring themes in most of Bakhtin's work is related to the construction of self-other relationships, society and the individual, and forces that unify or divide the group, the institution, or the society. The dialogic battle, Bakhtin (1984) argues, is between the centripetal and centrifugal forces of language and life. The centripetal forces unite and impose norms, regulation, and the monological discourse of dominant social groups. Working with and against them are the centrifugal forces that are trying to interrupt the unifying forces of language.

The centrifugal forces are the forces of heteroglossia that stratify and offer multiple, fragmentary, and decentralized views of the world. The

Indian accents of Deepali and her friends are part of the centrifugal forces of everyday life that cause small interruptions and ripples in the normative, centripetal forces. The Indian accent is positioned low on its attractiveness level, which has important consequences for its speakers.

Naina, a thirty-nine-year-old real estate agent, never imagined that her Indian accent would prevent her from obtaining a prospective client. She began the interview by stating that she had never felt like an outsider, a non-American, or a non-Indian. Naina emphasized that she no longer cared whether someone thought of her as an Indian or an American. Anjali, my cointerviewer, questioned her to find out whether she had had any issues with "differences" at work.

> The only thing I have to say, which happened four or five months ago, was a lady called at my work. This is voice recorded, and I answered the phone, and she wanted to sell her house and she didn't speak. After she spoke with me, she spoke to my manager, and said, "I don't want to work with somebody with an accent. I don't want to work with her. I want somebody else."

This marker of having an accent not only symbolizes foreignness but also may be interpreted as a mark of incompetence and inefficiency.

"You Talk Differently When You Come from India": Thick Accents

During their interviews, many men and women remarked that when they first came to the United States, they tried to "Americanize" their accents. Many were upset and irritated when their American friends and colleagues would ask them to repeat their statements: "Can you say that again?" or "What was that?" In response to these negative evaluations of their accents, several participants pronounced some English words with an American accent, rolling their r's and using American slang.[6] They cultivated, improvised, and acquired an American accent for various reasons, but the main one was that many Indians wanted to be told that they spoke clearly. During my early years as a graduate student, I had an American friend, Tom, who became a sort of ad hoc arbitrator for deciding whose Indian accent was American and whose was not. Tom would hang out with my Indian friends, listen, and then decide who had the most pronounced accent. Indians' attention to their accent in their first years in America carries racial overtones and, for many, is the first marker of cultural difference.

Their accents take on new meanings when Indian students leave graduate school and seek employment in the corporate or academic world. Rekha, a social worker for the State Department, came to the United States in the mid-1980s and spoke about the "look" she would get from other social workers when she talked in the staff meeting. "You feel different, and you are, but then, lots of times in meetings when you start talking people will look at you because they hear a different accent. You look different and you feel different, but you get used to it." The combination of "looking different," "speaking differently," and "feeling different" made Rekha aware of her own difference. Although she does contribute to staff meetings, it took many years before she felt comfortable speaking in her own Indian accent. Rekha emphasized that she was one of only a few nonwhite social workers in her office, and when she spoke in staff meetings, she would feel a rush of "difference" all over her body. But over time, she got used to the glances and the awkward feeling of not belonging.

> Because first of all, it takes a while to start to talk to people. Well, you can talk to people, but you talk differently, you know, when you come from India. The way we communicate in India is a little bit different than how they talk to each other. You can meet an American woman who will tell you her life story within seconds. And in that way, we are shy when we come here. And you have to learn how to talk. And before that, you cannot really go out and talk. It was very difficult—the first two years.

Learning how to talk in America does not mean learning English grammar. Instead, many of the participants were proud of telling me that "Indian English" was more grammatically correct than American English. Most of the Indians in my study were schooled in colonial British English and had acquired their advanced degrees in the United States. But they needed to learn certain phrases that were uniquely American. Learning to speak American English was an attempt to be seen as "normal" and culturally competent members of a new society.

Language socialization researchers see the impact of language on everyday, mundane, routine communication in two ways. First, we learn language in the process of becoming culturally competent members of our society. Second, in the process of learning language, we learn about our community's cultural practices (Bhatia 2001; Schieffelin and Ochs 1986). Like Rekha, many Indian participants suggested that experimenting with their accents was a way to acquire linguistic and cultural capital at their workplaces. Linguistic capital is often subsumed under cultural capital and is defined in terms of its "market value." Bourdieu (1994) made the case that in a linguistic market, some linguistic products have more value than others. In his view, people become competent speakers when they reproduce speech acts that have been assigned a high value in the markets. Thus, an agent's position in this social space is determined by the different amounts of linguistic capital that he or she possesses or is capable of producing.

For example, these differences in linguistic capital are reflected in how we use language in everyday communication. Language use and social class go hand in hand and produce what Hanks (1996) refers to as *communicative practices*. Our communicative practices and speech style, variation, pitch, accent, grammar, and vocabulary not only reveal the quantity of our linguistic capital but also give us access to the society's material and symbolic riches.

"The Way an American Would Approach the Word": Accent-Reduction Courses

Most corporations are aware of the power of using communicative practices that increase their profits and normalize the "voice" of their marketing practices. During my interviews, one of the participants told me that his company gave its foreign employees an opportunity to Americanize their accents by enrolling in an accent-reduction course. Rohan, who works as an expert on chip designs for the computer corporation, described the accent-reduction course:

> R: I don't know, but I mean obviously . . . being foreign over here, you
> know you are different. That's a given fact of life. . . . [My company] has a
> lot of non-English-speaking employees, and a lot of them have a need for

real language skills. I am part of a task force that evaluates vendors. They hired . . . they want to bring in a vendor to help people improve their communication. I was a part of a task force that evaluated the vendors. One of the guys on my task force admitted going to an accent-reduction course just so he could feel more a part of the picture. He eventually said that it didn't work for him, the accent-reduction course.

I: What is this accent-reduction course?

R: They actually work with you in a way. The person is a professor of speech from Yale's language department. He made me speak a certain word and showed how our inflections and stuff are different from other people. The way Americans pronounce words are different. These guys take a very technical approach to helping you switch your accent. I think this is a very useless exercise.

I was not surprised that accent-reduction courses existed, but I was curious to know how this course helped immigrants become competent professional workers. How did people with accents feel about this course? The irony was not lost on me that, on one hand, the multinational computer company aggressively promotes diversity and, on the other hand, subtly suggests to its foreign-born employees that they should erase their diversity. Several Indian participants of the diaspora were ambivalent about the benefits of the accent-reduction course. They expressed their feeling marginalized by telling me that those Indians who went to these accent-reduction courses and changed their accents were either "selling out" or giving up their authentic "Indian" selves.

Rohan resisted this course right from the beginning and explained his reasons for not enrolling: "Really, learning a language is something so . . . I don't think I could ever change my accent and wouldn't even bother changing it. . . . You know, the differences are not going away. You can dye your hair blue or red or gold or [wear] blue glasses." Rohan realized that changing his accent would not hide his identity as an Indian. Even changing his hair color to blond, blue, or red would not hide his "real Indian, brown self." Of course, the notion of authenticity brings up the question of whether there is a real Indian self, but the general point is that language, accents, and cultural identities are intertwined. When tinkering with one's accent, one may also fundamentally shift one's sense of self and cultural identity.

Characterizing language as giving meaning to human experience is obviously not a new idea, as several philosophers of language have commented on the relationship between language and human experience (Burke 1966; Cassirer 1955; Whorf 1956). Arguing against cognitive theories of selfhood, several scholars in the field of discursive psychology also maintain that concepts of personhood are not "internal entities" that a person expresses through language. Rather, notions of selfhood are understood as a product of language-based practices, with moral, social, and personal concepts seen as emerging from linguistic, discursive, and communicative practices (Edwards and Potter 1992; Harré and Gillett 1994; Shotter 1993).

A quick scan of any of the Web sites concerning accent reduction shows that the philosophy behind accent-reduction courses is that language and identity are separate and that one can modify one's accent without altering one's cultural identity. Many of these sites state that the courses focus on eliminating one's native accent. One site (www.accurateenglish.com) states, "Your language of origin and the thickness of your accent can determine the number of lessons needed." Many are targeted to international students and international employees and contain "testimonials" from their customers. Some suggest that after taking their course, many foreigners speak like well-educated Americans. Although the term *well-educated Americans* is not defined on these sites, presumably it refers to nonethnic Americans.

It is interesting that many of the Indian migrants I interviewed felt that speaking with an American accent was a step toward disowning their Indianness or buying into the American way of life. For example, Venkat told me that his skin color and hair, and his voice and language were visible properties that make him look Indian and that there was nothing intrinsically wrong with that. So to make these cultural properties invisible was to be ashamed of one's Indianness.

> The only disadvantage is the way I look. I can't change that. My language, I can't change that. My voice, I can't change that. The intonations that I have . . . When somebody speaks to me, they say, "You're not American, you know?" And I have not learned, or I have not tried to take on, those slang words or talk like an American. I don't believe in that. I don't like that.

For Venkat, the question is why he would want to have an American accent when being an Indian in research and science gives him certain advantages. But he was anxious to emphasize that like skin color and one's facial appearance, language and voice cannot be changed.

Poonam stated a similar view when I interviewed her immediately after September 11. Poonam's son had asked her to stop wearing the traditional *salwar-khameez* so she would not attract attention to herself. He feared that his mother would be mistaken for an Arab or Muslim woman and become the victim of a hate crime. But his request made her angry. "And I said, 'You know, what will I do with my face and my accent?' And he said, 'Yeah, you have a point.' And I said, 'No, I am, I am. And if it is at a disadvantage, it's their problem.'"

The Indian immigrants' narratives illustrate the varied dialogicality of marked otherness. Cultural markers such as religion, dress, physical appearance, and accents become the basis on which the story of difference and foreignness is formulated. These elaborate stories about marked otherness are part of the dialogical exchange between "self" and "other" and "us" and "them." These various assigned "I" positions are double-voiced. They are assigned by the other and then ventriloquated and given new meaning by the immigrant. The dialogue of marked otherness also raises questions about issues of belonging and home, as these markers of otherness undermine the Indian participants' notions of belonging. The diaspora thus becomes a ground for the inscriptions of racialized otherness and a place where many Indians share their stories of marginality and indulge in nostalgic memories of the familiar culture that they have left behind.

The dialogical relations between the assignor and the assignee shift meanings of otherness, foreignness, and alienation. The preceding stories of marked otherness show that language, dialect, and utterances become important to constructing meaning about self-other relationships between Indian immigrants and their American friends and neighbors. According to Bakhtin, language "exists on that creative borderzone or boundary between human consciousness, between self and an other. It is this responsive interaction between speakers, between self and other, that constitutes the capacity of language to produce meaning" (Morris 1994, p. 5). The accented English spoken by middle-class Indians disrupts the flow of the centripetal, uniform, and homogenous forces of culture.

These voices and utterances can be construed as belonging to the world of difference, stratification, or heteroglossia and oscillate between the world of the collective diaspora and the regular, or normal, world outside it. The tension between these two worlds creates a type of disruptive difference that is both profoundly alienating and painful.

Assignations of Disruptive Otherness

This section is a dialogical analysis of assignations of otherness that I describe as imperial, oppressive, and dominant. I call this type of assignation *disruptive* because these assignations have a powerful influence on the lives of the Indian migrants of this study. I discuss two types of dominant otherness. The first relates to parents reporting their feeling of being othered in the context of their children's lives. The second type is found in the Indian migrants' work life.

At the outset it is important to state that all forms of dialogicality are disruptive in one way or another. The dialogicality of generic and marked otherness is important to demonstrating otherness through race, cultural symbols, and ethnic stereotypes. Cultural markers such as the turban, *bindi,* and accents are used as material to construct and assign a status of "outsider" to the members of the Indian diaspora. However, the dialogicality in disruptive otherness is different from other types of dialogicality because it creates in the Indian immigrants disturbing and alienating feelings. Above all, this type of dialogicality is oppressively racist. The meanings and cultural assignations in the dialogicality of disruptive otherness have a lifelong impact on the lives of the people from the Indian diaspora.

Being Brown in "Solid White, American Suburbia": Racializing the Other

Many parents reported that their first encounter with difference was through their children. Neelam, for instance, told me that on her first day of kindergarten, her daughter, Smita, encountered difference in a way that significantly altered her sense of self. Smita wore a purple *bindi* to school and a boy ripped it from Smita's forehead and threw it down. Neelam recalled the incident, "Smita immediately went to him and said, 'You are not respecting my culture.'" Smita talked to Neelam about how this experience made her feel about her culture and her difference. After this experience, Smita apparently told Neelam, "It would be nice if we have people of Indian origin, who looked like they were from India in my school."

Similarly, Rohan remarked that he changed his daughter's lunch menu after she reported that one of her school friends said her chutney sandwiches smelled bad.

> I remember that once I gave her a chutney sandwich in elementary school and one of the girls held her nose, and Sheetal was very upset. I don't know what the girl said, but Sheetal basically told her, "You wouldn't know what chutney tastes like. You've never had chutney, so how can you make a judgment about it?" But after that we never have given the kids Indian food for lunch.

Rohan said that this was one of the most significant moments in understanding how his children differed from the other children in their classrooms. Rohan and his wife, Asha, decided to act strategically. From that moment on, they made sure that their children's lunches were vegetarian but still close to the typical American lunch. Both of Rohan's children were vegetarian, and he decided that one way to shield them from scornful remarks was to give them lunches that made them feel part of a group rather than excluded. "If you start pulling out an exotic lunch everyday, then it is going to give the whole sense that this kid is different." For Rohan, the move from the exotic to everyday involved repackaging Indian food in a way that fit in with the lunch practices of his children's white schoolmates.

Another important moment for Rohan occurred when his son, Sanjay, was having difficulty making friends in kindergarten. Rohan asked him whether he had made any new friends at school, and Sanjay replied that he did not feel comfortable in his classroom. Rohan recalled the incident.

> I can't describe the seriousness with which the kid spoke to me. He said, "I am trying to find a good person to make friends." That told me that the guy did not feel comfortable in his class. . . . The kid knew that he was different from the rest of the class.

Rohan continued, telling me that throughout Sanjay's elementary school years, he was the only nonwhite child in the class.

Rohan was sure that "Sanjay did not relate to his class" because he was seen and treated as different from the others. This racial experience translated into an experience of rejection for Sanjay and had a great impact on both father and son. I asked Rohan to explain how this racial incident affected Sanjay.

> What happened is that, I think, for the first couple of years, that none of the boys invited him to their birthday parties. Very few kids would invite him. He said that he knew he was being treated, being regarded as a different person. I think it is his dark complexion, too, that makes a difference.

The story that Rohan tells about his children is not unique. Many parents from the local diaspora report that preschool, kindergarten, or elementary school is one of the first places where their children became aware of being different, where many Indian children have their first encounter with racial slurs or racist comments. Such assignations of racial difference emerge from being the only nonwhite student in the class. In most cases, the Indian children are aware that their friends do not look like them, so they ask, "Why am I brown?" For example, Kajol told me that her son, Anand, in a Montessori school, was curious about his dark skin. "When he used to go to Montessori, he was the only nonwhite, only brown kid there, so once in a while, he'll come and ask me, 'Why am I darker than the others?'" Venkat's son, Vijay, is the only nonwhite boy on the swimming team, but he has much in common with the American students in his neighborhood. Nonetheless, as Venkat noted, "People always look at him as different." Venkat explains that his son is still too young to understand racism but that his older daughter, who is eleven years old, came home one day and asked him, "Why am I brown? Why do I have brown skin?"

How do we process these stories of Indian children encountering their differences for the first time? How do we make sense of these stories of difference in the context of the dialogical self? How do we contextualize these racial assignations? When children experience feelings of otherness through racial discrimination, ethnic prejudice, and rejection by their peers, parents are pushed to confront their own sense of difference in a new way. In some cases, they have to rethink their racial and ethnic identity in their new homeland. This does not mean that the parents' own encounters with otherness and difference do not lead them to question their own racial identity. Instead, encountering difference through their children intensifies parents' own sense of otherness and forces them to confront issues of race and ethnicity in a new, real way.

The disruptions created by assigning negative racial meanings to children are profound. The children feel marginalized and not part of the larger American culture. In order to understand the disruptive force of this type of othering, we also must understand how these external voices are connected to larger institutional and cultural ideologies. The voices that make children feel different reflect the asymmetrical dialogical relationship between the voices that assign meanings and those that appropriate them.

These stories—Smita's *bindi* being ripped off her forehead, Sanjay finding it difficult to make friends at school because of his dark complexion, disparaging comments about chutney sandwiches, and Anand's and Karishma's experiences with racism—illustrate the ways in which first-generation Indians are forced to confront their differences through their children.

Dominance relations concerning these foreign or exotic cultural markers help create uneven dialogical relationships between the multiple voices within the self. The voice of race is heavily privileged in the dialogicality of disruptive otherness, as the asymmetrical relationships between the children's voices and the voices assigned to them are grounded in racial and ethnic discourse. The communication among the various "I" positions is mostly conducted in a top-down, hierarchical format in which "I" positions are connected to the privilege and power of whiteness. Second-generation children who live and go to school with a white majority do not always ask why they are brown. Several second-generation Indians experience, in subtle and not-so-subtle ways, the racism of the other, with whiteness serving as the norm around which racial difference is either mocked or ignored. Within the larger framework of the dialogical self, both the professional, middle-class migrants and their second-generation children internalize the voices representing the dominant majority.

Being "othered" or "racialized" accentuates the pain of dislocation and displacement of many non-Western, second-generation immigrants.

The external positions and voices that are marked and assigned to "brown" girls are internalized or appropriated. But as DasGupta and Dasgupta (1998) remind us, the white standard of beauty is not the only issue affecting Indian girls' "sexual self-concept." Because many teenaged South Asian American girls also are subject to the West's fascination with the exotic and "mysterious" East, they say they feel caught in the dual metaphor of the "other" as both "ugly" and "exotic."

Parents can examine their own racial understanding when their children encounter otherness and difference that is both domineering and disruptive. The following are two cases in which the concept of disruptive otherness operates in different spheres of the diaspora.

"In India Maybe That Wouldn't Have Happened": *Children under the White Gaze*

Hema told me that her children's skin color prevented them from getting attention from their teacher.

> I felt like, you know, my daughter was not getting as much attention as others get, you know. Like others, the other children, are, you know, on teachers' arms, literally, you know. But I don't think, I've ever seen my son or daughter in any teacher's arms. . . . I used to think, like, you know, maybe if they were [white]. . . . Say, maybe they would be in teachers' arms, too.

Hema would routinely drop off and pick up her daughter from the school, and often her daughter's teacher was surrounded by mostly white students. She felt that if her daughter were white and blond, she would receive more attention. Hema says that her daughter is well dressed, clean, and neat but that she has never seen her daughter in a teacher's arms: "You know, I mean, she's nicely dressed, and, you know, all they care is, you know, who's cute and who's pretty and all that stuff right then. . . . I think if she were in India, maybe that wouldn't have happened." This is an instance of disruptive otherness, in which Hema believes that the teachers equate whiteness with attractiveness.

According to Hema, intelligence, not skin color, should attract the teacher's attention, that if her daughter were in India, in her own culture, she would be getting more attention. The disruptive force of this otherness lies in Hema's imagined world in India where her daughter would receive equal attention from her teachers.

Hema's experiences are disruptive and paralyzing because she constantly worries about how this uneven, racially charged environment is affecting her children. The thought of her daughter in a classroom in India appeals to Hema because it is filled with diasporic longings and nostalgia about the home that she left behind. India serves as an instrument for imagining a world where her children do not feel different.

The disruptive difference constructed for the children and their parents also is filtered through the invisible markers of whiteness supporting the "investments" in that whiteness (Lipsitz 1998). Although token browns and token blacks are given space, eventually the components of otherness are culturally regulated. In some cases, otherness is allowed to flash for a moment and then made to stand silent. The temporary "I" positions of power and centrality assigned to these token roles and tasks are dialogically connected to the assignor, the person who controls the otherness. The dominant voices that shape the construction of disruptive otherness also influence the acculturation trajectories of parents and their work lives.

Otherness at Work and in Daily Life

The stories of disruptive otherness in the everyday work lives of the members of the local diaspora show that otherness is not only given a linguistic name but also is acted on in ways that affect their emotional lives. Here, otherness is not just labeled or marked but also is often regarded as unwanted and unappealing. Furthermore, some of the events reflect racial and ethnic discrimination that goes beyond expressions of prejudice and bias.

"He Just Didn't Want Us Here": Outsiders in a Gated Community

While Poonam and Abhishek Mittal were building a house in an expensive area in Old Lyme, Connecticut, one of their neighbors filed a lawsuit against them for allegedly cutting down trees that opened up an unobstructed view of his master bedroom. For the Mittals, this house symbolized the culmination of three decades of struggle and hard work in the United States. More than anything else, the house showed that they had succeeded in American society. After thirty years in the computer and technology industry, Abhishek had become an upper-level manager and was the director of wireless integration services at a computer company in Norwich. Poonam, who had a doctorate in botany, had given up her research and academic career to become a full-time caretaker for her children. When her children began school and she had more free time, she started her own business, opening a bookstore that carried many international titles. Poonam's business did well and also gave her a sense of purpose and direction.

Poonam and Abhishek were looking forward to a peaceful retired life in this new house, so when they found out that they were being sued by their neighbor, they were bewildered, angry, and shocked. Recalling their exasperation, Poonam said, "He just didn't want us here. There were two trees. When they were taken down, his master bedroom . . . the view became totally clear. And so he wanted to find an excuse to stop us, and he thought he could." The Mittal family was one of the few nonwhite families that had recently moved into this expensive, gated neighborhood. Poonam told me that her neighbor was willing to go to great lengths to make sure that nonwhite families did not move into this area.

At the time of the interview, Poonam was reading Katherine Graham's autobiography, which she used to explain her own situation. Katherine Graham, the owner of the *Washington Post,* recounted the anti-Semitism she faced during her years at the newspaper. Poonam talked enthusiastically about the book.

> It's a beautiful book. She was Jewish, and she is so honest with the kind of discrimination she experienced and all that she and her father and family had to bear in the fifties. It is so clear—it is no different than the racial discrimination in the sixties and seventies—what we see.

Poonam has not seen much change in the racial relations among different groups in the United States in the last thirty years. She said that the months she and Abhishek spent filing papers in court and finding a lawyer to defend them were painful and difficult. When I asked her how she felt about being driven out of her neighborhood because she was not white, Poonam paused (there was an awkward silence) and then she replied: "You feel humiliated." The humiliation "comes and stares at your face. And you have difficulty. I mean—it was, like, very embarrassing, very humiliating. Um, . . . Those were very difficult months." Poonam said that the humiliation stemmed from the fact her neighbors were "playing" on her difference.

The Mittals were one of the few Indian or nonwhite families that had moved into this neighborhood, and their presence threatened some of the residents. According to Poonam, her white neighbors did not think an Indian family deserved to live there. She also noted that initially the neighborhood was divided on this issue, but as the legal battle escalated, more people began supporting her neighbor in court.

Poonam was quick to point out that she and her husband eventually won the case but that winning brought no joy, as the ordeal made them realize that their wealth, education, and other professional achievements had not made them immune to racism in the United States.

Before all this happened, Poonam believed that professional education, class status, hard work, and wealth would guarantee them a well-deserved part of the American dream. Although they knew that their race, accent, nationality, and brownness would prevent them from being fully accepted in American society, they did not realize that these differences would bring so much pain and misery. Poonam believes that she has everything that her rich neighbors have, except the "superiority" of being white. Although Poonam did not use the term *white privilege*, my conversation with her led me to believe that she was unwittingly using this concept to understand her situation.

In a much-cited article, Peggy McIntosh describes white privilege:

> I have come to see white privilege as an invisible package of unearned assets which I can count on cashing in each day, but about which I was "meant" to remain oblivious. White privilege is like an invisible weightless knapsack of special provisions, assurances, tools, maps, guides, codebooks, passports, visas, clothes, compass, emergency gear, and blank checks. (1997, p. 291)

Furthermore, McIntosh argues that white privilege is produced and passed on from generation to generation through a societal and institutional system. This privilege "confers dominance" and permission to control, ignore, and regulate people who are not white (McIntosh 1997, p. 296). Those who have white privilege, McIntosh notes, "were given cultural permission not to hear voices of people of other races, or a tepid cultural tolerance for hearing or acting on such voices" (p. 295). An integral part of having the voice of white privilege is that such persons feel at home in any neighborhood because they feel entitled to and are part of the established norm.

Poonam was trying to convey to me the idea that she was wealthy but lacked the privileges, entitlements, and assets that come with wealth. The legal case against them was intended to preserve the whiteness of the neighborhood. The Mittals were therefore not entitled to the benefits of white privilege, and their otherness was seen as interfering with the shared homogeneity of their mostly white neighbors.

While Poonam and Abhishek were fighting for their right to build a house in their neighborhood, Abhishek also began to have problems on the work front. At the beginning of his career when Abhishek was moving up the corporate ladder, he firmly believed in the culture of American meritocracy and that things like job discrimination and glass ceilings did not exist. But after being passed over for promotion to the upper-level management in his computer company, he now believes that his ethnicity and skin color held him back.

> It is the glass ceiling. I, for many years, used to say it doesn't exist. I would even have arguments with my friends, "It does not exist." But then about fifteen years ago, as I started moving up, I smashed my head *right* there. You know, it's true. When I stand up and speak, I've got an accent—we talked about it. I don't know what the football results are—don't forget that is important for bonding.[7]

The couple's legal case and Abhishek's difficulties at work took an emotional toll on Poonam. She confessed that she finally realized that people who are affluent and from the dominant group wear a *Mullammaa*, an Urdu word for "mask." The true face behind the *Mullammaa* is revealed only after one gets to know well the person from the majority culture, "When you deal with them a little bit more, you really see the inside out first."

I: So what is *Mullammaa*? It is an Urdu word?

P: *Mullammaa*[8] is an Urdu word: *Mullammaa chatakey bhaitna* [to hide behind a mask].

I: *Achha*, it means *ankhen odke*?

P: Yeah, *Mullammaa aisa hotha hain ki yeh* [just a mask], *aap laga deejiye na, upar, face ke upar* [so your face becomes different].

I found the concept of *Mullammaa* interesting, and I asked Poonam to elaborate. What did the unmasking process reveal to her, and what did she find hidden behind the *Mullammaa*?

Poonam immediately blurted out, "It's a, it's a degree of supremacy that they feel. We are better, kind of. You think, when you think of whiteness, you think of people down." She was implying that whiteness refers to a certain hierarchy in which people who belong to the white culture or race are on the top and the others are further down. I asked her to explain what she meant by "supremacy." Poonam paused and then explained using the concept of class in the Indian context. "It comes from, I think, it is something *jaise aap agar aap Indian hai. Mujhe ek* example *yaadh hai* [If you are Indian, you will know. I remember an example now].

Poonam recalled an incident during her childhood in Pune, India. "Um, we used to live very modestly, and my sister, Sharmila, was very bright. She had topped in high school in Holyoke. My sister is now the chairman of the zoology department in Pune University." Poonam explained that Simi Kapoor, a classmate of Sharmila's, befriended her sister because she wanted to be with a student who was bright and smart, so she could learn math and science and acquire new skills. "You know *upar aayegi usko*, you know *matlabh se* [So she could come up. There was a selfish motive too]." Simi Kapoor was the daughter of an IAS officer [Indian Administrative Service] who lived in a palatial, government house. The mansion had a huge manicured front lawn at the front and seemed like a palace to Poonam. Being a high-level government official, Simi's father had a retinue of servants and *chaprasis* [peons]. Simi would visit Poonam's home during final exams to study with her sister.

One day Simi's chauffeur dropped her off at Poonam's house so they could have extra study time together. Because the chauffer had to leave his work early that day, Simi's father himself drove to pick up his daughter in a white Ambassador.[9] When Simi's father stopped in front of their house, Poonam saw an agitated expression on his face.

> And the expression on his face. He did not come in the house. And the expression on his face I will never forget. You know like—it's just awful, and I have never forgotten that. It was almost like coming down for him, coming down. "My daughter is here in this?" And he called—I went out—and he said, "Where is Simi?" And I said, "*Abhi aa rahi hai*" [She is coming right away]. He said, "*Jaldhi bulaiye. Jaldhi bulao*" [Call her quickly]. "*Bulake*" [I called], and then we raced. He didn't give us a chance, though. That was a very humiliating experience, and those things you never forget, because before that I had never felt that. . . . My mother was a principal in this college, and we, by virtue of being, you know, . . . known in the university, and my mother was always in touch with professors of actual research. She, our whole family, was known as the family of academicians. So to put us down, our pride down, it was very hurting.

According to Poonam, Simi's father was angry and disgusted by being in a "dirty" environment. Poonam's house was in a *gully* (narrow lane) in Pune; the street was battered and run-down, and Simi's father was aghast that his daughter was in such a place. Poonam told me that the expression in Simi's father's eyes was similar to the expression of the neighbor who sued her and her husband.

Poonam says that when she sees her neighbor, she remembers the disgusted expression on Simi's father's face when he drove that "white Ambassador" to her house. Poonam believed that her family had professional status as academicians and when Simi's father indicated to them that her family's class was inferior, it was very humiliating for her. Through these incidents, Poonam felt that the *Mullammaa*—first Simi's father's and then her neighbor's—were removed.

Simi's father's condescending expression and her neighbor's lawsuit made Poonam feel inferior. She recalls Simi's father's expression and his statement "*Jaldi bulayae*" [Call her quickly] as the point at which he was unmasked and his real feelings were revealed to Poonam and her family. Poonam's experiences with her neighbor also taught her that she and her husband were not entitled to the same privileges as their white neighbors.

Poonam's desire to have access to white privilege does not, however, mean that she wants to be white.

Several Indians in my study gave accounts of open discrimination against them. Others suggested that discrimination was to be expected because they were foreigners in the United States. Arjun, for example, told me that because he was a foreigner, a "nonwhite," he was not promoted in his job beyond a certain level. Similarly, Venkat declared, "I can categorically say a person with my background, my experience, my education and my capabilities . . . would have reached much higher." Although many of the participants had good, professional, well-paying jobs and were aware of their relative privileges, for others, the consequences of being different or being Indian were severe.

"Yes, Yes, I Was Not Allowed to Wear a Sari":
Reprimanding Otherness

Rani began by recalling a series of incidents in which she had faced direct racism, personal humiliation, and rejection. The first incident took place in Northern California, where she was refused accommodation in a motel because the motel owners thought she was black or Hispanic. She said, "Because [it was] summertime, I get more tan, but in the winter, I'm lighter skinned." The motel receptionist thought Rani was Hispanic and told her to go "two blocks down. . . . And there is a black guy who runs the inn." After being told to look elsewhere, Rani reminded the woman at the reception desk that there was a vacancy sign outside the motel.

Despite her persistence, Rani was not given a room at that motel. As she observed, "From that time on, I started feeling the strong nuances of discrimination." She told me that she had tried to ignore these discriminatory incidents but that she was "breaking down, feeling little by little angry." When her husband moved to Connecticut for a new job, she followed him and began looking for work in the area.

In the early 1980s, Rani found a job as an associate director of the Kingston school system in Kingston, Connecticut. Rani said, "And the director who hired me was very supportive. But I found the maximum discrimination or waves of lack of acceptance from the parents and the board of education members." Because Rani has a PhD in psychology, I was surprised that she felt unaccepted by the school board. I was also confused by her phrase "waves of discrimination."

Rani supervised seven employees in middle management, and she believed that these people could not accept an Indian woman as their boss. "I also had seven people under me who had a very difficult time. . . . They are not like you. . . . [I] found that they have difficulty with me being a woman, and then to be an Indian woman." I asked Rani whether she recalled a specific incident that made her feel discriminated against. Rani noted that her boss constantly told her to "play down" her Indian culture. One day, Rani decided to wear a sari to work, which upset her supervisor, who promptly asked her to go home and change into a Western dress.

> My supervisor gave me a very hard time, that you're not supposed to do that. And then he says he's going to write a report about it and blah, blah, blah. . . . Yes, yes, I was not allowed to wear a sari. And actually he almost told me, since my home was not very far, "Go home and change!" So since that time, I never wore a sari at work. So that tells you the Indian aspects I could not express at work.

This incident was a clear-cut case in which Rani's otherness was suppressed or disrupted.

The sari is a cultural symbol of difference and also an important part of Rani's dialogical self. She regularly wears a sari at home and also at certain Indian events. To Rani, her supervisor's telling her to go home and change was a move to neutralize her difference. To me, Rani's supervisor's actions were a move to manage and regulate that part of the dialogical self that shows difference.

This management of otherness also means suppression of a voice that is an important component of Rani's cultural identity. By asking Rani to change her ethnic outfit, the supervisor wanted to "play down" Rani's Indianness or the voice that constructs the plurality of Rani's dialogical self. Although this incident clearly was racist, Rani could do little about it.

The sari may be acceptable to wear at international evenings at Rani's school or at home, but during the workday, it is considered an inappropriate display of ethnicity. Rani's boss interpreted her wearing a sari to work as defying regular cultural norms. Why did he object? First, her sari made Rani seem interested in "her own" culture and not ready to fit in with the others. Second, Rani's boss probably thought that others would see her as different, a difference would make her unapproachable and not a team player. Third, Rani's sari might be seen as a difference symbolizing inefficiency and incompetence at the workplace. I wondered whether Rani's boss was a product of the 1980s work culture, which conceived of diversity on a narrow basis, and whether this had changed in the public schools. Even though Rani resigned from the Kingston public school system in the mid-1980s, I still asked, "Has anything changed in the last twenty years?"

> In their ability to see other cultures, it has changed, yes. But in terms of workforce, I have seen a friend of mine who is no longer here. She is in Dallas now. She was not wearing American dress, she was wearing saris only. She was good. They were putting her in the back of the department store, so she's not visible. She was not a customer-service person and she was not at the catalogue front section, she was more like put away in the back on the computer or something.

Although Rani's friend, who regularly wore a sari to work, was allowed to display her cultural difference, that difference was made invisible by putting her in the back of the store where her customers could not see her. In this instance, diversity was confined to an invisible physical place.

Rani was fighting an uphill battle on several fronts, so she decided to take a semester off from her job and go home to India. Her boss's attitude and the oppressive working conditions had made her bitter and angry, and she decided to reconnect with her spiritual roots and to find balance and peace. When she returned from India to the Kingston school system, she found that her workplace had changed dramatically.

In her absence, she had been assigned new duties that previously were not part of her job description. Rani felt increasingly isolated, and the "me-against-them and vice-versa" demoralized her. I asked Rani to give an example of this "me-against-them feeling." She responded by saying that the feeling of not belonging at this school was present right from the beginning.

Before the sari incident, when the members of Kingston's school board were deciding whether or not to give Rani the job, one of the board members made the following remark, "Why do we have to go to get this person? Why can't we get somebody from the community?" Rani was present in the room when these and other similar remarks were made. Another board member interjected, "Why can't you promote somebody from within, or why can't you find anybody from the community itself?" Although Rani had been living in the same community for many years, she was not seen as belonging there. The dialogicality of disruptive otherness revolves here around the question of community and belonging. Who is an insider, and who is an outsider? Who is in the center, and who is on the margin? Postcolonial theorists like Frankenberg and Mani allege that race, gender, and class are crucial signifiers of our locations and positions in the center or the margin of society. Through them, we identify ourselves and our selfhood and we are identified by others. Many Indians feel that their professional status as doctors, teachers, software engineers, managers, and directors puts them in certain positions of authority and that some Americans are resistant to accepting this authority.

5

∎   ∎   ∎   ∎   ∎   ∎   ∎   ∎   ∎

Racism and Glass Ceilings

Repositioning Difference

When examining the construction of South Asian American identity, we must focus on the "tension between assignation and assertion that sociologists suggest shape racial identity, the negotiation that identity categories bring with them and those to which they are assigned" (Koshy 1998, p. 285). Waters showed (1999) how the Caribbean transnational migrants in New York must constantly negotiate their multiple identities as West Indian, black, and American. Most of the respondents in Mary Waters's study came to terms with being black and West Indian while still looking for ways to distance themselves from black Americans. Using Koshy's and Visweswaran's studies of South Asian racial formation and Waters's (1990, 1999) work on racial and ethnic identity choices, this chapter analyzes the different identity discourses that professional Indians use to assert their own racial identity. How do they make sense of their racial assignations? What kinds of strategic voices do they use to counter these assignations of difference at the workplace or at home? How do they reinterpret markers of difference such as brown skin, accent, *bindi*, and sari to represent their sense of difference in their diaspora?

I demonstrate how the participants used three forms of dialogicality to understand their racial assignations. I call these categories of understanding *assertions* because they are deliberate acts. The three forms are (1) assertions of sameness, (2) assertions of individual merit, and (3) assertions of universality.

Assertions of Sameness

Venkat began his interview by telling me that he had reached many of his goals, that he had earned a doctoral degree in management, and that he was the director of the eastern region for sales and marketing in the PC division at the local multinational computer company. Venkat wanted to stress that his "Indianness" played an insignificant role in his accomplishments, that it was his talent, hard work, and persistence that had made him successful: "I did my PhD, and everything I did, I was successful. Every career or otherwise, endeavors I have taken I've done them well, and it has nothing to do with whether I am Indian or not." Venkat believed that his nationality did not put him at a disadvantage over his white coworkers because all of them experienced some form of discrimination and prejudice.

> If I was a white American male, you know, maybe there would be prejudice because I'm too short. So, it doesn't really matter. It doesn't really matter. Everybody has their own, you know, pet peeve, I guess. So being an Indian, I don't think it put me at a different spot. Or at least, that's how I feel.

Venkat is the same man who mentioned that he was seen as "Indian" and therefore "different" by many of his coworkers, that his being foreign and having an accent would prevent him from achieving his full potential in corporate America.

During our conversations, I recalled his earlier statements from the interview and asked Venkat whether or not he thought being Indian had ever kept him from being promoted to a specific upper-level management position. Venkat replied that his Indian values, cultural habits, and educational foundations had prepared him well to meet the challenges of his workplace and that his being "different" had never affected his work life.

Yeah, there is discrimination, because you are Indian, but, OK, suppose you are a white American, OK. No difference whether your name . . . or if you have a Jewish name. I know for sure a friend of mine, Schwiekert, it's a German name. He did not get a job in a company because the guy who was interviewing him thought he was Jewish. He's a white blonde, blue eyes, can't get more white.

As I wrote earlier, Venkat told me that "had it not been for his Indian-ness," he would have risen much higher in his career. He was also disturbed about his son's and daughter's experiences with racism in their school. His daughter had once asked him, "Why am I brown?" So I was surprised when Venkat told me that his Indianness had had no adverse effects on his work life. What were the reasons for these contradictions and inconsistencies in Venkat's interview?

In fact, many of the interviews presented such contradictions, with many of the participants simultaneously accepting and rejecting their differences. We could call these contradictions rejection, denial, or justification, but they really are strategically asserted voices of the self. Many of the Indians I interviewed tried to convert their difference into sameness. That is, they wanted to establish their identity as being similar to that of the dominant majority. This kind of assertion is based on a dialogical relationship in which they have a strategic identification with the voice representing the dominant majority. Venkat established sameness by equating his experience of discrimination or prejudice with the experiences of the dominant majority, in order to form a strategic alliance with it.

Such assertions were most commonly made by Indian professionals who felt equal to their white counterparts in regard to professional education, talent, skill, ambition, and work ethic. Part of this strategic identification with the voice of the dominant majority is muting or back-grounding their Indianness. Instead of asking my participants how they asserted their identities at work, I framed my questions as open-ended statements: "As an Indian, nonwhite person living and working in America, I experience . . ."

The participants completed their statements in several ways, but many said they did not experience anything different from what their white American colleagues did. For example, Kishore observed, "I can't say that I experience anything different. I think I experience just like most of my cohorts at work." How should we interpret this contradictory discourse about "sameness of identity?"

On the one hand, many Indian professionals have clearly articulated that they did not reach the highest positions in their company because they were Indian; yet they were not willing to be considered as having racialized identities. Most of the participants were eager to point out that their experience at work had been identical to that of most of the other employees in their company. This simultaneous acceptance and rejection of their difference can be described as a "double-voiced" discourse between the individual's speaking voice and the majority's dominant voice.

Hermans and Kempen argue that "each word that is spoken by an individual speaker is 'double voiced': a word has always two directions, both towards the object of speech and toward a word originating from another person's speech" (1993, p. 77). The Indian migrants' attempt to establish sameness with the dominant majority represents a move toward the other direction. The voice of the other originates from a group, society, or institute and tends to occupy a strong presence in the mind of those from the minority groups. Thus, the Indian migrants' move toward establishing a strategic alliance with the powerful majority is also a move toward establishing some kind of "interactional dominance" among multiple voices.

Drawing on Linell's concept of power in dialogical relations, Hermans and Kempen noted that interactional dominance

> deals with pattern of asymmetry in terms of initiative–response structure. The dominant party is the one who makes the most invitatory moves: the contributions that strongly determine the unfolding local context. The subordinate party allows, or must allow, his or her contributions to be directed, controlled or inhibited by the interlocutors' moves. (1993, p. 75)

The Indian immigrants' move toward establishing equality with the dominant majority thus is an attempt to reposition the interactional dominance of their many interior voices. These immigrants identified with their white colleagues and were representing themselves as no longer the subordinate party whose voices were controlled and regulated by the hegemonic majority. This repositioning of self in relation to the dominant other implies that the participants are acting as agents recreating and reshaping their assignations. Such back-and-forth play between the voices of difference and the voices of sameness also implies that the participants were foregrounding or backgrounding their Indianness strategically.

Living in the Lab World: Espousing Science and Sameness

Another significant dialogical strategy that the participants used to establish sameness with their white coworkers at work was to enact the voice of the objective scientist rather the voice of an Indian. Most of these Indians worked at a local computer company as scientists, researchers, or engineers with doctoral degrees in computer science. Other Indians worked in local hospitals as doctors or taught as professors of engineering, medicine, biology, and biochemistry at local colleges and universities. Several of them regarded themselves as scientists involved in the universal scientific process of experimentation, discovery, and testing[1] and believed that their race or culture had nothing to do with their work. Furthermore, many of the Indians in this study did not see their colleagues as Indians or Americans but just as scientists.

Abhishek's story illustrates this duality. He divided his life into two chapters. The first chapter covered the first fifteen years of his life. During that time, he said,

> I worked very hard in the laboratory doing this stuff. I was lucky—made some major discoveries—and so that was one part. Then the second part was when I became very comfortable with my surroundings. I never looked at these guys as Americans, I was . . . because I was in the lab . . . you've got to understand that it is still a different world.

Part of Abhishek's biography of being an Indian immigrant has some noticeable developmental shifts. In the first fifteen years or so, he defined himself as a scientist who was working with other engineers and scientists, whom he did not see as American. One of the main emphases of his interviews was that he had strategically positioned himself as a scientist who happened to be from India.[2]

By backgrounding his Indian ethnicity and foregrounding his role as a scientist, Abhishek aligned himself with other Americans. The world of the scientific lab, according to him, considers race, class, and gender as extraneous to scientific knowledge. When Abhishek was in the formative stages of his career, he believed that science was a great equalizer and that his expertise in chemical engineering and later as a leader in management made him the equal of his American counterparts. Because he was clearly defined by his role as a scientist in the lab, Abhishek did not believe in reproducing "Indian culture" or sticking to certain Indian traditions. But toward the end of his career, Abhishek ran into the "glass ceiling" that he had believed did not exist. About a decade into his career, he realized that his foreignness or Indianness had been a serious obstacle in his being promoted to the highest positions in the company, that his belief that being a good scientist was enough to guarantee him promotions, rewards, and entry into the highest echelons of the corporate world was erroneous. He had hit the "glass ceiling with a bang." Indeed, Abhishek believed that his difference was used against him in his promotion reviews.

At the time of the interview, Abhishek acknowledged that it was time to show his "culture" to the world. His daughter's wedding turned out to be an opportune moment to showcase the richness of his Indian culture. My cointerviewer, Anjali, asked Abhishek whether it was his idea to have a big wedding. He said that although it was a family decision, in the end he also wanted to make a statement to his colleagues about the depth of his culture:

> I was completely happy with it because that's what she wanted, and it was an opportunity to show, here, what people do. What our culture was all about. Now, I've told you, spent so much telling you I didn't care about culture, but, here, but here I'm going to show you what India is.

Abhishek was aware that in this interview he had talked about the division between the technical and universal world of being a scientist and his personal world of being a foreigner, a migrant, and a well-educated scientist. "Yeah, because I am no longer a scientist, it's very different. And I'm no longer a scientist where I'd be willing to hide all that. And, so, I'm now an individual and I'm going to show them."[3]

What is noteworthy here is that Abhishek began to recognize himself as an individual after he had stopped being a scientist. He equated his becoming an individual not with the sense of self-discovery but with his sense of individuality as rooted in his difference. I saw this shift with many Indian scientists and engineers, who arrived in the country with the idea that the universality of science and mathematics would automatically protect them from the politics of racism.

I spoke about this issue with Arun, a chemistry professor at a local university in Connecticut. He saw the world of chemistry as belonging to the technical realm governed by universal principles. Although the non-technical realm had some universal features, it also contained messy politics. Arun explained, "At work, one doesn't have to do anything because the subject that I happened to be teaching is kind of universal. Both in the technical and nontechnical sense it is universal and so we don't have to do anything." When I asked him to talk about the politics of teaching in the nontechnical sense, Arun replied,

> If they [students] respect you, and I've seen that in spite of our strong ac-
> cent you have the respect of the students, and it has happened more than
> two or three times that someone would change a section from an Ameri-
> can instructor to an Indian instructor just because the person felt that he's
> a good teacher. And sometimes, of course, the Americans would resent
> [that] . . . and they will tell the chairman straight away, "Oh that, I don't
> like him. He's a lousy teacher." And so the chairman also knows why the
> person has switched sections.

Arun is suggesting that although one may teach the principles of universal knowledge, one cannot separate the medium from the message. Arun's accent, brown face, and foreignness are part of his presentation as a chemistry professor. Students who do sign up for his course therefore do so despite Arun's ethnicity.

Arun takes this as an assertion of his identity not only as an Indian professor but also as a good teacher. On other occasions, he told me that students are put off by his foreignness and accent and have preconceived notions about his teaching abilities based on his looks. These identifications are strategic because they reveal how professional participants use their multiple voices and shifting "I" positions to reconstruct meanings about their difference. Many Indian professionals use these dialogical strategies, choices, and tactics to understand their racial identities and to cope with their sense of difference in the work world. Seeing themselves primarily as scientists or engineers allows them to create sameness with their American coworkers and also gives them a conceptual framework for describing their identities that transcend culture, race, and gender issues. These dialogical strategies also reveal that despite experiencing racism and discrimination, many Indians are ambivalent about their racial identity and often are reluctant to see themselves as raced, "brown people."

Assertions of Individual Merit

The second approach that the participants in my study used was to describe their performance in the work world as connected to individual merit and not to socioeconomic background or class. In other words, the participants invoked the rhetoric of meritocracy when describing their success at work. Raju summarized this idea well: "I firmly believe that being of Indian origin or looking different has nothing to do with the way you go about your life, your professional life, career development. It has nothing to do with that." He felt that his belief in Sikhism, his turban, and his otherness had nothing to with his success as a scientist, although on several occasions, he acknowledged that he also might be desensitized to how people reacted to his difference. As a scientist, he believed that the lab world made him immune to discrimination. Raju was very aware of his sense of difference, but he did not view talents, work ethic, and personal ambition as connected to this. He strongly believed that individual effort, hard work, and merit did pay off in this country.

"There Is Racism, but Do I Personally Believe in That?": American Karma

To many Indian professionals, the idea that they are different and that it is preventing them from succeeding is self-destructive and self-defeatist. According to most of my participants, accepting that their difference has prevented them from achieving success is seen as acknowledging that they will always be behind their white counterparts.

For Vivek, although this strategic identification with his Indian culture meant that he was seen as different in the workplace, it was not something that affected him or his individual performance. As he emphasized, "There is racism . . . , but do I personally believe in that? No, I don't." I was puzzled by how Vivek could acknowledge that racism exists and yet not believe in it. I asked more questions to clarify his position on racism. He replied:

> And that's my personal philosophy. You know, people talk of glass ceilings. I personally never talk of glass ceilings in the workplace because my belief that the moment I've talked about it and I start accepting it, then I have already lost the battle. But then it's not the case that I don't realize that I probably work a lot harder to get the same thing that somebody . . . who is a white American or a black American. I think it depends on what situation you are in. I'm always . . . I've had to always prove a little a bit more than somebody who is [white].

Vivek recognizes that he is different and that because he is different, he has to work harder than his white colleagues. But he does not personally believe in racism or discrimination.

What are the consequences of admitting that one is different? Vivek believes that if he admits he is different, it will hurt his career. According to Vivek, talking about Indianness, racism, glass ceilings, or skin color in the workplace just makes his foreignness more visible. He is afraid that if he emphasizes his difference, he will see all the obstacles that he faces at work through the lens of racism. One of his main fears is that he will internalize the idea of a different self so deeply that it will transform his ideological belief in human talent and merit.

One of his strategies is to acknowledge that because of his difference, he has to work much harder than his white or black American coworkers do. Vivek also is afraid that by acknowledging that his difference will prevent him from reaching his fullest potential in the workplace, he actually will fail—that his acknowledgment will become a self-fulfilling prophecy. His story of coming to America and succeeding through hard work and merits would be tarnished if he accepted the idea that he was different.

Like many other Indian professionals, Vivek feels that he is a beneficiary of American meritocracy and the educational and professional opportunities that America has given him. He feels that America helped him succeed despite his difference. Many of the Indian professionals in my study genuinely believe in the greatness of American individualism and the educational and work-related opportunities it provides.

"That Is the Bottom Line": Merit Transcends Color

Neeta echoed Vivek's thinking, making it clear that she never allowed her Indianness to distract her from her goal of becoming a medical doctor. "In my profession," Neeta explained, "I worked hard and this country gave me the opportunity to grow the way I could grow. I'm not sure whether I could have grown any better anywhere else in the world." Neeta continued by praising the advanced medical knowledge in American hospitals. Although her medical degree was from India, it was in the United States that she became a "professional" medical doctor and researcher. She did this by being a resident at a good hospital, by attending several medical conferences, and by having access to the world's most sophisticated network of medical knowledge. In America, she learned that her work identity required keeping her class, religion, and ethnicity outside the work space. Neeta never saw herself as an Indian woman doctor, but instead as a professional doctor whose skills, experience, competence, and education mattered.

> That is the bottom line. To me, it never made a difference. Even if somebody did say anything, probably I didn't, it didn't phase me. But it never, nobody ever talked to me about anything, or I felt that I was not white, different face. It never came across my mind. Never ever.

Neeta's two children were raised in the United States and are studying also to become doctors. She was asked whether while growing up in a white suburban neighborhood, her children had ever experienced any racism or told her that they felt different in school.

Neeta remarked that she never talked with her children about racism or issues related to difference. "In our family, nobody talked about white, black, or brown or discrimination in the family. So the children did not feel or talk about it at home either. Probably they didn't feel because we didn't feel it, so they didn't see it." Neeta decided that if parents did not feel different, then their children would not feel different either. It is important to say here that Neeta's comments do not suggest that her back-grounding or muting of difference means that she wants to pass as a white person or believes that she is white.

On the contrary, many of my Indian participants maintained that try-ing to pass as white only complicated their acculturation process because both Indians and whites could detect the mask of whiteness. Rather, Neeta was identifying with the same values and norms as those of many middle-class whites in their work world. Indeed, many of the participants stressed that hard work and determination were the foundation of one's professional development and that matters of race and ethnicity were ex-ternal variables that had nothing to do with competence or skill. From a dialogical perspective, the idea that individual merit should be seen as separate from one's race and ethnicity shows that the voice making the statement is indeed speaking from a privileged position. The Indian par-ticipants in my study were, after all, part of an elite, professional body of people who earned good salaries and were highly regarded in society. This privilege of being in a dominant, powerful position allows profes-sional Indian immigrants to separate the "voice of culture" from the "voice of the individual."

Hermans argues (1996) that the role of dominance or "social power" is important to the construction of the dialogical self, that since the voices and positions of the dialogical selves are relatively autonomous, some "individual" voices can dominate and overpower other voices. Sim-ilarly, Sampson notes that we should be aware of how dominant groups often maintain their power positions by engaging in monologues that "masquerade" as dialogues. He cautions about such masquerading be-cause he believes that "those in power manage the portrayals of the other and so manage who they will be" (1993, p. 143). According to Her-mans, the

> notion of social power or dominance is an intrinsic feature of the dialogical processes and, moreover, closely associated with the position a person oc-cupies in a particular institution. As such, dominance is an indispensable concept for the analysis of cultural processes. Dominance relations orga-nize and constrain not only the dialogical interactions within societies and groups, but also the interactions between different cultural groups. (1993, p. 143)

Many professional Indians in this study felt that if they accepted their sense of difference, they would be unable to fulfill their potential. By suggesting that racism exists but denying that it is part of their lives, the Indian professionals establish sameness with the dominant majority and avoid confronting their difference directly. It also reinforces the voice that says they are powerful and have made it on their own. These men and women of the Indian diaspora believe that they worked hard to get into highly competitive universities in India and succeeded on their own merit to be admitted to American graduate schools. Now, in the American workplace they believe that they are, once again, succeeding entirely through their own talents, which allows them to feel that they are powerful agents in the world and are in charge of their lives.

"It Probably Is Just Ourselves": Indianness as a Constraint

According to Hermans, power positions in "asymmetrical" dialogical communication are structured both horizontally and vertically. That is, on the one hand, communication can occur horizontally, from one "I" position (here) to another "I" position (there), and vice versa. On the other hand, communication can be vertically structured, with movement between "I" positions from up to down, and vice versa. These asymmetrical relationships between different voices and positions can be seen as "reproductions of institutionally established provisions and constraints on communicative activities" (Hermans 1996, p. 45).

Similarly, Wertsch contends that these asymmetrical relations and constraints force us to "privilege" one voice over another (1991, p. 124). Valsiner refers to this privileging of one voice over another as *domination*. In some cases, he notes, such domination can quickly transform into complete "expropriation," the extinction and erasure of all voices. On such occasions, Valsiner argues, the dialogical self becomes completely "monologized" and one-dimensional (2000, p. 9).

Several Indian participants in my study were more than willing to talk about how their initiative, enterprise, and talents had made them successful. I was eager to know how they would respond to stories of individuals who had left their jobs because they faced blatant racism in their workplace and/or were not promoted because of their skin color, cultural values, or foreignness.

I told Kishore, an IIT engineer, that IIT graduates enjoy a cultlike status in America. These graduates are expected to go very far, perhaps to the top of their field. Kishore responded by saying that some of the aura and mythology about being an IIT graduate are true. His strong education in the fundamentals of science and mathematics made his graduate work in the United States very easy. He said he got A's in his courses and felt that he was a successful doctoral student. But he also felt that he had not gone as far as he should have. Kishore said that many top Indian professionals are successful at what they do but not as successful as their white American counterparts are.

I asked Kishore what prevents many professional Indians from rising to the top segment of their society. Despite their excellent education and equal talent, these immigrants are not on the same level as Americans. Kishore replied,

> It probably is just ourselves. I think we still hold on to some of our things really very tightly, uh, I would say. I mean, just to give an example, we spend a lot of time, we have parties and stuff like that, and then we chat and then we talk, and we spend a whole lot of time doing that.

I asked Kishore, "How does interacting and socializing with other Indians prevent these professional Indians from reaching the top? What about the inequalities in the system?" He remarked that there are no intrinsic problems with Indians socializing with one another. Many ethnic communities do that in their diasporic enclaves. But this "hanging out" with one another, he observed, prevented Indians from breaking out of their comfort zone and becoming part of the networks of powerful people at work.

Kishore told me that Indians could be more professional in their approach to work by becoming part of professional societies and understanding how the system works. He emphasized, "And, so, if you're an engineer, you might spend a little bit more time in the engineering professional associations. And that might give you a little bit more of an insight as to where some other things are happening." Basically, Kishore felt that Indians were not good at networking with other white Americans and did not understand how the professional culture operated in national conferences and meetings and the workplace. With this in mind, I asked Kishore, "What is the responsibility of the corporate institution toward professional Indians?"

Kishore placed the blame mainly on Indians' lack of initiative in getting good mentorship at work. He said that "Indians lack mentorship in their professional organizations. It's related to really taking somebody under your wings, and that is less likely to happen with Indians. . . . You need to have a, probably a guide, a mentor, or somebody who can actually, you know, just sort of give you some guidance." Kishore agreed that Indians were less likely to have the kind of mentorship as their white American counterparts did, but he blamed Indians for not taking the initiative to get it. He was very resistant to the idea that somehow the corporate system, institutional racism, or other political factors might be responsible for Indians not reaching the top management at the ABC Computer Corporation. He thinks that Indians hold on to their views and traditions too strongly and do not try to become part of the top network of core powerful professionals. They carry their difference with them to their workplace rather than trying to assimilate with the rest of the workforce.

"Recognize You're an Indian!": The Rise of Indian Individualism

Most Indians were ready to take responsibility for their success and also to blame only themselves for not making it to the top. Their belief in merit, initiative, and enterprise was consistent with the idea of the larger narrative that in America, merit and action can help overcome obstacles in life and at work. This philosophy, rooted in the idea of "American individualism," surfaced quite often in my interviews.

Venkat, who is in the marketing team at ABC, told me that he has been unable to reach the top position in his company despite his talent and hard work. "And why would that be? Would it be because you are not white?" I asked. Venkat felt the main reason that he was not at the top of his profession was because he is not white. "Number two," he remarked, "is, as I told you before, the ways in which probably our tradition has modified our behaviors. I'm not as boisterous as them; I'm not as open as them. I don't try hard to fit into the American mold; it's a little difficult." From Venkat's point of view, it was clear that his so-called Indian values and tradition had helped him get to the place where he wanted to be but that at the same time, these Indian traditions and behaviors also prevented him from reaching the top-level positions in his company. The idea that one must modify one's behaviors to fit the American "mold" seems to show that it is up to the individual to reach the top of the corporate ladder. The idea that one's competence, skills, and professionalism should be devoid of one's history, class, race, or gender is a view shared by many Indian professionals. Kishore and many other Indian professional hold two, conflicting, views of work and their culture.

On one hand, Kishore believes that his Indianness prevented him from getting to where he should be on the corporate ladder. On the other hand, if he changed too much and became like "them," white Americans, he would run the risk of losing his authentic "Indian" self. I asked Kishore whether he knew Indians who had acquired "American behaviors" in order to get to the top of their profession.

> Yes, there are people I know who try to do that, but it sounds too hollow, they should recognize who you are! Recognize you're an Indian! You can't change that. Just using slang doesn't make you American. Just wearing clothes the way they do doesn't make you American. So you have to take a medium in between. Play on your Indianness, the uniqueness of being an Indian. Use all that value that you have gained and you've learned and acquired and invite some of the American values that will help you and then take that as a package for yourself and go ahead. I mean, that's what's important.

Kishore believed that this idea of packaging Indian tradition with American work values was a sure way of becoming successful, but the two ideas seemed to conflict.

Kishore and many other Indians from the local diaspora with whom I talked were aware that if one colored one's hair blond or used slang or acted like an American, it would come across as hollow and superficial. Thus retaining one's Indianness and yet acquiring American work traits creates tension, which was clearly visible to me in the participants' responses. But many of my participants were not directly aware of the paradoxes and ambiguities in their efforts to integrate the asymmetrical power relations, conflicting voices, and contested cultural codes under which they were operating. These Indians believed that ultimately their talent, ambition, and hard work would lead them to success and that factors like race and gender would only hinder their efforts.

Indeed, Kishore felt that a middle way, taking values from both cultures without sacrificing one's core Indian self, was best.

> I can't just sit here and complain that, oh, Americans don't make me feel welcome or this is their responsibility. One must ask, "So what have I done as an Indian to be more accepted in the American community? Have I taken the steps to do that, or have I invited Americans into my home, or have I shared with them some of my values?" I have done that. Because you can't, you can't just sit on your high horse and say, you know, "Well, they're not really accepting of me."

Kishore clearly put the burden on himself of becoming assimilated and accepted by the larger American culture. He firmly believes that there are limitations to being a foreigner or a nonwhite working professional but that one must work hard to transcend those limitations by not believing in them. Kishore and many other of my participants maintain a separation between success in the workplace and culture and believe that their performance at work should not be defined by cultural norms but by determination, talent, aptitude, and merit.

This idea that success in the workplace is self-determined also resonated with Abhishek, who worked at ABC Computer Corporation for thirty years. He told me that at the peak of his career, when he was rapidly moving through the different management divisions, he should have taken the initiative to socialize more with his colleagues from work. He did not play golf with his superiors, attend cocktail parties, or invite his colleagues to his home. His "Indianness" put a distance between him and his colleagues, and he feels that is why he hit the glass ceiling. By contrast, he interacted mostly with Indians and felt more comfortable inviting them to his house. Abhishek remarked, "That's failure which I told you. Which, I mean, we used to get invited to the American homes . . . and then, we're supposed to call them back, but we would hesitate to do that. Then that bond was not going to develop to that extent." Abhishek mentioned that at the early stages in his career, he had a small, modestly decorated house. He felt self-conscious about inviting Americans to his home, although he felt that he did not have to worry about his Indian friends. Abhishek remarked to me that it was easier to be with Indians because all one had to do was cook and mingle.

Almost all the Indians who participated in this study were successful at their work, but they also found themselves unable to break through the "glass ceiling" at their workplace. They were aware that their accents, brown skin, and "foreign behavior" were partially responsible for their slow progress. But rather than talk about racial discrimination, institutional racism, and inequities in the system, they were much more likely to internalize their perceived failure by blaming their own actions. The very few Indians who did break through promotion barriers felt that it was entirely because of their own effort that they were able to achieve such success in America.

According to Archana, one must "cultivate a sense of pride" in oneself because people who "think that you need to be white in order to succeed are foolish in the extreme." Strategically identifying with the majority group does not mean becoming white. Instead, Indianness is seen as having shifting meanings depending on the cultural context. It is perfectly fine to wear Indian clothes and saris if one is celebrating Asian heritage day or entertaining white colleagues at home. The properties of Indianness are spatialized and bounded and kept very private. They are not allowed to extend into the public realm unless they are accepted by the majority as well. In some circumstances, they claim to speak with a voice of difference that reflects their superior culture: the participants in my study say that they are products of a five-thousand-year-old civilization. In other instances, they are afraid that displaying their ethnicity or ancient heritage by wearing a sari or a saree or *salwar khameez* to work would hurt their chances of being promoted.

For many professional Indians in my study, the best way to deal with this paradox was to display their difference only at home or when the context seemed appropriate, say, at an Asian heritage celebration. For Naina, the idea is to appeal to something beyond the cultural constitution of self, to invoke a universal self beyond cultural labels like whiteness or Indianness. Naina says that she is not an Indian or an American but "me." The idea of a universal "I" or a "me" shared by everyone is a strong sentiment running through the gamut of responses provided by many of the Indians in my study.

Assertions of Universality

Difference is often asserted by appealing to universal claims, which reflect an understanding of difference that can be best described as falling into the category of strategic universalism. Many of the participants in my study agree that they are racially and ethnically different and are considered the "other" in U.S. society, but they also believe that racism and inequality are universal facets of human nature. Some participants felt they also had to contend with issues of inequality, injustice, and discrimination in India and that being the "other" in the United States was not new. The second part of this strategy is to say that even though issues of difference are manifested equally in both societies, the overall quality of life is much superior in America. The participants in my study believe in the inherent goodness of America as an open, tolerant, and free society and feel that their talents, skills, and education have been rewarded by the American system. For instance, Raju began by telling me that there are racists in every country due to a "lack of exposure, education, or narrow-minded thinking. And I don't think, you know, that's going to be any different" in other places.

A story often repeated in the Indian communities is about an Indian student coming to the United States for the first time with fifty dollars (the figure varied) in his pocket and very little knowledge of American culture. The student then enrolls in a graduate program at an American university and gets an advanced degree in computer science, engineering, medicine, microbiology, biochemistry, sociology, psychology, or management. This student is usually in the top of his class, and after finishing his degree, he gets a good job, goes back to India to marry a professional Indian woman, saves money, buys a house, is promoted, saves more money, and sends the children to the best schools in the area.

For many Indian professionals, success came as a result of their educational qualifications, competence, disciplined hard work, and cultural values, and on some level they felt grateful for the opportunities they had in America. Even though they faced racial discrimination as foreign migrants, they felt that America had given them a better deal than their own country would have given them.[4]

"I Have Felt Racial Differences More in an Indian Climate": Desi Racism

Most of the local professionals of the diaspora believed that the system had worked to their advantage despite their facing inequality and racial discrimination.[5] Many members of the community were more comfortable with the idea of being seen as belonging to a different cultural group than as belonging to a different racial group. With this in mind, I asked Kishore, an IIT engineer and a successful professional, whether he had experienced any racial inequalities at work. I said, "I've heard from Indian immigrants here that no matter how successful you are, you can never be part of the American culture. How do you feel about that?"

Kishore began by admitting that some elements of discrimination were present in this society but that there were different levels of racism. He acknowledged that one's foreignness or skin color might prevent one from reaching a certain level in the workplace, but he felt that the same was true in India. Kishore reminded me of the rampant regional and provincial discrimination in India's private and public companies and in the government and even the universities. According to Kishore, people everywhere prefer to promote their friends and family members, so America is not unique in this way.

There are those very same barriers because there are companies that may be predominantly Gujarati. Those may be companies that have predominantly Rajasthani employees, and there may be companies that may be predominantly Punjabi. If you're not one of those, then you would have the same issues. So, in terms of rising through the ranks, if you're working for a company, it may be, that's OK, but in order to get to the very top few spots, the CEOs and the CFOs, things like that, I think those things will definitely come into the picture, and exactly the same things come into the picture here. I would say, "Are you an Italian? Are you a Jew? Are you a Christian, Baptist? You know, those things come, you know. Are you a Republican? Are you a Democrat? I would say there are different things that come into play.

Kishore deems India and America as similar and then universalizes the concept of racial inequality, stating that racism, prejudice, and provincialism exist in both India and America.

I next asked Kishore, "If religion and your community affiliations play a role in India, do you think race plays as important a role here?" He quickly answered that although he had not traveled around the whole world, "I would say it's probably the least in America. You'll probably find it more in the U.K., more in Germany, more in Europe. More in many other places." Kishore's response illustrates the assertions of universality used by many professional Indians. As part of this strategy, they first invoke their differences and incidents of racial discrimination in order to establish equality between the systems in Indian and America. That is, they compare India and America to show the pervasive regional and communal bias in the Indian workforce and then describe the American work culture as being very open. Their next step is to compare racial politics in the United States with that of other European countries, pointing out that America is the best place to work.

Many of my participants saw America as a good and fair society and India as corrupt and bureaucratic. Prashant said that people in America are "very open." He continued, "It's just amazing. Even in India, if a foreigner goes, people stare at that person." Prashant's response was contradictory. In the earlier part of the interview, he talked about feeling "out of place" in America, so I asked how he reconciled his feelings of loneliness and alienation as a foreigner with his descriptions of America as an open place. How did he explain the racism he experienced as a foreign immigrant in the United States and yet talk about his workplace as being full of open and accepting people?

Prashant responded by saying that racism was relative:

> You know, you got to kind of compare that to what would be the scenario in other countries, and it'll be the reverse paradigm. It will be true in any other place. Probably more so, more so there, in India. As a matter of fact, I would say I have felt racial differences more in Indian climate because of comparisons between this religion versus that religion.

Prashant's response is a good illustration of the strategy of branding America as "inherently good" and yet finding identical issues of discrimination and racial intolerance in both countries. He did admit that there were more racial inequalities in India than in America, meaning that it was better to live in the United States than in his own country.

Prashant felt that one of the chief differences between racism in India and the United States was that racism was expressed more subtly in the America.[6] He considered racism and prejudice to be much more "out in the open" in India, whereas it was hard to "pin down" and deal with the subtle type of racism found in the United States. Nevertheless, Prashant felt that America was a far better place to live in than other countries.

Most of these comparative responses are based on the idea that discrimination is universal and that America is one of the more tolerant societies in the world. Other Indians explained the presence of racism and discrimination in all human beings through the concept of "human nature." An important element of this assertion is that we should not dwell on the differences between brown and between white people, Indian and American culture but, rather, should focus on our universal humanity. In the suburbs of Connecticut, this multicultural, liberal perspective was one of the most common ways of understanding racial, ethnic, and cultural differences. Many Indians in my study believe that we need to transcend categories of culture, nationality, and race and instead focus on the core universal humanity that makes us all human beings.

"What Is American, Anyway?": The Search for Core Humanity

Neeta grew up in England, studied in Delhi, and has lived in the United States for the past thirty years, and she agrees with the idea of universal humanity.

> I have come to realize that no matter what nationality you are, what color of skin you are, we all have the same principles. That's the bottom line, OK? At home, religion, dealing with human to human, we all have the same thing. But the way we present ourselves is slightly different. That's all it is.

According to Neeta, all of us have a core humanity on which our cultural identity is founded, and nothing else. We use concepts like nationality and race, which are artificial external categories used to present ourselves, but ultimately issues of difference evaporate under the common universal humanity. "To me," Neeta emphasized, "these labels don't mean anything." My cointerviewer, Anjali, asked Neeta to comment on the idea that real class and racial differences in the United States separate people. Did Neeta feel that some people are disadvantaged because of their skin color?

> No. Same. It's both the same, you know? How can they be different? They cannot be different; they are living in the same world. And if you're going to make them different, then you're going to torture them. And they're same. They have to accept, though, that their color will be different and all their stuff, but just leave that aside still. I've seen they're just the same. Believe me, OK?

Having a different skin color and all that "stuff" is not important to Neeta's universal worldview of humanity. She believes that if someone highlights the difference of another person, he or she is torturing that person with this sense of difference. What is the common thread of universal humanity that makes us all the same and, in some ways, equal to one another?

Asha told me that she did not sense any vast cultural differences when she arrived in the United States. She asked me, "What is 'American,' anyway?" and answered her own question:

> Yeah, an American is a white Anglo-Saxon, and that is what is American, but America isn't that anymore. And if you choose to think that way, then I think you're missing out a lot because. . . . When people say, "Oh, you know, X is an American," the first thing I want to say is, "Oh, what do you mean, white Anglo-Saxon?" Because America is, I mean, I am an American. I happen to have the citizenship, so it makes me just as much American as, as them.

The universal humanity here is based on citizenship and the questioning of the idea that only white Anglo-Saxons are Americans.

In Asha's mind, it is quite clear that Indians stand to lose if they focus exclusively on cultural differences. She believes that as human beings, we all are part of this American culture. Furthermore, "once we get to know

Americans, we realize how similar they are to us. They are after the same things as us. They want a comfortable life, house, job security and a good future for their kids." She does believe that there are cultural differences between Indians and Americans but that they are superficial.

Venkat echoed Asha. He feels that there are real differences between Indians and Americans in terms of language, religion, and traditions but that "at the bottom of it all, we are all human beings." As he asserted, "I don't consider myself really that different from this other American guy who's sitting next to me." He believes that ultimately both Indians and Americans want the same things: prosperity and well-being for themselves.

Kajol stated, "Being an Indian woman did not affect my promotions." She explained, "My relationship with all my colleagues are no different from, like, two white colleagues or anything. There's a universal humanity, and there are certain similarities. Like I said, a mother is a mother. It doesn't matter where she comes from." Kajol's relationships with her colleagues are the same as the relationship between two white colleagues. She found common links with Americans through her son, Anand. Most American mothers, according to Kajol, take pride in their children's school activities. Through motherhood, "a bond has opened up between different women," Kajol maintains, "a mother is a mother. It doesn't matter whether she's Indian or not."

The cultural and ritualistic responses to these various events are described as subtle and not worth taking too seriously. One participant, an Indian woman, Deepali, who has a PhD in genetics, argued that the shared universal humanity of Indians and Americans was based on similar genetic material. She used biology to explain the similar features of Indians and Americans.

Genetic work has shown that Indians are probably whites, and we know that, because for ten thousand years, you know, the white people have been coming into India. We Indians are everything. We are not white or black or brown. We are everything. We know that, but they don't, they have no historical knowledge.

The "they" to whom Deepali is referring are Americans. But she added that there are some cultural differences between the two groups:

Indians do not come on time to work, put our family before work, and have other faults, but we share the same genetic material. So, yeah, we've just waited and we've sown the ground. We know that we can do the job, but we do have our defects. We don't stick to time. We're not that, you know, we don't finish it, we don't work like they do in certain areas. Our work ethic is different and if our family comes first, our family will come first, which is not a bad thing. So there are some things which are different but . . .

One way of describing this universal humanity between Americans and Indians is to invoke the notion of being a citizen of the world. Another way is by appealing to the concept of human nature. Two examples illustrate this phenomenon.

"I Really View Myself as a Citizen of the World": *Appeals to Global Citizenship*

I asked Raju how he negotiated his identity as a Sikh who wears a turban, especially after September 11. Raju was quick to point out that he considers himself a Canadian and not an American. Several times in the interview he told me that his life in Canada had greatly influenced his cultural identity. But even though he regarded himself as a Canadian, he did not actively cultivate a sense of "Canadianness" or "Indianness" at home.

His answer perplexed me because he had devoted much of his interview to talking about being different and growing up different in various parts of the world. Raju remarked, "So if you want to know how I cultivate a sense of Canadianness, I really don't. I really view myself as a citizen of the world in its idealistic sense." Raju based this view of himself as a citizen of the world on the idea that categories and labels do not give people an identity. He also told me that "the fact that I'm living in America" does not necessarily put [me] in the category of "being an American." What mattered most is "that this is home to me now." Not surprisingly, this notion of being a citizen of the world is based on an individualistic view of the self.

What matters most to Raju is how he views himself. His physical appearance, skin color, and clothes do not contribute to his self; rather, it is his deeds and actions and contributions to society that matter. Nonetheless, during much of the interview he talked about his son's difficult choices because he wore a turban and because cultural symbols had an important impact on his identity.

Raju was acutely aware that especially after September 11, his turban would make him stand out as the "other." His family feared that both Raju and his son (who also wore a *patka* [a turban usually worn by young Sikh boys]) might be targets of hate crimes. How could Raju see himself as a citizen of the world while struggling with feelings of difference manifested through a cultural symbol of his religion, his turban? Raju's culture and religion were secondary to his identity as a citizen of the world. To him, nationality and ethnicity were superficial labels that interfered in getting to know people on their own terms. I found these contradictions in an overwhelming majority of the participants in my study. They were preoccupied with defining, actively asserting, and constructing a cultural identity that was undermined by their seeking a universal, cultureless world that brought people together because of their shared human condition.

The participants' appeal to human nature was another strategic tactic. Finding individual tendencies to use to discriminate against people was considered not only universal in all cultures but also part of human nature. Consider Kishore's and Vivek's responses to issues of difference.

"I Think It's Partly Human Nature": Appeals to Human Nature

My conversation with Kishore took an interesting turn when we were discussing issues of identity and difference. I asked him whether any of his children had experienced racism in school. Kishore did not answer my question directly but said that it was good for them to be different. "Because I didn't go through it, I would say it's lucky that they are in a place where diversity is valued so much." I promptly turned this around and asked him, "But at the same time, even though some diversity is valued, why do you think there are deeper issues of racial division in this country? Where does that come from?" Kishore responded, "I think, I think it's partly human nature, and I would say you can't totally eradicate everything." Vivek used a similar strategy to deal with difference and illustrated in his narrative the idea that human nature is responsible for all racism and inequality in the world.

Vivek is a successful scientist and teaches physics at a university in Connecticut. He believes that his success is a result of his work ethic, education, Indian values, and the many opportunities that living in America has given him. America is very accepting, he observed, and individuals who persevere can accomplish great things in this country. Earlier in our interview, Vivek made it quite clear that although he is aware that racism exists, he personally does not believe in it. He explains, "I still continue to get opportunities. I mean, I'm not talking purely about science. A lot of other things in life. And those whom I report to give me opportunities. Most of them are Americans. In fact, all of them are Americans."

Vivek tells me that one of the reasons he is offered these opportunities is because he does not internalize issues of racism and discrimination and makes sure that they do not become part of his life. "If you start believing in them, then these things, such as racism and discrimination, will happen to you." Working as a nonwhite, Indian person, Vivek says that he has experienced "good things" in America. He has been amply rewarded for his hard work. Nevertheless, even though Vivek had had much success—both personal and material—in the United States, I asked him if he had ever felt discriminated against: "I don't think I have faced it. . . . Personally, I don't think I have faced it. I may, there may have been some subtle, but not by anybody. . . . Not in the immediate working room that I have. I don't think it's important because I also believe it's human nature." Vivek thought that he may have experienced some subtle form of discrimination but that one should not dwell on such incidents because they are ultimately part of human nature. I asked Vivek to comment on those Indians or nonwhite Americans who are exposed to racism every day.

> Absolutely, there are people who experience racism, but you know, I think that's part of human nature. It doesn't matter where you are. Nowhere in the world you can . . . go to where there's not that division. Here it's based on color, and in India it's based on caste and religion. You go to Ireland, it's based on Catholics and Protestants. And you go to Africa, there are

different tribes that are fighting. I mean, it's very, it's inherent part of human nature."

I asked him to explain why racism is part of human nature. He was surprised by my request. He told me that he could not accuse whites of being racists, because "Indians are the most racist people" in the world. He mentioned that he was troubled by Indians' attitude toward black people in the United States. Vivek continued, in a sarcastic tone. These Indians, Vivek said, fly "into the United States, and somewhere in that twelve-hour or eighteen-hour journey, staying at different airports and landing here in New York or Boston or wherever, they learn to hate blacks." I asked Vivek why he did not hold the same views. He said that he is not that different from many Indians who come here, that most of the people with whom he works share his outlook on the world. These people, he notes, are very cosmopolitan.

Vivek then told me that he does not discriminate against people and does not have racist feelings about blacks because he was brought up by his parents to believe in the inherent equality of all people. It was not just a theory; his parents expected him to be kind to all people. I asked him to give me an example. Vivek explained, "We have *jammadarnis* [lower-caste people in India who clean toilets] who come and clean the bathrooms in our place, and nobody ever differentiated between them and any other servant or any other person coming into the house." The servants and toilet cleaners from lower castes all were given food on the same plates that Vivek's family ate from, and his parents treated even low-caste people with respect. His parents' attitudes deeply shaped his views of equality and difference in the United States. "Wherever I've gone, I've never considered myself any different from anybody else who's there. I'm competing for the same things, fighting for the same resources, and I'm going to get it."

Vivek does not consider himself different from others because he was taught to treat others as equals, and he expects that others will not single him out because he is different. This deep, internal belief in universal equality and the shared humanity of all people makes him feel that he can compete for the same job and have the same opportunities as other Americans do. Vivek reaffirmed this belief: "I always say there's only one religion that matters. People laugh at me when I tell them what it is. I say, it's humanity." I asked Vivek whether his belief in universal humanity was a way to distance or background his Indianness.

> I'm not erasing my Indianness, but when people think of me, when people look at me and my friends look at me, they don't think—"Oh there goes an Indian." They think, "There goes Vivek, who is an Indian." That's fine! I personally believe that I am a human being first and that's what I am. Anything else just doesn't matter.

When I told Vivek that a lot of people in this world know their humanity only through their religion or the cultural practices of their respective groups, he found that statement problematic. According to him, the concepts of universal humanity and human nature have no categories like Indian, American, religion, race, gender, and class. "One's ethnic background and race cannot be used as a factor in promoting people," he asserted. Vivek was not unaware that many people are denied promotion because of their color and that their talents are not recognized because of their cultural, racial, and ethnic backgrounds. However, he did not want to be "burdened" by those incidents and believed that it would not happen to him.

These were not the only dialogical tactics that my participants used to come to terms with their difference. Prashant remarked that issues of difference he faced at work or at home were largely due to the homogeneity of New England. He said that because New England was less diverse, nonwhite people stood out and their differences were more noticeable. He felt that this would not happen in places like New York or Los Angeles. In addition, how other Americans viewed him depended on their education and upbringing. Vishal stated that although he had not faced any discrimination at his workplace, instead he had faced "differentiation" as a nonwhite employer. I asked Vishal to explain the difference between the two concepts: "I will not say discrimination. I will say differentiation —more, that, uh, there is respect in general. But, uh, there is a lack of trust, a lack of total trust taken. Lots of my clients were there because they have worked with me for a long time." Many of his clients respected Vishal, but others were not able to trust him right away because he looked different. Vishal reiterated several times that he had to earn his clients' trust by working hard because they regarded him as a foreigner and were less likely to trust him. But he termed his clients' behavior "differentiation" rather than outright discrimination. Even though they respected him as a person, they were not sure that he had the skills to carry out the job.

6

■　■　■　■　■　■　■　■　■

Analyzing Assignations and Assertions

The Enigma of Brown Privilege

Bharati Mukherjee, a well-known Indian American novelist, published an article in which she wrote,

> I am less shocked, less outraged and shaken to my core, by a purse snatching in New York City in which I lost all of my dowry gold—everything I'd been given by my mother in marriage—than I was by a simple question asked of me in the summer of 1978 by three high-school boys on the Rosedale subway station platform in Toronto. Their question was, "Why don't you go back to Africa?" (Mukherjee 1981, p. 38)

Why is Mukherjee disturbed by being mistaken for an African woman? Why is she upset about being told to go back to Africa by three teenagers at a subway station?

Her reluctance to be seen as a person of color is a theme that surfaced often in my interviews. Most of these Indians have faced varying levels of racism and discrimination but have been able to carve out a place for themselves in the American middle-class suburban culture. They usually are perceived as the model minority and are not given the kind of negative reception in their communities that is usually reserved for other working-class, poor migrants. Instead, that these participants want to be seen as a group that is close to white culture and their distance from "blackness" is evident in the ethnographic data. This chapter describes the different ways in which Indians use assignations to locate their selves in their new world, the American suburb. On one hand, they strongly identify with their Indian ethnicity, but on the other hand, they distance themselves from their ethnicity and frame their cultural identity in terms of a universal human condition and universal human nature.

Migration, by its very nature of movement, has significant implications for how Indians view their personal and collective identity through the categories of nationality, ethnicity, and racial identity. According to Shukla, "Even if an ambivalence that already existed comes to fore or is newly articulated, the affective dimension of being Indian is changed by the diaspora and by being located in and through the processes of racialization, ethnicization, and nationalization" (2003, p. 10). How do Indians, as both a collective group and individuals, understand their racial and ethnic identities in their new homes? What processes of racialization and ethnicization do the assignations and assertions discussed in the previous chapters reveal? How can we explain the contradictory status of South Asians as "ambiguous nonwhites" (George 1997; Kibria 1998) and the ways in which this ambivalence about racial identity is demonstrated?

One way to understand these responses to migration—voices of assignations and assertions—is to situate them in the model minority discourse of the diaspora. I use the dialogical model of self to explain the ambiguities regarding the formation of racial identity in middle-class Indians. More specifically, I show how voice as an analytical concept allows us to understand the multiple, shifting, and often contradictory positions on the racial and ethnic identity formation of the professional, elite Indian diaspora in the United States.

The discourses of racial identity in the Indian diaspora also suggest that we need to rethink traditional notions of immigrant adaptation and acculturation in cross-cultural psychology. Traditionally, much of mainstream psychology has been occupied with developing universal, linear models and theories of immigrant identity, acculturation, and adaptation. For instance, cross-cultural psychologists have studied topics like acculturation and acculturative stress (Berry 1998), socialization and enculturation (Camilleri and Malewska-Peyre 1997), and bicultural identity (LaFromboise, Coleman, and Gerton 1998). This body of research, though commendable for bringing issues of immigrant identity to the table, has largely presented migration as a series of fixed phases and stages that do not account for new immigrants' culturally distinct and politically entrenched experiences.

The ongoing negotiations between the voices of assignation and those of assertion give us an alternative model for understanding the process of migrant acculturation. This dialogical model of acculturation illuminates how middle-class Indian migrants negotiate their hybrid sense of self in the context of cultural difference, racial politics, and increasing globalization and transnational communication (Bhatia 2004).

Between Assignations and Assertions of Racial Identity

A certain kind of exceptionalism has permeated the narrative of "South Asian–American racial formation" (Koshy 1998, p. 285). The narrative of exceptionalism feeds basically two conflicting views about South Asian identity in general and Indian American racial and ethnic identity in particular. One view, shared mostly by middle-class Indian Americans and reflected in the ideologies that operate in Indian American organizations, emphasizes "ethnicity and class and denies or mitigates the historical salience of race for South Asians in the United States. This position emphasizes the anomalous status of South Asian Americans among racial minorities and embraces the rhetoric of color-blind meritocracy" (Koshy 1998, p. 285). The second view, shared mostly by South Asian scholars, academics, and activists, "treats South-Asian color consciousness as equivalent to White racism and criticizes the immigrant community for denying its own blackness" (Koshy 1998, p. 285). These theorists and activists argue that South Asians should not be reluctant to see their identities in racial terms and should make a concerted effort to form political alliances with other racial minorities. One of the implications of these contrary and conflicting views of Indian American identity is that both these positions of racial and cultural identity are grounded in the language of choice, "thus inadvertently re-producing the American ideology of self-making and possibility in discussing one of the social arenas where it has been least applicable" (Koshy 1998, p. 285).

Koshy (1998) proposed that we explore the negotiations—the tensions and ambiguities—that South Asian individuals must undertake when certain identities are assigned to them by the majority groups. We also must examine the concept of identity that immigrants bring with them and reconstruct that identity in new cultural contexts. These acts of assignation and assertion by the Indian participants reveal that they are willing to acknowledge and reject their differences, often by moving between these two positions.

Amreekan Dreams: Living as the Model Minority

The 1990 census shows that Indians have the second highest median income, $49,309, of any group in the United States, just below the highest, earned by the Japanese (Rangaswamy 2000). For many Indian migrants, the fact that their median income is higher than that of the national average of $35,225 is a source of immense pride. Visweswaran (1997) underscored this point by stating that in 1985 the average income of an Indian family in the United States was about $80,000, and the 1990 census indicated that the Indian community's income reflected a "mean per capita level at 115% of the national average." The same census also stated that 50 percent of Asian Indian men and 34 percent of Asian Indian women held jobs in the professional and managerial sector of the economy. Many of these professional Indians, who migrated to the United States after 1965, earn large incomes, live in large suburban homes located primarily in white neighborhoods, drive luxury cars, and send their children to expensive private liberal arts colleges and Ivy League schools (Rangaswamy 2000). Kibria examined the effects of a model minority stereotype on second-generation Chinese and Korean Americans. "Asians in the United States have been popularly identified as the model minority, or a minority group that is primed for socioeconomic advancement and success. At the heart of their achievements are, it is said, their cultural predispositions, in particular a strong work ethic and an emphasis on education" (Kibria 2002, p. 131).

Throughout the 1980s and 1990s, professional, middle-class Indians began celebrating their status as one of the most successful migrant communities in the United States. They publicly proclaimed their model minority and economic status as a community on a par with that of middle-class white America. In short, they had arrived as a community and wanted recognition from white America as part of the American social fabric.

On hearing about the success of Indian immigrants in the United States, many politicians began to compare their achievements with those of other minorities, such as Hispanics and African Americans. The former Republican senator Phil Gramm, for example, stated, "Indians as an ethnic group had the highest per-capita income and highest average education level in the U.S. He said the U.S. needed more hard working and successful immigrants like Indians" (Visweswaran 1997, p. 5). In September 1997, the former Republican senator Jesse Helms addressed the Indian American Forum: "Indian Americans represent the best and the brightest the United States has to offer. You can go to the finest hospitals, you can go to the universities, you can go into business and there they are, people from India" (Prashad 2000, p. 7).

The model minority discourse perpetuated by Indian immigrants and reinforced by the validations of politicians like Phil Gramm and Jesse Helms overlooks the fact that in the 1980s many nonprofessional, working-class Indians also made their way into American society. Indeed, the uneven demographic profile of Indian migrants is "only now being corrected as nonprofessionals migrate to join families, as economic and/or political refugees; as workers in the transportation, and other trades; as small businessmen (running shops, motels and so on)" (Prashad 2000, p. 6).

The demographic profile of the Indian diaspora shows that most professional immigrants come from a middle-class background in India. Since only 10 percent of Indian citizens can afford to go universities and colleges in India, "it is not its poorest citizens who migrate to the United States but rather its most, sophisticated: people trained in economics, medicine, engineering or management" (Lessinger 1995, p. 11). Furthermore, what also distinguishes Indian professional immigrants from, say, their first-generation Chinese or Korean counterparts is their fluency in the English language. Other scholars have pointed out as well that because the model minority stereotype focuses on Asians' achievements, their success also invites resentment and hostility from mainstream America. In regard to the Chinese American diaspora, the model minority stereotype represents the opposite meanings of the Yellow Peril (see

Okhirio 1994). As Kibria found, "In both the model minority image and that of [the] yellow peril, Asian achievements takes on [an] inhuman, even species-different character" (2002, p. 133).

Another important component of the model minority discourse that is perpetuated in the Indian diaspora is the idea that Indian immigrants have the requisite cultural strategies to deal with the assignations of otherness bestowed on them. Many Indians, in general, believe that not only do they rely on their educational qualifications, skills, work ethic, and competence to excel at work but that they also can successfully reconstruct the meaning of otherness that is assigned to them. For example, recall how Priya dealt with being othered when Americans considered her as an exotic Indian woman. Her strategy to avoid this label was wearing a black Western dress and scarf. She wanted her friends and coworkers to see her as one of them and not as an "exotic Indian woman." Similarly, Poonam decided not to invite American guests to her daughter's wedding because they would not be able to participate in the ladies *sangeet, khana peena,* and *gana bajana.*

As a protective father, Rohan felt that it was necessary to intervene and control the ways in which his children were being othered. That is, he decided to repackage his daughter's Indian food to make it look similar to the lunches the American children were eating at school. All these examples point to the deeply held belief in the professional Indian community that they must deal with otherness not by directly fighting the racist depictions of ethnicity but by using careful strategies to frame their meaning of difference and constantly negotiating their difference by moving between voices of assignations and those of assertions. These middle-class Indians were willing to use their status as model minorities, their strong educational foundations, and their belief in the American dream to negotiate the terms of difference that were thrust upon them.

Belonging in and Claiming White Spaces

When Deepali and her family had just moved to the exclusive, mostly white suburbs of Old Lyme, her daughter Karishma did not get a single play date. According to Deepali, most of the parents in Old Lyme were seeing daughter's "color" and thus were reluctant to let their children associate with her. Deepali detected an indifferent attitude from the parents when she brought Karishma to school, but she was determined not to become a victim and be treated as second-class citizen.

Deepali frantically called all the parents of the children in her neighborhood and managed to get two play dates for her daughter. Because she actively sought out friends for her child, within a year of their arrival in Old Lyme, Karishma's social life had changed dramatically.

> A year later, on her birthday, there were forty people at her birthday party running all over the place. These are people from her preschool and her current classmates, and every one of them came. Not only because of those play dates, but because she turned out to be the best in the class, and the beautiful thing about [the Old Lyme] school system is that intellect is respected, and every mother wants her child to play with the child who is best in the class. And that's where we'll win out. Every child has been told by their parents, "Play with Karishma!" She gets phone calls from her friends, "How do I do this homework?" She's the one telling them, "This is how you write a Veterans Day essay." Her essay was so well written; it's still up on that wall. So, I think that's where we'll win out.

Deepali's response shows that Indians have to rely on their education and intelligence to become the model minority and make the dominant others, the majority, come to them. Karishma had lots of friends at her birthday party because of her intelligence, hard work, and determination to prove that she was the best student in her class.

The critical part of Deepali's interview was that Karishma's forty schoolmates were at her birthday not because of the play dates but because their parents realized that Karishma was a model student. The young girls in the neighborhood called Karishma to ask her for help with homework, and they consulted with her on writing a good essay. Deepali was proud to tell me that these are the same children who did not want to play with her daughter a year ago.

But what if Karishma—a brown, Indian girl—were not a model student? Would her friends still have accepted her, and would she still have had so many students at her home for her birthday party? If Karishma were a mediocre student, would her white friends still call her? If Karishma was not such a good reader and writer, would the parents in her

Old Lyme neighborhood still be eager to send their children to her house? Did Karishma have to prove that she is a model minority student in order to gain acceptance and approval from her friends? Deepali and I did not dwell on these questions, but it was hard for me to ignore them as Deepali was constructing the model minority discourse to explain her daughter's success.

The professional Indians in this study consider the use of intelligence and determination to be excellent tools for handling otherness and alienation from the larger American society. Even though Karishma had forty white children at her birthday party, Deepali was not trying to become white. By telling me that Karishma was accepted in their white neighborhood, Deepali was not trying to erase her Indianness or otherness. Instead, she was telling me that Indians have to work hard and be model citizens in the eyes of the majority in order to be considered equal to white Americans.

Karishma did not erase her Indianness or her otherness to gain acceptance from her peers; rather, she adopted the same social values regarding education and hard work as those of many upper-class Americans living in her neighborhood. Deepali was establishing "sameness" or equivalence with the majority by stating that she could be the other and still be equal in terms of power, economics, and middle-class values. An essential part of the model minority discourse is its emphasis on middle-class values and the different ways in which they offer immigrants both proximity and cultural recognition from upper- and middle-class Americans. Another part of the model minority discourse is the belief that Indians are a minority group, and so they have to work harder than others to prove that they belong in the same space that is occupied by the majority members of American culture.

By constantly reproducing the model minority discourse, many professional, post-1965 immigrants try to reposition their difference as being the same or equal to the dominant majority. This attempt to establish sameness by using a model minority discourse also means that many participants are reluctant to see themselves as racially distinct from white America. By attempting to position themselves as similar to the dominant majority, professional Indian immigrants also appeal to universal humanity, thus completely leveling the divergent historical and cultural conditions that have created these two cultures. For some Indians, it is important to believe that there are no major differences between Indians and Americans.

When I asked Venkat how he reconciled his views about universal humanity with the racism experienced by his family members in this country, he responded by saying that he drew strength from Indian/Hindu culture and traditions to cope with acts of prejudice and discrimination. Venkat also tried to establish a strategic alliance with the majority culture by saying that everyone experiences some form of racism or prejudice, thereby equating his experience of discrimination or prejudice with the experiences of the dominant majority. This is how Venkat formed a strategic alliance or a strategic identification with the dominant majority, seeing his voice and subject positioning as equal to those of white Americans by separating his role as scientist from his personal identity as an ethnic American.

Likewise, Abhishek, Arun, Kajol, Neeta, Raju, and Vivek all believe in the universal laws of science, and when they step into their labs as scientists and engineers, they feel like other Americans. By backgrounding their foreignness and foregrounding their roles as scientists and engineers and doctors, many of these elite Indian professionals try to align themselves with the majority white Americans.

When he was in the formative stages of his career, Abhishek believed that science was a great equalizer and that his expertise in engineering and management positioned him as equal to his American counterparts. Abhishek did not believe in bringing "Indian culture" into the lab or sticking to certain Indian traditions, because he had clearly defined his role as a scientist.

Like Abhishek, Raju is very aware of his sense of difference, but his individual talents, work ethic, and personal ambition are not embedded in his self-image as a Sikh and a member of a minority community. Raju believes strongly in the basic elements of the model minority discourse: the idea that hard work pays off in America. Similarly, the women of the Indian diaspora—Kajol, Naina, Neeta, and Rekha—invoked the philosophy of multiculturalism based on universal humanity, whose emphasis is on a core, bounded self that transcends the categories of color, caste, nationality, or ethnicity. These assertions of sameness, universal humanity, the great American nation, and meritocracy all are important elements that are used not only to create the model minority discourse but also to organize the collective life in the diaspora.

The Model Minority and the Greatness of America

An important part of the model minority discourse in the Indian diaspora is the belief that America has treated Indian immigrants benevolently and that they owe their success to America. The idea that the American dream is open to everyone, provided that one works for it, has an immense appeal to the Indian community. This belief that talent and ambition can overcome shortcomings and lead to success allows these immigrants to strategically background their brownness or ethnicity and make a case for a color-blind meritocracy.

This belief in color-blind meritocracy, however, means that professional Indians have to find a way to background their own color or sense of difference. Many professional Indians believe that their career achievements are based on their talents and not on their status as people of color. How do Indian migrants in the diaspora put aside their color when their employers see them as "brown"? These Indian employees are working in elite positions because of their talents and skills, but they also are aware that they bring "color" and "diversity" to their company.

What strategies do these professional Indians use to demonstrate their similarity to their white workers while still maintaining their identity as Indians? For Vivek, the way out of this dilemma is to identify strategically with his sense of difference. For him, racism and discrimination are meant to be "out there" and not something that affects him and his performance at work. Vivek accepts the model minority discourse by acknowledging that he is different but is immune from racism in society. That is, he sees racism as something that happens to others. He believes that the day he confronts racism and makes it valid for himself, he will stop being equal to the dominant majority.

In the previous chapter, Neeta noted that she never talked with her children about racism or issues related to difference. Talking about racism, according to Neeta, implies that she and her children are different and thus not equal to the majority culture. Neeta stated very clearly in her interview that in her family, no one ever talks about racism or about being white, black, or brown. She believes that her children do not feel different, and, as a result, they never feel the need to talk about being different.

What Neeta is leaving out from her discourse about difference is that her husband, Vishal, experienced both overt and subtle racism throughout the three decades he has lived in America. Consider an incident that I discuss in chapter 7. Immediately after an automobile accident on a Boston highway, a police officer asked Vishal's white employee and subordinate, "How come he is your boss?" Although Vishal clearly perceived the incident as a case of overt racism, he preferred to see the racism of his white clients as "differentiation" and not "discrimination." The implicit assumption here is that in this world of diversity and universal humanity, being different implies inferiority to the majority.

This is why we see Vishal, Neeta, Kishore, Vivek, and several others reluctant to use the language of racial difference to understand their sense of self. Kishore believes that racism is universal and that people everywhere promote their own people. As examples of racism, he pointed to the casteism and nepotism and the parochial work culture that exist in most of India. Furthermore, Kishore blames Indians for being unable to reach the top levels in corporate America. He thinks that their tendency to socialize with other Indians and their inability to network with elite Americans in their companies or at national conferences have created barriers to success.

Kishore maintains that professional Indians spend too much time with their own people at cultural festivals organized by the diaspora instead of strategically finding ways to help one another at work. Venkat echoed Kishore's suggestion: "I'm not as boisterous as them, I'm not as open as them. I don't try hard to fit into the American mold. It's a little difficult." From Venkat's point of view, it is clear that his so-called Indian values and traditions have helped him reach the place where he wanted to be on the corporate ladder, but at the same time, he believes that these Indian traditions and behaviors have prevented him from reaching the top-level positions in his company. The idea of having to modify one's cultural behaviors to fit the American "mold" seems to reflect the view held by many professional Indians that individual merit, personal ambition, internal motivation, and advanced professional skills are needed to get to the top of the corporate ladder. This collective belief in the discourse of individual meritocracy is an integral component of the model minority discourse circulating in the diaspora.

A benevolent notion of America is foregrounded in this belief of individual merit. This notion of a magnanimous America is created from the idea that racism exists in this society and also, in more dangerous forms, is a universal feature in almost every society. This idea of a benevolent and fair America, a nation that has always attracted immigrants from all parts of the world, is rooted in the material success of the model minority. This picture of America is grounded in the story of many Indian professionals' own material and financial success. They have all the requisite cultural and symbolic markers to prove that they are minorities, albeit privileged model minorities who are "higher up" than other minorities in the America.

The need to characterize America as a benevolent and magnanimous nation stems from the perception that minorities are located socially as foreigners and outsiders in this society. Mahalingam (2003, 2006) argues that social locations are created by the intersecting identities of race, class, and caste and that the differential power relations among the axes of these identities locate these outsiders as living on the margins. In order to "negate such hegemonic social representations, people at marginalized locations feel a stronger need to create a positive identity than do members of a dominant group" (Mahalingam 2006, p. 3). Many Indian participants do not belong to an oppressed or strongly marginalized group. But because they are an immigrant minority and have an ambivalent relationship with their racial identity, some of them tend to project an "idealized" identity of both the goodness of the "American nation" and their own status as a "model minority."

Social-Class Positions and Model Minority Discourse

Rangaswamy's 2000 demographic profile of the Indian diaspora in and around Chicago is relevant to the Indian diaspora of southeastern Connecticut. The ways in which professional Indians construct their image is closely tied to the idea that they are upper-and middle-class model minorities, who are vastly different from members of other ethnic communities. My interview with Archana, a British Indian woman with a doctorate in sociology who has lived in Connecticut for about fourteen years, touched on the model minority discourse.

Archana grew up in the 1960s in England and then moved to the United States in the 1990s when she married Ashok, who is in a top management position at the ABC Computer Company. Ashok and Archana live in a house in the rural community of Plainville, Connecticut. Because Archana grew up in England in the 1960s and 1970s, her sense of being the other, or a "person of color," was influenced by the overtly racist climate and tensions in many towns and cities in England.

When Archana first arrived in Plainville, a small, almost exclusively white, rural community, she was nervous about being one of only a few minorities in the neighborhood. She was afraid that her family would stand out. "So, it's like feeling, oh, I am kind of back in the 1960s in Britain—people looking at us." Archana was strongly shaped by the dominant images of Indianness in England in the 1960s and 1970s. As she told me, "Well, they always look down on us." It was clear to her that most British people in the 1960s and 1970s could not distinguish among Indians, Pakistanis, and Bangladeshis. She also added that British people in general regarded all South Asians as poor illiterates who lived in mud huts. In the 1960s in Britain, South Asians were seen through racist stereotypes and were accused of eating "smelly food" and displaying "lot of raucous behavior."

I asked Archana why she thought that South Asians experience such overt racism in England. Using a postcolonial analysis, Archana told me that Britain was coming out of a "postimperial" phase and had lost its power and prestige in the world and that looking down on South Asians was a way of recovering the glory of the imperial past.

Archana explained that in Britain during the 1960s, South Asians from all classes and educational backgrounds began arriving in Britain. But she mistakenly singled out Pakistani and Bangladeshi migrants as those mainly employed as labor workers and were generally low skilled. In contrast, Archana argued that Indians were in Britain to obtain degrees in higher education and that a majority were skilled professionals. Archana may have thought she was referring to the social class of South Asian migrants, but in my view, she also was explaining why Indian migrants in the United States came to be seen as a model minority.

Of course, we all, to them looked the same. We were all put in one basket —and all of us were called "Pakis." No matter what you look like, you know, you could have a PhD from MIT, you're still a "Paki." But in this country, it's not quite like that because, as far as I can tell, those Indians who have come here have tended to be professionals. So they get a bit more professional respect, and the lower rungs of strata in this country are essentially African Americans and Puerto Ricans. . . . So we are socially higher up the ladder in this country.

Archana was contrasting the social class of Indians in Britain and in America and was grateful not to be called a "Paki" in the United States. Her comments reinforce the view held by many Indians in the local diaspora that Indians are a model minority and are considered higher on the social ladder than many other racial groups.

Archana was happy to tell me that there are no "ghetto-like situations" for Indians here, as is the case for many Indians living in Britain. This is "something which I don't have an experience of in this country. There are no Bradfords and there are no Manchesters[1] in [the United States]." Archana's statement that there are no Indian ghettos in America distances the Indian community from other oppressed minorities.

What is the role of race in the Indian immigrants' subjective understanding of their identity as a group? Their responses show that sometimes they directly resist identifying themselves in racial terms or that their view of their racial identities may be ambiguous. Prashad writes that Indians in the United States are aware that they are not part of mainstream American "white" culture but that they are not "black" either. On one hand, *desis* have denied their "blackness" in America, "partly out of a desire for class mobility." But on the other hand, "Indians have formed political connections with other minority groups to express solidarity, but mostly the alliances with minorities groups have been formed to gain some of the resources for advancement guaranteed to historically oppressed minorities by the states" (Prashad 2000, pp. 94–99).

Understanding Desi Ambivalence about Color

Indian Americans are comfortable with the idea that they differ from mainstream America in regard to culture and ethnicity, but not in regard to their racial identity. According to George, "What is refused by nearly all upper and middle class South Asians is not so much a specific racial identity but the very idea of being raced. The only identity that is acknowledged is the cultural and ethnic one of being no more and no less than 'Indian American'" (1997, p. 29).

The Indian immigrants' reluctance to be cast as persons of color—as having a racial identity—can be explained in several ways. George states that many South Asians living in the United States want to make themselves racially invisible by constructing their personhood in terms of class and cultural formations. For example, many Indian Americans represent themselves to Americans as being from the glorious ancient Indian civilization, the spiritual and cultural East, or the pure Aryan race.

Such a stance, George noted, is intended to reposition their negative portrayal as "immigrants of color" to a positive ascription of belonging to a superior culture. This stance is intended to distance Indian Americans from other people and communities of color residing in the United States. "Recognizing this commonality across ethnicity supplied by brownness of one's skin requires that one surrender the comfort offered by a seemingly race-free but culturally value-loaded Indianness" (George 1997, p. 43).

The other strategic move made by many Indians in the diaspora is to find ways to hide, overcome, or transcend all markers of difference that are present in the self. In this case, they overcome their sense of difference by changing their accent and replacing traditional, ethnic clothes (such as saris) with T-shirts and blue jeans. These strategies, according to George, should be read as "symptomatic of the upper-caste South Asian determination to occupy a position that is simultaneously privileged and unmarked: the place of invisibility" (1997, p. 45). This desire to occupy the place of invisibility and to be seen as "Aryan" is demonstrated repeatedly in the history of Indian migration to the United States.

Color Me Aryan, White, Olive, Black, or Brown

Mazumdar's pioneering article "Racist Response to Racism: The Aryan Myth and South Asians in the United States" (1989) analyzes the ways in which South Asians insist on seeing themselves as "Aryans of pure stock," even though the dominant majority perceives them to be black or people of color. In reference to Indian migration to the United States, Mazumdar cites the case of Bhagat Singh Thind, who was a Hindu born in Punjab and came to the United States in 1913. Under the 1906 naturalization law, Thind brought a case to the U.S. Supreme Court that he was Caucasian and therefore white and entitled to U.S. citizenship.

Jensen writes that Thind and his attorneys argued their case by using both the "traditional combination of anthropological evidence and judicial precedent." Indians were Aryans and therefore Caucasians, according to anthropologists, and the courts had agreed that the term *Caucasian* *meant* "white." But the government took a different position in its arguments. Its case was based on refuting the anthropologists' arguments, that "white should be interpreted according to the usage of the common man and, in that usage Indians were not white . . . and in view of most common people 'white was not synonymous with Caucasians'" (Jensen 1988, p. 258). The government won the case, and Thind's failure to win in court had several repercussions for other Indians and South Asians in the United States.

Subsequently, all South Asians who had been granted U.S. citizenship in the 1920s lost it. For several reasons, Mazumdar found the desire of many Indian migrants to be seen as "Caucasian" and therefore "white" to be troubling.

> What concerns us here is the premise on which the struggle for citizenship was based. South Asians see themselves as "Aryan" and therefore Caucasian and white despite the fact they had plenty of evidence to the contrary. The self-perception prevents the immigrants from making common cause with other Asians who were barred from citizenship on the grounds of race—such as Japanese immigrants after the judgements in the Ozawa case. Instead of challenging racism, the South Asian struggle became an individualized and personalized mission to prove that they were of pure Aryan stock. (Mazumdar 1989, p. 50)

This desire to appear white or Aryan did not disappear with the influx of professionals migrating from India or with the passage of the 1965 Immigration and Nationality Act.

Mazumdar cited a survey conducted in 1975 on how professional migrants described their own racial identity. "Fifteen of the respondents stated they were 'Aryan' in some measure. Five people replied Indians are

Caucasians, six stated Indians are not Caucasians, while five others stated 'some Indians are white.'" Mazumdar then looked at another survey conducted in 1976 of 159 Indians living in Chicago. The survey asked the respondents, "What do you consider your skin color to be?" Mazumdar suggests that the responses are similar to those from the Indian immigrants in the New York community. "Eleven percent in this sample chose 'white' as their skin color, 70 percent wrote 'brown.' A further 8 percent, obviously dark-skinned, were willing to use terms such as olive and blue to describe themselves, rather than use the term 'black.' Only 3 percent identified their skin color as black." The interesting part of this survey is that 44 percent of the sample of 159 Indians surveyed talked about being discriminated against in America. Approximately half the discriminatory incidents were related to being "passed over for raises and promotions in favor of white Americans" (Mazumdar 1989, pp. 51–52). Other incidents were related to not being able to rent apartments or buy houses available on the market.

It is important to remember that the idea of denying, erasing, or muting one's racial identity is not tantamount to a "straightforward desire for whiteness" (George 1997, p. 42). Drawing on Kibria's 1998 work, George tells us that the confusion about racial identity in the South Asian diaspora can best be described by using the term "ambiguous non-whites," as it "allows for an identity as non-white and as white (because it is ambiguous): in either case the racial marker around which identity revolves is white" (George 1997, p. 43).

Maira's 2002 work on the second-generation Indian American youth culture in New York City shows some parallels between the strategies used by first-generation and second-generation Indian Americans to understand their racial identity. Some of the Indian American youths in this study emphasized their ethnic identity in response to racial ambiguities they had experienced. According to Maira,

> The discourse of ethnic identity, according to some youth, is a way to resolve or perhaps deflect the question of racial positioning. These moves reflect broader patterns of emphasizing ethnicity that some critics view as attempts to position Indian Americans outside the racial stratification of the United States and to deflect identification with less privileged minority groups of color. (2002, p. 67)

The assertions of racial identity by middle-class Indians thus can be construed as strategies or "ethnic choices" to cope with the acculturation struggles of Indian immigrants in the new world.

"Ethnic Options" and "Racial Choices" in the Indian Diaspora

Another way to understand and analyze the responses of assignation and assertions by the participants of this study is to situate them in accordance with Mary Waters's book *Ethnic Options* (1990). She writes that most white Americans adopt a "symbolic ethnicity" to define themselves because this type of ethnicity makes them feel special and also gives them a sense of community and belonging. Indeed, Waters argues that for many white Americans, being ethnic is a leisure-time activity and they feel they can easily move in and out of their ethnic roles as needed. For most white Americans, becoming ethnic is seen as a matter of personal choice, and they are free to choose among different ancestries. But Waters pointed out that the participants in her study assumed that everyone else also could choose their ethnicity if they wanted to. Symbolic ethnicity is appealing to most white Americans because

> being ethnic makes them feel unique and special and not just "vanilla," as one respondent put it. They are not like everyone else. At the same time, being ethnic gives them a sense of belonging to a collectivity. It is the best of all worlds: they can claim to be unique and special while simultaneously finding the community and conformity with others that they also crave. But that "community" is also a type that will not interfere with a person's individuality. The closest this type of ethnic identity brings a person to "group activity" is something like Saint Patrick's Day parade. (Waters 1990, pp. 151–52)

The concept of symbolic ethnicity as Waters describes it cannot be applied directly to the participants in my study. But it can be used as an important analytical device to understand the assignations and assertions of the Indian migrants. As we have seen, they do not have a personal choice in framing the meanings of ethnicity assigned to them. Waters contends that "the social and political sequences for being Asian or Hispanic or black are not symbolic for the most part, or voluntary. They are real and often hurtful" (1990, p. 156). The different types of otherness—generic, marked, and disruptive—that are assigned to the Indians in the southeastern diaspora by their white colleagues and coworkers exemplifies Waters's point.

Even though all the Indians in this study have had some experience with racism, discrimination, prejudice, and otherness, they are nonetheless ambiguous about their own racial identity. Many are aware of their differences but have great difficulty seeing themselves as belonging to a racial group, like the Hispanics and the African Americans.

My point is that the participants' assertions of sameness, individual merit, and universal humanity can be construed as a desire for "symbolic ethnicity." Based on my analysis of their assertions, I believe that the participants in my study want to be able make the choice of backgrounding or foregrounding their Indian ethnicity. They want to be able to construct meanings about their personhood in terms of their Indian ethnicity or through the language of universal humanity, sameness, and human nature. Most of the professional Indians with whom I spoke want to be in a position in which they can choose to invoke the type of symbolic ethnicity that Waters described.

I am not arguing that these Indian participants want to erase or completely deny their ethnicity. Instead, they are invested in their cultural identity as Indians and are proud to be part of the "Indian" cultural heritage, yet they also do not want any costs associated with having Indian ethnicity or being brown. They want to be in a position in which the *bindis,* saris, Diwali rituals, thick accents, and stereotypic images associated with India, such as being dirty and poor, are not subject to racist evaluations. These Indians want to retain their cultural roots and feel that they can enjoy their ethnicity in the same way that the subjects of Waters's study do. They also want to be able, if necessary, to present themselves as being a person or an individual without necessarily having to attach ethnic meanings to their personhood or identity. The desire to see themselves as similar or equal to their white counterparts is to want a normative status for Indian ethnicity that is similar or equal to German or French ancestry. This quest for normative status does not mean that the participants are not aware of the divergent political and cultural histories of Indian or German ethnicity. They know that they are brown, with roots in an Eastern culture, and that their homeland is in the Third World, but they do not want their "Indianness" or brownness marked and given the status of being inferior and on the margins of society. Through their discourse of sameness, these participants want to be able to invoke their Indian ethnicity without having to feel that their ethnicity is a psychological burden that invites acts of hatred, racism, and prejudice.

Paradoxically, many Indians do not recognize that they are already speaking from a position of privilege when they cast their identities in terms of the universal human condition. Most of the Indians of the local diaspora with whom I spoke are able to resist the assignation of otherness and racism by invoking universal humanity, human nature, and individual merit. According to Waters,

> Symbolic ethnicity is not just something associated with generational movement. It is alone very much dependent on social mobility. As long as racial or ethnic identity is associated with class stratification, or as long as ascriptive characteristics are used to assign rewards in a society, ethnic identity will be much more complex than individual choice and selective personal and familial enjoyment of tradition. (1990, p. 165)

The social-class position of the Indian migrants of this study, their education, and their sense of being part of an elite segment of the society already have granted them the privilege of being in a position in which they can make universal assertions of their identity. For example, as mentioned before, Abhishek, Arun, Kajol, Neeta, Raju, and Vivek believe in the universal laws of science, and when they step into their jobs as professionals, they think that they are like other Americans. Their Indianness, foreignness, or otherness is bracketed, and, for that time, they feel that they are on par with their American colleagues. By backgrounding their foreignness and foregrounding their roles as professionals, many of these Indian professionals are aligning themselves with the majority white Americans.

Based on the Indian migrants' responses and assertions, we could argue that they want the same privileges that are associated with "symbolic ethnicity" but that still frame their sense of self in terms of Indian culture, religious practices, and the meanings of otherness assigned to them. That is, they want to be able to invoke their "ethnic option" without having to suffer the political and psychological consequences associated with being different in America. Having "Indian ethnicity" does have important material and psychological consequences for middle-class Indian immigrants. It affects their social networks, their choice of spouses, the places where they live, and the way they organize their life in the diaspora. Waters sees race as playing an important part in the construction of symbolic ethnicity.

> Americans who have a symbolic ethnicity continue to think of ethnicity—as well as race—as being biologically rooted. They enjoy many choices themselves, but they continue to ascribe identities to others—especially those whom they identify by skin color. Thus a person with a black skin who had some Irish ancestry would have to work very hard to present him or herself as Irish—and in many important ways he/she would be denied that option. (Waters 1990, p. 167)

The different assertions of the professional Indians in this study tell us that they are involved in an ongoing negotiation with their ethnicity.

The findings of my study fit well with Mary Waters's work on Caribbean immigrants living in New York. In her book *Black Identities,* she shows that both first- and second-generation West Indians simultaneously identify with black Americans and also try to distance themselves from black identities. For most of the participants in her study, being West Indian and black means a continuing, painful negotiation with their multiple identities as black, West Indian, and American. Most of them strongly identified with being black and Jamaican or West Indian. But this did not mean that "strongly identified West Indians did not distance themselves from blacks or believe strongly that they did not want to be identified with American blacks or confused with them" (1999, p. 64). Instead, these Caribbean participants pointed out that

> they were superior to black Americans, and they were disappointed and dismayed at the behaviors and the characteristics they associated with black Americans. Although some adopted the term "American" as part of their identity, referring to themselves as Jamaican American or West Indian American, they did not want to be seen as simply "black American" be-

cause for most of them assimilation to black America was downward mobility. (Waters 1999, p. 65)

The Indian migrants' negotiations with their ethnicity and brownness are not the same as the West Indian immigrants' negotiations with blackness. In both studies, however, the migrants show an affinity and identification with their ethnicity and also make active and agentive efforts to distance themselves from that ethnicity. Waters points out that the West Indian immigrants in her study gave African Americans the status of the "other" and that this status was important in shaping their meaning of what it means to be both black and West Indian in America.

I should emphasize here that my participants' assertions of sameness and universal humanity would not be accepted by the majority culture of U.S. society. Although they want to have the privilege of attaching universal meanings to their sense of self, their ability to attach unlimited meanings to their ethnicity is constrained by their marginal status. These Indian migrants are marked as other and have been assigned certain types of identities by their coworkers and friends. They reconstruct the negative ascriptions of their racial identities and express their agency and choice in repackaging their sense of difference. But they do not have the freedom or the power to attach any kind of meaning they want to their ethnicity. They may construct their ethnicity through multiple, layered, and contradictory reference points, but the framing of their identities is governed by their sociocultural history and their position in the socioeconomic and racial structures of American society. Waters explained:

Racial and ethnic identities are not zero-sum entities; it is possible to hold several at any one time, and they are very clearly situational. In one situation a person can feel very American, at another time Irish, and yet another time white—one could hold all identities simultaneously. But the recognition of the multiplicity and situationality of social identities does not mean that people are free to choose any identity they want or to attach any meaning they want to their identity. History and current power relations create and shape the opportunities people face in their day-to-day lives, giving some people "ethnic options" and other "racial labels." There are also shared or contested meanings attached to different groups that affect individual's way of thinking about themselves. (1999, p. 47)

On one level, Indian participants' multiple negations with race, class, and culture are about their ambivalent relationship with their racial identity and their position as persons of color. On another level, the participants' assignations and assertions also pertain to their struggle to acculturate in a society in which "otherness" is constructed as a problem. These dialogical strategies reveal conflicting and contradictory voices and show us that Indian transnational migrants do not follow a linear path in becoming assimilated or acculturated in their host country. Indian migrants' acts of assertion and assignation are not progressive acts of assimilation into the "melting pot" of American culture. Rather, their acculturation into U.S. society is marked by shifts, disruptions, and selective assimilation.

Identity Construction in Other Immigrant Groups

How do the assimilation processes of other immigrant groups differ? This section compares the assimilation processes of "privileged" minorities of Indian diaspora and other "unprivileged migrant" groups.

Portes and Rumbaut (2001) argue that three factors are vital to understanding the acculturation trajectories of contemporary migrants. The first factor is their educational background, fluency in the English language, and economic and class status in their homeland. The second factor refers to the social policies of the host government and the historical and contemporary perceptions and attitudes of the mainstream society toward a particular immigrant group. The third factor is the immigrants' social presence and networks and their family structure. The educational background of the immigrant groups and their social class back home are the "social" and "cultural" capital that they bring with them, which has an enormous impact on their economic assimilation. Although all three factors help determine how immigrants will assimilate into the larger mainstream American society, the second factor is the most relevant to shaping the acculturation outcomes of many nonwhite immigrants, especially of those immigrant groups who have little social and cultural capital and are not white.

Even though the Indian diaspora is racially distinct from the larger American mainstream, professional Indian Americans have an abundance of human-cultural capital acquired through their advanced education, knowledge of the English language, and social class in their home country. The low political profile of the Indian diaspora also gives them a degree of invisibility that shields them from the scrutiny of the larger mainstream culture. What happens to the acculturation experiences of those migrant groups that are not white, have little human capital, and have had difficulty becoming incorporated in the larger American society?

The Mexican migrant community in the United States is one of the groups that is not white, has lower levels of education, and usually faces a negative reception in the United States. It provides a picture that contrasts with that of the Indian diaspora.

Portes and Rumbaut offer three reasons that make the Mexican immigrants unique: (1) Mexicans have been immigrating to the United States for more than a century and are one of few migrant groups to continuously migrate over such a long time. They also are the only group of migrants to have been part of both the classical period of American immigration and the transnational migration of the late twentieth century. (2) Mexican migrants "come from the only less-developed country sharing a land-border with the United States" (Portes and Rumbaut 2001, p. 277). This shared geographic border has also resulted in the recruitment of massive, cheap Mexican labor and services for U.S. companies. The nature of such low-wage, low-skilled labor continues to generate only little human capital for this group. Despite their long history of migration to the United States, Mexicans still earn little and continue to be economically disadvantaged.

The categories of race and ethnicity have permeated as well the migration experiences of many contemporary, non-European migrants. Stephen Cornell and Douglas Hartman argue that race and ethnicity are interrelated categories that are constantly transforming the meaning of identities in American society. "Are immigrants, then, racial outsiders whose fates will be determined by powerful others, external others? Or are they ethnic agents free to choose their own identities and futures?" (Cornell and Hartman 2004, p. 36). Clearly, though, there are limits to reorganizing the identity that is given to migrants. The process of readopting and reconstituting the meaning of a label or category assigned to a migrant group does not allow completely free play and choice. Rather, external constraints govern this process of reconstructing a group's identity.

A long-standing sociological concept suggests that if newly arriving immigrants share several characteristics with the mainstream groups, then their reception in the host country will be positive (Portes and Rumbaut 2001). Thus, if foreign migrants are similar to the mainstream population in racial appearance, language, social class, and religion, their integration into the larger society will be both positive and rapid. For example, most of the educated immigrants from northern Europe are able to integrate quickly into the larger U.S. society mainly because of their racial similarities to white Americans and their strategic use of their social class and their education.

Migration theorists also claim that European migrants such as Poles, Italians, and Irish were initially regarded as belonging to different races. Although these groups faced prejudice and discrimination in the American society, their "phenotypical similarities" to the majority, native populations of the United States eventually allowed them to become integrated into the American fabric. Some theorists have noted that the influence of race trumps the influence of social class, religion, and education in America. Portes and Rumbaut (2001) explain this position:

> Regardless of their class origin or knowledge of English, nonwhite immigrants face greater obstacles in gaining access to the white middle class mainstream and may receive lower returns for their education and work experience. A racial gradient continues to exist in U.S. culture so that the darker a person's skin is, the greater is the social distance from dominant groups and the more difficult it is to make his or her personal qualifications count. (2001, p. 47)

The powerful and profoundly influential role of race in American society has been well articulated by Omi and Winant (1994) through the concept of "racial formation." The phenomenon of race and the racialization of groups permeate the entire social life of the American society, both psychologically and socially. Social structures, social networks, and individual and group identities are closely connected to, and shaped by, the legacy of racial and racial meanings in the United States.

This process of actively reordering and transforming intergroup relations along race and ethnic lines is illustrated in Alba and Nee's (2003) concept of network mechanisms. They observe that through a system of social rewards and punishments, group members use network mechanisms to enforce and maintain certain rules in their community, in order to improve the status and image of their own group.

For example, Alba and Nee state that the Chinese American migrant community living in the Mississippi Delta in the 1870s collectively decided to conform to whites' customs and social norms in order to avoid being treated like blacks. That is, they used their network mechanisms to change the racial meanings attached to being Chinese. According to Alba and Nee,

> Social pressure was brought to bear on merchants with black wives to leave them, and those who refused were ostracized from ethnic associations and events. The children of mixed Chinese–African American marriages were also socially excluded from the Chinese community to demonstrate that the Chinese accepted the norms against racial mixing. Eventually, the strategy succeeded. Despite de jure segregation, Chinese American families moved into white residential neighborhoods and their children gained admission into white schools. (2003, p. 44)

Similarly, Irish groups also collectively distanced themselves from blacks to avoid being called "shanty Irish."

The group strategy of using network mechanisms applies to both racial and ethnic dimensions. Alba and Nee note that "assimilated German Jews encouraged the acculturation of eastern European Jews through their charitable activities in the immigrant neighbourhoods of New York City, lest the impoverished eastern European Jews blemish the favourable image of the American Jewish community" (2003, p. 45). The acculturation processes of these migrant groups involved a dynamic reorganization of race, ethnicity, nationality, language, and class. Some of these migrant communities actively changed the identities that were given to them, but other migrant groups found it difficult to change the identities that were assigned by others. The acculturation processes of some of the migrant groups seemed predetermined given their social class, paucity of cultural capital, and educational background. But other groups were able to use their cultural capital strategically to assimilate on their own terms. In any case, for many of these new migrant groups, acculturation to the United States is not a simple process of arriving as foreigners and eventually integrating into both the mainstream society and their ethnic communities.

Culture, Self, and Acculturation in Psychology

The field of psychology in general and cross-cultural psychology in particular offer several models that explain acculturation-related issues. Cross-cultural psychology researchers study topics such as acculturation and acculturative stress (Berry 1998), socialization and enculturation (Camilleri and Malewska-Peyre 1997), intergroup relations across cultures (Gudykunst and Bond 1997), cross-cultural differences in work values (Hofstede 1980), individualism and collectivism across cultures (Kagitçibasi 1997), and bicultural identity (LaFromboise, Coleman, and Gerton 1998).

Prominent in acculturation research is the model of acculturation strategies proposed by Berry and his colleagues (e.g., Berry 1980, 1985, 1990, 1997; Berry et al. 1987, 1989; Berry and Sam 1997). Their prolific output, and the fact that several major introductory books on psychology (e.g., Halonen and Santrock 1996; Tavris and Wade 1997; Westen 1997) cite them extensively, indicates that their model has had much influence on the subject of acculturation in American psychology. Acculturation strategies refer to the plan or the method that individuals use in responding to stress-inducing new cultural contexts. Berry and his colleagues propose a fourfold classification of "assimilation," "separation," "integration," and "marginalization." People who decide not to maintain their cultural identity by seeking contact in their daily interactions with the dominant group are using an *assimilation strategy*. When persons from the nondominant group "place a value on holding on to their original culture" (Berry and Sam 1997, p. 297) and do not seek contact with the dominant group, they are pursuing a *separation* strategy. People who express an interest in maintaining strong ties in their everyday life with both their ethnic group and the dominant group are using an *integration* strategy. Finally, when persons "lose cultural and psychological contact with both their traditional culture and the larger society," they are using a *marginalization* strategy (Berry 1998, p. 119).

The optimal acculturation strategy for immigrants is said to be integration, which "appears to be a consistent predictor of more positive outcomes than the three alternatives" (Berry and Sam 1997, p. 318). Integration implies both the preservation of and contact with the home culture, or the "country of origin," and an active involvement with the host culture, or the "country of settlement." Central to the theory of the integration strategy is the assumption of universality. Berry and his colleagues assert that although there are "substantial variations in the life circumstances of the cultural groups that experience acculturation, the psychological processes that operate during acculturation are essentially the same for all the groups; that is, we adopt a *universalist perspective* on acculturation" (Berry and Sam 1997, p. 296). In other words, immigrants' acculturation strategies reveal the underlying psychological processes that unfold during their adaptation to new cultural contexts. This position has dominated acculturation research for almost three decades in psychology and has provided an important theoretical basis for research carried under the larger rubric of cross-cultural psychology (see Segall, Lonner, and Berry 1998).

Classifying culture as an "antecedent" variable and the properties of the self as universal, natural, and pregiven is a view important to shaping acculturation research in cross-cultural psychology. Thus for Berry and his colleagues, culture and history are variables that enable the "display" of the previously given properties of the acculturating self, but these very variables are not thought to be inextricably interwoven with the self. The historical and political aspects of immigration rarely enter the discussion, and when they do, they are classified as group variables.

Acculturation and Formation of Identity as Multivoiced

In contrast to cross-cultural psychologists' model of acculturation, the responses by the Indian participants in my study suggest ongoing and simultaneous dialogical negotiations with the voices of assignations and assertions. Their acculturation processes exemplify the dynamic interplay among the multiplicity of voices and also point to the voices' political, cultural, and historical foundation. The Indian participants' acculturation struggles are linked to and constituted by going back and forth between multiple homes, societies, identities, and languages.

The responses of the Indian participants in the diaspora do not fit in the category of either being fully assimilated into or being completely separated from American culture. Rather, the acculturation process and construction of cultural and racial identities in the diaspora, as previously stated, involve constant processes of negotiation, intervention, and mediation with a larger set of political and historical practices.

Assimilation or integration is not an option for many first-generation Indian immigrants like Abhishek or Rani, because they were described as the racial and cultural other as soon as they arrived in America. The identity that they negotiated in the diaspora began the moment they were marked as the other. For example, Abhishek, Deepali, Rohan, Priya, Prashant, Neeta, Naina, and Kajol recalled how other people's voices had constructed their identity and that those voices influenced their diasporic experiences in the United States. We have seen how this otherness is constructed by assigning exotic or negative cultural meanings to *bindis,* saris, and "thick accents." In many cases, the construction of otherness was downright racist and extremely disruptive to the children and families of the Indian diaspora.

Venkat recalled painful occasions when both his children asked him why they were brown and different from white children. Neelam talked about how her daughter's *bindi* was ripped off by a six-year-old boy on the first day of school. Rohan spoke at length about how some Indian employees felt subtle pressure from their bosses to reduce their "thick accents" so they could switch from working in the technical field to the management level. Accent-reduction courses, they felt, would make them a "better fit" for midlevel management positions at ABC Computer Corporation.

Rani told her story of not being admitted to a motel because the receptionist thought she was Hispanic or black and being asked to go to a motel that was run by African Americans. Poonam recalled the very difficult years when she battled with her neighbors in court in order to live on an exclusive property in Old Lyme. We also heard from several professionals who believed they were not promoted to top-level management positions in their companies because they were seen as foreigners, outsiders who were unable to network and socialize with the elite workforce in their corporation.

The professionals of the Indian diaspora are privileged minorities who have doctoral degrees and large incomes and who own houses in suburban, upper-middle-class neighborhoods. But they still consider themselves migrants or outsiders even after two or three decades in America.

The acculturation experiences of professional Indians is shaped by their class back home, their advanced education, their success in America, the colonial and postcolonial history of India, and the history of multicultural discourse about race and otherness in America. In responding to these assignations, the professional Indians in my study reconstructed and reframed their identities by making assertions of sameness, universal humanity, and human nature. These two voices of assignation and assertion clearly show that Indians are neither assimilated into the American culture nor completely marginalized or separated from the mainstream culture.

The Indian immigrants' movement between voices of assignation and assertion reveals their simultaneous acceptance and rejection of racial otherness. Many were quick to acknowledge the numerous racist and discriminatory incidents they experienced in the United States. Nonetheless, they still were ambivalent about seeing themselves as racial others.

The participants made several attempts to show that they were not racial others but were exactly the same as their white counterparts. In their conversations about their acculturation experiences, most professional Indians tried to reposition their identities as equivalent to those of their American coworkers and neighbors, by invoking arguments about human nature, the universal human experience, and the greatness of America. This reframing of their identity reveals a double-voiced, contradictory discourse about their general acculturation experiences and, more specifically, their acculturation as it relates to their racial and cultural otherness.

Appropriating Voices of Otherness

One part of Deepali's interview is a good example of the ambivalent movement between voices of assignations and voices of assertions pertaining to issues of racial identity. Deepali, who has a doctoral degree in genetics, recalled one occasion as a graduate student when she was clearly treated as the other.

> All the time I feel like a foreigner, and uh, it's one of the times I felt was when I was doing my PhD. I was one of the best students there, but when it came to photographing for the catalog, which they were going to send out to get more students, they photographed the white students. And my professor would look at me and laugh. The photographer would come, and she would put the white student there in a lab coat to be photographed

doing my job, you know? And she knew I understood, but she wouldn't tell it to me. . . . You do not send out a picture of me when you're trying to get more students. Even to India, they would send a catalog, but it would be a white person in the picture.

This was Deepali's first experience of feeling like a minority. As a research assistant to her professor, she did all the lab work, but when it came to taking photographs of the lab for the university catalog, the university decided to use the face of a white student.

Deepali stressed that the image of America is closely tied to that of white Americans. I asked Deepali whether she thought she would be featured in the catalog that was going to nonwhite students.

No, they couldn't afford that. So there's just one white picture, and it would be a white person. And now, I understand. When I have to send people out for sales, like when I'm trying to get business for the company, I myself choose a white person. The lectures will be given by a white person, and there's something about that when you're trying to get the business. You need the white person, but the actual technical work will be done by the Indian maybe or Chinese maybe, the other ones that actually know the subject better. But to give the sales stuff, it will be a white person. And that's what's surprising. Uh, you know . . . even I will do that myself. So, I will rather stay in the background to get the business, and that's surprising me, myself. . . . You'll see . . . they'll put a white face on all the ethnic-run motels—you will never know they're the owners. There will be a white face at every motel, the hotels. There will be a white face at all the restaurants, but when you go to the restaurants, the hostess is an Indian because there they are going for an Indian experience. That's what they are selling. So there, when you are selling something, you have to use the white person, and you have to give it all the support. The knowledge base comes from the foreigners, maybe.

Deepali's long response is worth noting because it reflects the ambivalence and contradiction of her acculturation experiences.

The experience of being othered stands out in Deepali's memory because she feels that her foreignness and Indianness were used against her. This incident was, in her mind, clearly racist and discriminatory. Deepali experienced anguish about the incident, but she reacted by internalizing the voices of otherness assigned to her sense of self.

One of the lessons that Deepali learned from this incident is that for marketing or sales, one should choose a white person, because it is good for business. Almost fifteen years after the incident in graduate school, Deepali still holds to the same system of belief that made her feel like an outsider.

Deepali believes that it a good marketing strategy by the Patel community, which runs most of the United States' motel chains, that it often employs a white person as the receptionist at the front desk of their motels. Most of their customers are white, and, Deepali explains, most white people feel comfortable talking to a white receptionist, who "looks" like them.

Deepali also pointed out that some places, such as ethnic restaurants, where the receptionist or the host who is greeting the customers must be ethnic because white customers expect to have an "ethnic experience." So when white customers are paying for an "Indian experience," an Indian face is appropriate. But an Indian face is not usually suited to a small firm's direct marketing or sales. In my interview, Deepali saw herself and all Indians as nonwhite foreigners, or racial others, but she also was part of a system that, perhaps inadvertently, was reproducing the experience of inequality that was going along with the construction of otherness.

Based on the cross-cultural psychologists' models of acculturation, Abhishek, Deepali, and Venkat, after having been in America for nearly two or three decades, would be expected to have assimilated into American society. But their voices of assignation and assertion tell a different story. They speak with the double-voice of being both privileged and marginalized, assimilated and separated, racialized and othered, and seen as a model minority.

Acculturation as a Dialogical Process

In contrast to the universal models of acculturation in cross-cultural psychology, the dialogical view of acculturation does not insist that conflicting voices need to be replaced by harmonious voices. Rather, a dialogical approach to acculturation emphasizes that asymmetrical power relations between conflicting voices and "I" positions are part of the diasporic self. Viewed from a dialogical perspective, acculturation and the construction of hybridity are not necessarily a series of phases during which one goes from being less acculturated to more acculturated over time. Instead, I suggest that several voices compete and that we need to think of acculturation as a process and not as a product. This process is not moving toward an end that can be captured by fixed categories but is revolving and interminable, with an emphasis on multiplicity, conflict, and contradiction (see Bhatia 2004; Bhatia and Ram 2001a). The dialogical view of acculturation, with its accompanying voices of assignation and assertion produced by the Indian diaspora, challenges three assumptions of the dominant theories of acculturation in cross-cultural psychology.[2]

The first assumption relates to theories about integration struggles. One of the assumptions inherent in the integration strategy proposed by traditional acculturation theorists is that immigrants can somehow "positively" assimilate the values and ideologies of both the dominant, mainstream group and their own ethnic group. Remember that the concept of "acculturation strategies" and "bicultural competence" assumes that all immigrants can achieve a happy, balanced blend that entails "becoming effective in the new culture and remaining competent in his or her culture of origin" (LaFromboise, Coleman, and Gerton 1998, p. 148). Those immigrants who do not reach this goal are considered to be experiencing higher acculturative stress (Berry 1998) and are not as physically or psychologically healthy (LaFromboise, Coleman, and Gerton 1998).

But as we have seen in this study, the acculturation experiences of Indian immigrants living in the diaspora are constructed through a back-and-forth play between the different voices of being both privileged and marginalized. This study also indicates a simultaneous acceptance and rejection of racial otherness in the Indian diaspora. These Indians' status as a model minority has assured them part of the American dream in the suburban enclaves of America, where they own houses and the requisite middle-class material comforts and send their children to expensive colleges and universities. On the surface, it would appear that these professional Indians have "made it" in America and have integrated into the larger society. Their stories of disruptive otherness, or experiences with racism and prejudice, however, have forced them to reposition their identities as cultural others, and they have carved out an isolated space for themselves in the suburban diaspora. These different voices represent the multiple, shifting, and often conflicting cultural selves in the diaspora.

Why Use the Concept of Voice to Understand the Concept of Acculturation?

The concept of voice allows us to focus on the idea that the Indian participants' racial and cultural identity emerges through a dialogical process that is constantly moving back and forth between incompatible cultural positions. Rather than posit migrant identity as an allocation of different cultural components in a fortuitous, congenial amalgam, the concept of voice allows us to emphasize immigrants' constant contradiction, struggle, and negotiation between different cultural selves. It is this process of negotiation and contestation between different voices that complicates the study of identity in the diaspora.

The diasporic identity of Indians in this study is not fixed by a singular, essential "trait," "attitude," or a personality "attribute." Rather, through acts of assignation and assertion, their multiple and often contradictory voices illustrate that acculturation in the United States is a highly contested process rather than an either/or phenomenon of marginalization or assimilation (see Hasnat 1998; Khan 1998). Thus, the concept of voice allows us to claim that Indian immigrants attempt to rework the different voices related to their racial and cultural otherness. Their heritage or ethnicity does not entail a movement toward assimilation or marginalization or separation and integration in a new culture. Instead, there is an ongoing, simultaneous dialogical movement between the voices of feeling that are at once assimilated, integrated, privileged, and marginalized.[3]

The acculturation experiences of the professional, middle-class, post-1965 Indian immigrants are structured primarily through the voices of assignation and assertion, and these contradictory voices challenge the idea that they can be "biculturally efficient" by integrating the cultural voices on both sides. To think that the acculturation process is merely "culture shedding" or "some behavioral shift" or the "unlearning of one's previous repertoire"—as much of the scholarship on acculturation in psychology demonstrates—implies that one can float in and out of cultures, shedding one's history and politics and replacing them with new cultural and political "behaviors" whenever needed. Advocating the strategy of "integration" as an end point or examining acculturation in terms of universal categories overlooks the multiple, contested, and sometimes painful voices associated with "living in between" cultures.

The second reason why the concept of voice is useful in analyzing the Indian participants' double-voiced responses is that it demonstrates the asymmetrical relationship of power between different cultural components of the self. Being othered or racialized is part of many non-European/non-Western immigrants' acculturation experiences, which are tightly knit with their evolving conceptions of a hyphenated, fractured, and in-between selfhood. An important question not in Berry and his colleagues' discussion of "integration strategy" is how issues of conflict, power, and asymmetry affect many diasporic immigrants' acculturation processes. For example, Berry and his colleagues view the concept of integration as implicitly assuming that both the majority and minority cultures have equal status and power.

Furthermore, it is not clear what the term *integration* means exactly. How does one know when one is "integrated," or not, into the host culture? Who decides whether an immigrant is pursuing a strategy of marginalization, integration, or separation? Radhakrishnan (1996) suggests that the notion of multiple, hyphenated, and hybridized identities of the diaspora challenges the idea of a blissful marriage or an integration of the cultures between the hyphen. Recognizing the difficulty of understanding the diasporic identity, Radhakrishnan raises a series of insightful questions:

> When someone speaks as an Asian-American, who is exactly speaking? If we dwell in the hyphen, who represents the hyphen: the Asian or the American, or can the hyphen speak for itself without creating an imbalance between the Asian and American components. . . . True, both components have status, but which has the power and the potential to read and interpret the other on its terms? If the Asian is to be Americanized, will the American submit to Asianization? (Radhakrishnan 1996, p. 211)

The identity of middle-class Indians in the local diaspora is made up of different voices in an asymmetrical relationship with each other. Although most professional Indians try to counter the racist assignations made by many Americans by asserting that they are equal to the dominant majority, the voices of assignation and the voices of assertion have an inherently unequal relationship of power.

The assignations of marked otherness, generic otherness, and disruptive otherness are deeply painful and agonizing to Indian immigrants.[4]

The racist assignations made by many Americans about their saris, *bindis,* food, customs, accents, and skin color cannot be fully countered by acts of assertion. The Indian participants' assertion of being equal to the dominant majority of Americans is their way of shoring up their sense of otherness, but it does not integrate the Indians into the larger majority.

Thus, the concept of voice not only highlights the multiplicity of a single person's selves but also allows us to foreground their tensions, contradictions, and asymmetrical power relationships. Thinking about race and nationality as part of the shifting voices of the migrant self forces us to abandon universal models of acculturation. Although integration and bicultural competency may be worthy goals, I contend that for most people living in contemporary diasporas, their negotiation with multiple cultural sites is fluid, dynamic, interminable, and often unstable. When we adhere to universal models of acculturation, we undervalue both the asymmetrical relations of power within the diasporic communities and the inequities and injustices faced by certain immigrant groups from the dominant culture as a result of their nationality, race, or gender.

The Indian participants' voices of assignation and assertion challenge the idea that all immigrants' acculturation processes can be placed into one of the four classifications of acculturation strategies (assimilation, integration, separation, and marginalization) developed by cross-cultural psychologists, such as Berry and his colleagues. In addition, Josephs explained that while a voice can contain a reference to a "social label," it also is imbued with "personal meaning" (2002, pp. 162–63).

Thus, the primarily Hindu–Indian American voices are developed through the immigrants' personal constructions of their ongoing experiences of being seen as members of a model minority community and their ambiguous view of their racial identity. Furthermore, these voices do not stand alone but talk to one another, inform one another, suppress one another, and animate one another. This polyphony of different voices constructs and shapes the Indian acculturation experiences as fluid, dynamic, contextual, contingent, and not fixed and singular as reflected in the universal and linear concepts of marginalization, integration, and separation.

7

■　■　■　■　■　■　■　■　■

Imagining Homes

Identity in Transnational Diaspora

During my fieldwork in suburban Connecticut, Vishal and I discussed the concept of "America return" in the 1960s and 1970s. I told him that it was quite common for the entire family to go to the Mumbai airport when someone was returning from America or England. The families would hire a Matador van, and some fifteen to seventeen people would wait for the family member to come out of the arrival gate at the airport. Vishal interjected, "*Vilayat jaa raha hain, vilayat aa . . . garland lekhe khade huin ay hain*" (laughs). That is, every time somebody was either going to, or coming from, abroad, family members would go to the airport with garlands to say farewell or welcome him or her back home. Vishal, who has lived in the United States for thirty-five years, remarked that back in the 1960s and 1970s it was a big occasion for the family to go and meet someone at the airport.

Well, you know that's the time when I came also—and my, father and everybody used to come from Delhi, and he was such a, he was an old man, but still he would insist on coming—my father, mother, brothers, everybody would be there at the airport. [Today] nobody is at the airport!

Vishal's statement that these days family members are not at airports for arrivals or departures signifies just how commonplace such travel has become. For many middle-class families and their extended families and relatives in India, "going home," back to India, is now an annual affair. Many first- and second-generation Indian immigrants travel home every year to keep their contact with the home culture alive. The real and imagined home that exists over there as "back home" helps create the cultural and physical space of the home that is "over here" in the Indian diaspora. In this concluding chapter, I focus on some of the themes that emerge from the ethnography of the Indian diaspora: home, racial ambivalence, acculturation, and culture and development.

Home: Memories, Community, and Imaginary Locations

Capturing the essence of how migrants remember home, Salman Rushdie (1991) wrote, "Our physical alienation from India almost inevitably means that we will not be capable of reclaiming precisely the thing that was lost; that we will, in short, create fictions, not actual cities or villages, but invisible ones, imaginary homelands, Indias of the mind" (1991, p. 10). Nostalgia in the Indian community now does not build up as a collection of memories that were left behind decades ago. Instead, for contemporary Indian migrants, the concept of home is present in their lives through routine visits to India, Bollywood films, the Internet, transatlantic travel, and the existence of little Indias all across the cities of the United States.

For many migrant groups, the global movement of capital, labor, goods, people, ideas, and culture has enabled the creation of transnational spaces and diasporic communities. In these spaces, home, language, and self refer to multiple dwellings, making a qualitative distinction between contemporary immigrants and those of the early twentieth century (Glick Schiller, Basch, and Szanton Blanc 1995). The story of the earlier form of immigration includes images of permanent displacement and a complete break from the homeland and a difficult transition to a new language and life in a new world. The journey required a movement away from one's culture and customs and a step toward a new ethnic identity and then an eventual assimilation into the "melting pot" of the majority culture. But the new migrants of the Indian diaspora, like many other new migrant groups, paint a different picture.

The post-1965 suburban Indian diasporas have both created and transformed social networks, circuits of capital and commodities, and cultural practices and rituals in the country of their settlement and their home society. The participants in my study referred to home as both a physical and a psychological space. As the children of these participants grew older, it became important to keep a sense of home life through the maintenance of Indian traditions. Most of the participants visited India once a year, and the children were introduced to both their family members and cousins and their ways of life in India. The meaning of India and Indian culture gradually shifted as they carved out lives in the American suburbs. Accordingly, the Indian community in southeastern Connecticut is a transnational diaspora with multiple linkages to India. Its members live in a transnational psychological space, vacillating between their lives in American suburbs and their imagined ideas about India. Just as the cultural meaning of home is continually revised in the diaspora, so are notions of both Americanness and Indianness.

The interviews in the ethnography illustrate that once the husbands and wives of the Indian diaspora have children and are professionally employed, earning high salaries, they postpone the idea of going back home to India, although never completely. But now, faced with the prospect of raising their children in America, home begins to take on a different meaning. These Indian immigrants now live in dual societies and inhabit multiple homes, roles, identities, and languages. Their networks and ideas of belonging transcend national boundaries that bring together the local and the global and the home and the host country into a single "social field." Glick Schiller, Basch, and Szanton Blanc (1995) defined the new immigrants as transmigrants whose pattern of activities is structured around multiple and continuous linkages across the national borders. My interviews and the ethnographic data provide a contrasting account of how two different groups of Indian immigrants reinvented and reconstructed their identities as they moved from the culture of their homeland to their new homes in the United States.

How is this simultaneous linkage and embeddedness of self and identity in multiple social fields constituted and reconstituted? The new transnational migration has realigned the conception of majority and minority communities, as well as the concomitant concepts of assimilation, resistance, adaptations, and ethnicity associated with it (Clifford 1994). Several scholars distinguish diasporas from immigrant communities. They describe the latter as temporary communities whose inhabitants do feel the loss of their homeland but essentially follow a linear assimilation in which typically three generations, through hard work and struggle, attain the identity of ethnic Americans and build a new home in a new world (Clifford 1994). Nations that follow the assimilationist ideology apply these narratives to immigrant communities, as opposed to diasporic communities.

The Indian participants use the space of home or the inside/private culture as a site to imagine Indian culture and to perform and enact the identity of being Indian with other family and community members. The complex and multilayered process of creating Indian culture in the diaspora included practicing aspects of the home culture such as *puja* (prayer) and rituals, watching Bollywood and Hindi films, and participating in other social and cultural practices. The community events are imagined, recreated, and personalized in the home space in order to activate old memories and to show affiliation and identification with Indian culture. Such enactments and performances play an important role in constructing an agentive, dialogical self that moves between the distinct culture space of home and the outside space of whiteness or American culture. The Hindu-Indian diaspora uses the home space to create and promote a concept of a unified, Indian nation, culture, and community. The home space is used by the family and the community to organize various social and religious days to transmit Hindu culture for their second-generation native and foreign-born Indian Americans. This space is strategically used by the Indian diaspora to uphold and instantiate for their children the model minority discourses that are then used in the popular culture to describe and regulate the various Asian communities. The inside, private home space of the Indian diaspora allows Indian Americans to enact their cultural identities with the larger collective diaspora, but their contact with the outside world—with their neighbors, colleagues, coworkers, and the larger American culture—also plays a significant role in shaping their racial identity as privileged minorities.

Identity: Racial Ambivalence

Indian immigrants of this study both displayed and resisted certain forms of identity to define their sense of "who they are" in the United States. This ambivalence about racial identity is closely linked to the production of culture in transnational diasporas. The politics of race and class manifested through assignations and assertions of racial identity in the India diaspora is intrinsically tied to the construction of "culture" in the Indian diaspora. And the definition of cultures "as composed of seriously contested codes and representations" (Clifford 1986, p. 2) is clearly visible in the Indian diasporic space, such as what it means to be a brown-skinned minority.

For example, Vishal runs a successful management consulting company in Groton, Connecticut, and has many American employees working under him. His firm has offices in several major cities in New England. He recalled an incident that illustrates the various forms of otherness. Vishal and his employee, Harry, a white American, were driving at night from Boston to New London when they had a terrible accident on the highway. Although the car was totaled, somehow both of them survived. After the accident, a state trooper arrived and took them to a hospital in Boston, where they were examined and given permission to go home. Vishal and Harry decided to go to Harry's apartment in Boston.

At the apartment, Vishal and Harry discussed the accident. Harry said, "That trooper was a real racist." Vishal asked why, and Harry explained, "He [the trooper] could not believe that you are my boss. He asked me, 'How come he is your boss?'" Vishal explained:

> It was weird. It was around 4:00 A.M. or 5:00 A.M. when we came back to Boston and to his apartment, and, uh, he was telling me, you know. . . . What he asked me, he says, "Who is this guy and all this and that." He says, "Oh, this is my boss." [The trooper] says immediately, he says, "How come he's your boss?" Yeah, and this fellow is a total racist, and, uh, he is just pointing all that out to me.

Vishal did not feel angry because his employee, Harry, came to his defense and clearly saw the trooper as a racist, but the incident was deeply etched in Vishal's mind. It was evident that the state trooper was not used to seeing men of color in positions of authority. Upon learning that Vishal, a person of color, was the boss of a white man, the trooper's worldview was momentarily turned upside down. This example demonstrates that despite achieving tremendous economic success in the United States, professionals from the Indian diaspora still are subjected to varying levels of racism and discrimination in their workplace and their suburban communities.

My study shows that the members of this Indian diaspora have an ambivalent desire to seek proximity to white culture because it signifies success and represents the norm. Accordingly, they fear that positioning their identity in terms of their racial identity would hold them back from achieving professional and material success. In addition, some of these Indians bring their prejudice against dark-skinned people from home, where *gora/kala* (black-white) distinctions are deeply entrenched in society. Indeed, in much of South Asia, "light skin" is seen as more desirable than dark skin, and many cosmetic products sell on the promise of changing one's "dark complexion" to a "fair complexion." However, the Indian participants' relationship to whiteness cannot be construed as simply a desire to "become white," as they also see whiteness as something from which they need to distance themselves, because it symbolizes "colonization," "coldness," "rationality," "promiscuity," "immorality," and "Western materialism." The dialogical model of identity shows how Indian immigrants express multiple, alternating, and often paradoxical "voices" as they encounter cultural and racial differences and diversity at the workplace. The Indian community's responses to racism are indeed agentive acts that are used to reposition the immigrants' feelings of otherness, but by no means are they as powerful as the disruptive assignations thrust upon them by the majority culture.

What is not fully acknowledged by middle-class members of the Indian diaspora is that their education, fluency in English, and social-class values acquired at home gave them an edge in their early years as graduate students in U.S. universities. That is, the foundation of their success in America was laid at home and helped them move ahead of many other migrant groups that had been in the United States much longer.

In addition, owing to their desire to portray themselves as a successful minority group, members of the Indian diaspora resist forming any kind of "oppositional politics" or creating political organizations that highlight the racism and discrimination they experience. Many professional Indians also distance themselves from other minority groups such as African Americans and Latinos because of the apparent class and racial differences. Their responses to other minority groups in the United States and their refusal to form alliances based on minority experiences of racism and class oppression are largely based on their own class standings in the larger class/caste structure in India. Those Indians who base their lives on the model minority discourse are less likely to forge alliances with other racial minorities in the United States. That is, these migrants are far more comfortable with the idea of being from an "ethnic" group shaped by the concept of "Indian nation" and "culture" rather than having a racial identity.

A small number of Indian and other South Asian migrants, however, have defied the mainstream minority discourse and have spoken out about the experiences of "minorities within minorities." Several scholars have documented the experiences of these marginalized minorities of the South Asian diaspora, such as domestic workers, oppressed women, gays and lesbians, and working-class migrants (DasGupta and Dasgupta 1998; Dasgupta 2006; Koshy 1998; Maira 2002; Maira and Srikanth 1996; Mathew 2005; Prashad 2000; Purkayastha 2005; Visweswaran 1997). This critical scholarship has questioned the "gender and race neutral accounts of immigrant experiences, the separation between the public sphere, convention sites of resistance, access to citizenship as an unqualified boon, and the success story itself" (Dasgupta 2006, p. 29).

Unruly Immigrants, by Monisha Dasgupta, is one of the first detailed ethnographic studies of organizations supporting South Asian immigrants who face problems of gender discrimination, homophobia, domestic violence, poverty, and racism. Dasgupta conducted interviews with seventeen core members of seven organizations that were mainly located in the East coast. The seven organizations that are the subject of her book are Manavi, Saakhi for South Asian Women, South Asian Women for Action (SAWA), South Asian Lesbian and Gay Association (SALAGA), Massachusetts Area South Asian Lambda Association (MASALA), New York Taxi Workers Alliance (NYTWA) formerly known as the Lease Drivers Coalition (LDC) and Andolan. The emergence of these organizations was a response to the middle- and upper-class South Asian communities' embrace of the model minority discourse, nationalistic and assimilationist perspectives, and their refusal to acknowledge the racism, sexism, and elitism in their communities. The larger mainstream South Asian community has positioned itself as having an identity based on a particular culture and traditions, and this construction of cultural identity focuses on "ethnicity not race, culture not power, sex roles not gender and sexuality, groups and individuals and not institutional structures" (Dasgupta 2006, p. 26).

The politics of the upper-class, mainstream South Asian immigrants is emblematic of what Dasgupta call "place-taking politics," which does not acknowledge or address problems like poverty, domestic violence, racism, homophobia, and xenophobia in the large South Asian migrant community. Rather, their politics is largely concerned with succeeding in America and finding ways to assimilate and adapt to the system's larger structures. In contrast, the seven organizations studied in this book are engaged in what Dasgupta calls "space-making politics," a type of politics that agitates for social reforms that create "structures and resources that transform daily life into an arena of political contest" (2006, p. 11). These organizations provide social and economic support to marginalized men and women of the South Asian communities while simultaneously working to change the larger American institutions such as legal and social services, law enforcement and immigration agencies, and public policy workers.

The larger Indian diaspora in the United States can overcome its ambivalence about its experience of racism and racial identity by engaging in the kind of "space-making politics" that Dasgupta defined in her book. The racist assignations made by many Americans about Indians' saris, *bindis,* food, customs, accents, and skin color cannot be fully countered by acts of assertions based on concepts of universal humanity, human conditions, and appeals to "human nature." The Indian participants' assertion of being equal to the dominant majority of Americans is their way of shoring up their sense of self, but this does not in any way allow them full integration into the society or the larger majority. They need to initiate a difficult but necessary dialogue in their own communities about their class and racial politics. The Indian diaspora needs to find a way to reimagine itself as a collective body of migrants that includes the marginalized minorities. The migrants' reinterpretations of their cultural and racial identity should also be built on forming coalitions and alliances with other racial and ethnic minorities and migrant groups such as African Americans, Latinos, and other Asian Americans.

Acculturation: Living on the Margins and in the Center

Acculturation is a key component in understanding the interplay of migration, culture, and psychology. My study shows that the acculturation experiences of Indian immigrants living in the diaspora are constructed through back-and-forth actions between being both privileged and marginalized. This finding challenges the psychological models of acculturation formulated by the prominent cross-cultural psychologists Berry and his colleagues.

I have shown that many Indian immigrants living in the diaspora cannot consciously and freely choose one of Berry's acculturation strategies because they are restricted by their skin color, accent, and their status as foreigners and outsiders in the system. Moreover, the participants' responses demonstrate that migrant communities do not necessarily follow a linear, finite progression toward acculturation. Rather, they must constantly negotiate between past and present, home and diaspora, self and other, renovated memories, and imagined communities, and narratives of home.

The integration metaphor dominant in cross-cultural psychology assumes that we live in a multicultural society "where a large number of distinguishable ethnic groups, all cooperating within a larger system" live in a mosaic-like system (Berry 1998, p. 118). The assumption that immigrants can choose to internalize the value orientations of both their ethnic group and the dominant group is based on the notion that the United States is a plural society. This plural, multicultural society is based on "core values and traditional institutions but also many cultural variations . . . accepted as valued characteristics of the society" (Berry 1998, p. 118). The pivotal words in this quotation are "but also," which refer indirectly to two points. The first is that some sets of cultural practices reflect the essence of the American society, and the second is that "other" sets of cultural practices exist on the side or the boundaries, which are considered marginal and usually are associated with minority experiences.

The asymmetrical relationship between core and peripheral values is important to defining the experiences of the participants living in the Indian diaspora. Their strategies to cope with racism show that we need to view the acculturation process not in terms of fixed models but as negotiated, historical, and political practices. Acculturation is not moving from home to host culture as though these are hermetically sealed spaces. Rather, it is a complex process that involves multiple, contradictory, and conflicting voices. In turn, these voices are shaped by the history and politics of colonization, race, casteism, and class differences and are rooted in transnational connections.

The ethnographic data reveal that the various identities in the Indian diaspora do not coalesce into a harmonious "integration" free from tension and conflicts. Instead, the disparate elements of the participant's multicultural identity are filled with moments of alienation and fragmentation. Using her research on Asian Indian women immigrants, Hegde demonstrated that cultural relocation and the unfolding of migrant identities involve a constant negotiation with old and new environments. Such mediations of selfhood are never finite, complete, or benign. Instead, she illustrates that "the theme of being other continually echoes in the lives of immigrants, displacing and deferring their sense of coherence about self" (1998, p. 51). Lavie and Swedenburg (1996), however, point out that the notion of boundaryless identities, or "geographies of identities," is by no means a postmodern pastiche of many identities or a multicultural celebration of diversity. Originally, the notion of the borderland identity was used to refer to the Chicano women who lived and worked in the boundary region between the United States and Mexico. Lavie and Swedenburg (1996) emphasize that the notion of borders, like that of the diaspora, is not a place with "imaginative interminglings and happy hybridities" for us to celebrate (p. 15). Rather, they use warlike metaphors to suggest that borders are like "minefields, mobile territories of constant clashes" where "formations of violence" continuously signify "zones of loss, alienation," and pain.

Psychology has rarely shown any interest in problematizing the politics inherent in the acculturation process of hybrid migrants who occupy multiple racial and cultural positions constantly at odds with each other. Questions about history, inclusion, and authority are necessary in order to expose the hegemonic construction of any discourse, especially when we consider that in most of psychology, the term *cultural* is defined as nothing more than a set of variables that are used for "empirical" demonstrations. This study shows that the term *culture* is not a static variable but symbolizes multiple realities that are painful, alienating, and filled with ambiguities and ambivalences about one's racial and cultural identity.

In my study, I provide an alternative model of acculturation, a dialogical process that can be used to understand how the participants negotiate their movement between the contradictory voices of assignation and assertion. These voices are dialogical because the other—representing these voices—plays a powerful role in how the middle-class Indians living in the suburbs of southeastern Connecticut situate their identities in the larger culture. The theoretical framework of the dialogical self is relevant here because it shows how the immigrants appropriate the words, language, and evaluations of the other. The concept of acculturation as multivoiced allows us to think of it as a dialogical process rooted in history, culture, and politics.

Culture: Development in the Context of Migration

The findings of this research illustrate that the migration and displacement of people across the different parts of the globe should be central to the field of psychology. The construction of transnational selves across the First World is global and plural, but the theories used in American psychology continue to examine notions of self and identity using local frameworks. These local, conceptual frameworks, while useful in many respects, have failed to address the conflict and complexity that these hybrid identities have come to represent.

In addition, the concepts of culture and self need to be problematized and reconfigured in the context of a global and transnational cultural psychology. Although the field of psychology has focused on the mutual constitution of culture and self, it has not investigated the complexities associated with the formation of the selves and identities created in the borderland and the postcolonial diasporas. If cultural psychology—or any psychology anchored in the politics of culture—is to be relevant to the contemporary global world, it must pay attention to the ways in which diasporic, hyphenated, and hybridized identities are being formed across First World metropolitan areas.

We know that concepts such as race, class, and gender are intricately woven into the fabric of cultures and that their meanings are recreated in the diasporic spaces. But psychology has yet to explore how the concepts making up culture acquire new meanings in the context of migration and globalization. My interviews with middle-class Indian professional migrants illustrate how the rapid formation of diasporas as transnational communities, the collusion between the First and Third World spaces, the spread of global contexts, the creation of hybrid identities, and the movement of highly skilled labor, people, ideas, commodities, and artifacts across international borders have led to new configurations of culture and self.

In the early 1990s, about 8 million South Asians, 22 million Chinese, 11 million Jews, 300 million Africans, and 350 million Europeans were living as migrant populations (van der Veer 1992, p. 1). These global movements and globalization impulses (variously motivated) have thus forced us to abandon seamless conceptions of similarities and differences among national cultures in favor of hybridized, diasporized, and heterogeneous notions of culture (Hall 1993, p. 356). In other words, "culture," however we wish to interpret it, cannot be understood as circumscribed by national boundaries. Instead, the configuration of culture as transcending space and time has led to the formation of a selfhood that is often characterized as multiple, fractured, dual, fragmentary, shifting, and hybridized. The investigation of these identities is critical because they not only affect much of our population but also provide an area in which psychology has an opportunity to remake itself as a field that continues to be relevant to a world that is rapidly becoming transnational, diverse, and global.

Many Indians in the Connecticut diaspora reported that their identity underwent a developmental shift when they were transformed into "people of color" after they arrived in the United States. Their racial identity also affected how they socialized their children as second-generation Indian Americans. Most parents preferred to socialize their children through the prism of "Indian culture" and "desi traditions" rather than a framework emphasizing race or race-related matters.

In particular, the gender identities of most women and girls in the Indian community changed. Some women were able to break free from the traditional gender roles in India, to have professional careers and also a greater input in household affairs and the daily organization of family routines. But both professional and nonprofessional women were still mainly responsible for preserving the traditional Indian culture and thus the basic developmental blueprint for their children.

This blueprint was generally defined by following religious customs and rituals and recreating authentic "Indian" culture at home. According to Mani, "It comes as no surprise that the burden of negotiating life in the new world is borne disproportionately by women, whose behaviors and desires, real or imagined, become the litmus test for the South Asian community's anxieties or sense of well being" (1994, p. 34). Thus in addition to the immigrant women, the second-generation daughters of the community also must live up to the idealized models of Indian womanhood, but they often form their sense of self based on static mythologized and idealized images of India. When second-generation Indian American women question such idealized Indian traditions, the "guardians of community" often interpret these questions as challenging the integrity of Indian traditions. For example, when these second-generation immigrant women began dating men from both inside and outside their group, made independent sexual choices, and rejected the system of arranged marriages, they were "policed with the stick of tradition" (Mani 1994, p. 34). Such policing occurs with the "close monitoring" of their behavior, and when these women transgress the boundaries of tradition, they are seen as Western and "un-Indian."

Clearly, immigrants seek connectedness or relatedness to their community by participating in religious rituals and other social events that enable them to feel they belong. But such retreats into their community by no means suggest that the immigrant's journey from the majority culture to the minority culture and vice versa is an undisturbed, balanced, and effortless journey. On the contrary, for most immigrants, this developmental process is marked by incompatibilities, conflicts, and asymmetries between their immigrant culture and the host culture, their homeland and their adopted land, the majority and the minority culture, and the mainstream and ethnic cultures. The hybridity of cultures influencing the development of migrant selves provides an important avenue to theorize about the reconstruction of migrant identity. The "incommensurable elements" making up the hybrid patterns of contemporary transnational migrants have been used to critique essentialized notions of cultural difference (Bhabha 1994, p. 219).

In summary, the idea of living in a diaspora with a hyphenated identity and inhabiting a "double consciousness" has forced us to redefine the development of the migrant identity as a negotiated and a contested process rather than as a movement toward a fixed, singular, developmental end goal. Such developmental processes lead to multiple end goals, manifested through localized power struggles and asymmetrical relationships of privileges in diaspora communities. These ideological struggles in community practices often pertain to defining the normative identity of which cultural standards should prevail. Such struggles help determine not only how we live generally but also how we should discuss issues of immigration, acculturation, and selfhood. The concept of hybridity allows us to explore the politics of identity construction from multiple and conflicting developmental goals. It also enables us to analyze how new identities are being constructed as a result of travel and movement between "here" and "there," home and elsewhere, *des* (home) and *pardes* (abroad), and the center and the periphery. Given that such psychological terms as *bicultural competency* and *integration strategy* assume that both host and immigrant cultures share equal status and power, the concept of hybridity becomes important as well to understanding the contested aspects of human development. Rather than describing only one developmental end state of acculturation for all immigrants, the hybridity perspective helps us understand how immigrants living in postcolonial and diasporic locations are negotiating and reconciling conflicting histories and incompatible subject positions.

Notes

Note to the Introduction

1. *Pujas* are performed by priest and lay Hindus through devotional songs and prayer to express faith, gratefulness, love, and offerings to a deity.

Notes to Chapter 1

1. All the participants' names, their places of residence in the suburbs of southeastern Connecticut, their professional occupations, and the names of their businesses or firms and companies have been changed in order to protect their identities.

2. All the interviews for this study were conducted primarily in English. Since most of my participants were fluent in English, I have tried to keep the language structure and syntax as close as possible to the participant's own language, although many of these excerpts had to be edited for clarity, grammar, and coherence.

3. "The holy dot or *bindi* (also known as *kumkum, mangalya, tilak, sindhoor* and by other names) is an auspicious makeup worn by young Hindu girls and women on their forehead. The term is derived from *bindu*, the Sanskrit word for a dot or a point. It is usually a red dot made with vermilion (finely powdered bright red mercuric sulphide). Considered a blessed symbol of Uma or Parvati, a bindi signifies female energy (*shakti*) and is believed to protect women and their husbands. Traditionally a symbol of marriage, it has now become a decorative item and is worn today by unmarried girls and women of other religions as well.

No longer restricted in color or shape, bindis today are seen in many colors and designs and are manufactured with self-adhesives and felt" (http://www.kamat .com/kalranga/women/bindi.htm).

4. *Desi* is a colloquial Hindi word that is etymologically connected to the word *Desh*. *Desi* refers to first- and second-generation families who have origins in South Asia. For a detailed discussion of the changing conceptions of the label "South Asians" in the United States, see Bahri and Vasudeva 1996.

5. The quotation marks around "Indianness," "Indian culture," and "Indian identity" indicate that they do not have a fixed definition. Rather, these terms have overlapping meanings and were used by the participants to invoke a particular form of "Indianness" that is tied to their identity.

6. Most of the Indians who participated in this study worked for a local, multinational corporation, which I have called the ABC Computer Corporation, to protect their privacy and identity.

7. While growing up in the town of Ambarnath in Maharashtra, India, I had friends from working-class families whose parents told them that an IIT education would guarantee them success and social mobility in India. Many parents selected schools and colleges for their children that specifically trained their students for the IIT entrance examination.

8. "I" refers to the interviewer, and "A" is the first initial of the participant's name.

9. I want to emphasize here is that diasporic identity is not just about abstract concepts but the fact that they are rooted in the lived experiences of difference and otherness. The construction of diasporas reminds us again and again, according to Hall, that we cannot go on defining "identities as two histories, one over here, over there, never having spoken to another, not having to do with one another" (1991a, p. 9). Such a definition of identity, he asserts, "is simply not tenable any longer in a globalized world. It is just not tenable any longer." This new type of transnational selfhood and the experiences accompanying them have forced us to "reconceptualize fundamentally the politics of self, community, solidarity, identity and cultural difference of living in a global world" (Hall 1991a, p. 9).

10. The critical literature on migrant identities is closely connected to thirty years of feminist scholarship emanating from literary criticism, the philosophy of science, and postcolonial and cultural studies. This body of literature has shown that gender indeed influences our society, institutions, cultural practices, subjectivities, selves and identities, nation, and our readings of other selves and identities, texts, and contexts. Early feminist theories about self, originating mainly from North America, focused on the liberation of the universal, monolithic woman. The construction of this unified female subject was seen as tied to masculine histories, privileges, regimes, powers, and the ever-present male gaze. In the late 1970s and early 1980s, feminists rooted in their various ethnic, racial, postcolonial, and sexual locations were quick to interrogate the monolithic category called "woman" (Moraga and Anzaldua 1983). *This Bridge Called My Back,* pub-

lished in early 1980s, is now considered part of the inaugural moment that created a significant paradigm shift in how race, class, and sexuality entered the equation of writing about and defining the category of a woman in America (see Behar 1995). The editors of the book write that *This Bridge Called My Back* is intended to reflect an "uncompromised definition of feminism by women of color in the U.S." (Moraga and Anzaldua 1983, p. xxiii).

11. Although the theoretical positions in the ever-expanding field of postcolonial studies are diverse, common themes and issues bind them together. For instance, postcolonial theorists challenge and question how dominant groups, particularly those from the "First World," represent and construct meanings regarding groups with less power, particularly "subjects" from the "Third World." In other words, postcolonial theories focus on cultural representations, discourses, positioning, and power.

12. For a complex discussion of which migrant groups are considered postcolonial and how the term *postcolonial* has been extended to include many groups and nations, see Fabricant 1998 and Sharpe 1995.

13. I contend that it is important to study how these shifting and hybrid are *contrapuntally* constructed. Bammer notes that from a postcolonial perspective, national and cultural identities are constructed through the "result of historically negotiated" processes that need to be "understood relationally." Furthermore, she emphasizes that these historically negotiated relationships are "inherently and in multiple ways unequal" (1998, p. 23). The unequal relationship she mentions refers to that between the "colony and the empire" (p. 23). Borrowing from Edward Said (1993), she argues that both the marginalized and the privileged, the colonized and the colonist, in many ways formed and shaped each other. The history of the colonizer and the colonized evolved with each other, and the unequal relationship of power that accompanied such an overlapping relationship, according to Said (1993, p. 51), should be viewed "contrapuntally." He observed that the term *essentialization* refers to the idea that identities are not fixed by some core, singular, essential, universal properties. Rather, they are contested, multiple, and shifting and are embedded in various cultural and historical practices. Bammer clarifies the term *contrapuntal ensembles* using an example from French Algerian history. She suggests that any understanding of contemporary "Frenchness" is as "informed by its relationship to Algeria, in other words, as is Algerianness by its involvement in French history" (1998, p. 24). But she contends that the idea of cultural identity as consisting of contrapuntal ensembles is an "inherently contested site," a site in which one is constantly negotiating and renegotiating one's position vis-à-vis the other.

14. In the 1960s and 1970s, cross-cultural studies significantly shifted their representations of other non-Western populations. This was a marked shift not so much in "redefining" non-Westerners on their own terms but more in studying the "development" of the non-Western subject in light of the emerging postcolonial, Third World economic contexts. In his analysis of cross-cultural research

conducted in Europe and North America after World War II, Richards points out that although cross-cultural psychologists were "nonracialist," the stance adopted by many of them "remained often unwittingly, Euro-centric" (1997, p. 226).

15. Although Clifford and Marcus's *Writing Culture* was lauded for its path-breaking, critical evaluation of the canonical concepts in anthropology, it excluded the feminist voices in anthropology. Later, however, feminist writing in anthropology made up for the absence of women's voices in *Writing Culture* and featured how issues of gender, race, privilege, accountability, and voice are tied to the ethnographic process of writing about culture. The book *Women Writing Culture* was one of the first feminist responses to or revision of *Writing Culture*. Clifford and Marcus omitted the work of feminist scholars on the grounds that "feminism had not contributed much to the theoretical analyses of ethnographies as texts" (Clifford 1986, p. 20). In addition, Clifford wrote that feminist ethnographies of culture have "not produced either unconventional forms of writing or a developed reflection on ethnographic textuality as such" (1986, p. 21). In the introduction to *Women Writing Culture,* Behar (1995) writes that Clifford's statements made many women anthropologists angry and sad. The impact of these statements was immense. Behar notes that "no two pages in the history of anthropological writing have created as much anguish among feminist readers as did James Clifford's uneasy statements justifying the absence of women anthologists from the project writing culture" (Behar 1995, p. 4). One of this objectives of *Women Writing Culture* was to go beyond formulating a feminist response to *Writing Culture* and to create a strong intellectual foundation for a feminist anthropology that spoke to issues of race, sexuality, morality, history, culture, difference, multiculturalism, and the canon.

Notes to Chapter 3

1. The Hindi term *des* or *desh* refers to the Indian nation or the home in India or within the boundaries of South Asia. *Pardes* refers to a foreign country or the home located abroad.

2. It is important to note here that Clifford (1994) believes that we must acknowledge the strong influence of Jewish history on our understanding of the term *diaspora* but must refrain from making that history a "definitive" model.

3. Many of the scholars cited here work from an interdisciplinary postcolonial and cultural studies perspective and describe the disaporic condition as emerging from colonial and neocolonial contexts.

4. *Sepoy* or *sipahi* was the rank given to native Indian soldiers recruited to fight for the British army in India. In 1857, the sepoys, who were Hindus, Muslims, or Sikhs, initiated one of the first social uprisings against the British colonial government.

5. For a detailed discussion of the bidirectional relationship among law, immigration, race, and society in United States, see López 1996.

6. Some of the participants in my study also reported that they experienced subtle racism and discrimination in their early years as graduate students in the United States but were able to recognize those incidents as racist only much later, especially after they had joined the workforce.

7. *Babu* usually refers to those middle-class men who work in the Indian government's large bureaucracy, and brown *shaibs* is a label given to those upper-class, British-educated Indians who mimic the lifestyle and cultural habits of the ruling upper-class segment of British society.

8. Some Indian students applying to graduate schools in the United States think that they should not be required to take the TOEFL (test of English as a foreign language) exams because of their fluency in the English language.

9. Enid Blyton, a well-known British writer, was the author of the children's series *The Famous Five*. Many generations of English-speaking South Asian children read her books.

10. Biggles was an action hero and fighter pilot created by the British author W. E. John. He created the children's book series *Biggles* during World War I and continued writing books based on the character Biggles until the 1960s.

11. Some women in the local community came to the United States for graduate school, so marriage was not a priority for them until they had established their careers.

Notes to Chapter 4

1. A number of other scholars interested in examining the mutual constitution of the relationship between culture and development have examined differences between the concept of appropriation and internalization (see Aukrust 2001; Nicolopoulou and Weintraub 1998; Olson 1998; Valsiner 1998).

2. Josephs's article "The Hopi in Me" (2002) provides an illuminating analysis of the concept of voice in the dialogical self. In particular, it shows how the creation of individual voices are connected to the social, ideational, and material aspects of culture.

3. It is important to mention that from a Bakhtinian point of view, "Edward Said," the narrator of his memoir, emerges as a transformed person in the process of having a *dialogue* about his own selves. The memoir actually enables him to enter into a dialogical reflexivity with the different parts of his diasporic selves, thereby reworking and reconstituting the varied parts of "Edward Said" in a way that new meanings about his identity are established.

4. The *pagadi* became the focus of my interview with Raju because I had interviewed him immediately after the events of September 11. Although Raju went to work every day in the weeks after September 11, he was reluctant to go anywhere else because he feared that someone might mistake him as an Arab.

5. Convent schools in India were started by British Christian missionaries to instruct Indian children in the English language. These schools often employed

"nuns" and "fathers" to teach the children and run the day-to-day operations. In postcolonial India, these schools were ones the most sought after by middle-class, urban parents because of their emphasis on discipline, academic performance, and a strong English-language curriculum.

6. During my graduate school years, one Indian student was fond of pointing to those Indian students whom he thought had acquired an "American accent" right after receiving their visas in Madras, Mumbai, or Delhi.

7. Abhishek and several other male Indian professionals told me that not knowing much about American sports put them at a serious disadvantage at the workplace. Most of the Indian immigrants I spoke to did not follow American sports such as football, baseball, and basketball and thus felt left out at work when their American colleagues bonded over them.

8. As I was analyzing Poonam's interview, I realized the word *Mullammaa* needed clarification. So I called Poonam and asked her to explain it by using it in context. The next day, I received the following e-mail from her:

> After I talked to you, I called a friend who is reasonably familiar with the Urdu language. She told me a thing or two about the word "Mullammaa." The best anomaly she could think of is equivalent to when our parents got their "peetal pots and pans covered with 'kalai' done by hawkers going by our houses yelling 'kalai karva lo.'"

Abhishek got on to his favorite subject "Internet for all the world's problems!!"

> Urdu: Mulammaa = gilded (English); overlay or overspread with a thin covering of gold = give an air and agreeable external appearance to; = a cover for the face? = masquerade?

He went to two sites for this: eBazm.com and Urduseek.com: I hope it will help you.

9. "Ambassador" is the brand name of a car that was used until the 1990s by many high-level government officials in India such as IAS officers and police commissioners, so the white-color car became a "status symbol" representing power and success.

Notes to Chapter 5

1. Several participants in my study were very interested in knowing the "methodology" I was going to use to analyze the results of my study. When I said that I would be using qualitative/ethnographic methods to frame the questions, they appeared skeptical about the validity of this study. But at the same time, these scientists also encouraged me to have in-depth conversations with a large group of Indians. Some of these scientist-participants were convinced that the "scientific method" was the most important method but still encouraged me to use conversation and in-depth interviews as my key methodological tools.

2. It is important to mention here that even when they were in India, some of these Indian participants defined themselves as being scientists, above any-

thing else. In the United States, however, these participants seemed to have constructed an identity for themselves solely in terms of being a scientist.

3. The idea that "Indian culture" had to be strategically displayed to Americans came up quite often in the interviews. One participant suggested to me that Indians must not lose their image as being "exotic" and "spiritual" people. In this case, being seen as belonging to an exotic culture was equated with being visible.

4. Several participants in my study told me that if they had lived in India, they would have had to wrestle with some of the same issues related to discrimination that they now confronted in the United States.

5. *Desi* refers to people of South Asian origin who have ancestors or roots in countries such as Bangladesh, India, the Maldives, Nepal, Pakistan, and Sri Lanka.

6. In my interviews, many participants pointed out that color or racial differences such as *gora aur kala* (white and black) also exist in India. To prove their point, some of them asked me to check out the racist descriptions used by men and women in matrimonial columns in Indian newspapers, such as *India Abroad* or the *Times of India*.

Notes to Chapter 6

1. In the 1960s and 1970s, most of the South Asians who migrated to England lived in the cities of Bradford, Manchester, and Southall. Since then, South Asians have created "Little Indias" and "Little Pakistans" in these cities, and, as a result, these towns have been described as "ghettos" for brown people. In the last five years, places like Bradford have also been the site of some of the worst race-related riots in the history of modern Britain.

2. In our paper on second-generation Indian women (Bhatia and Ram in press), we describe a model of acculturation that is culturally specific, dynamic, and historically and politically situated. We focus on three forms of dialogicality—polyphonization, expropriation, and ventriloquation—to demonstrate how hybrid selves and hyphenated identities were constructed in the South Asian diaspora.

3. It is important to examine the relations between these different voices. Valsiner notes that in order to understand the specific dialogical processes in the movement of the "I" positions of the self, we need to raise two important questions. First, "How are the 'I' positions changed?" and, second, "what is the whole range of dialogical relations between the constructed voices"? (2000, p. 4).

4. In my interviews with first-generation migrants, issues of sexuality were mentioned only in regard to their second-generation children. Sexuality is an issue, among others, that complicates the issues of self and identity in the second-generation South Asian American diaspora. Sayantini DasGupta and her first-generation immigrant mother Shamita Das Dasgupta (1998), using their own personal experiences, write that for many young, second-generation South Asian girls, coming of age in America has been a very painful process. Sayantini DasGupta

recalls that growing up in an almost all-white, midwestern American suburb, she was one of the few " brown" girls. Growing up among an "ocean of blonde hair and blue eyes," her feelings about her appearance, she notes, were "particularly low" (1998, p. 121). Not being able to live up to the "unattainable" images of *Charlie's Angels* and the golden-haired girls of *The Brady Bunch* and facing "repeated and constant" racial slurs at school, like "nigger," "injun," and "hindoo" combined with a lack of role models, she recalls a "perpetual feeling of self-loathing" (DasGupta and Dasgupta 1998, p. 121). For many non-Western, second-generation immigrants, being "othered" or "racialized" accentuates the pain of dislocation and displacement. The external positions and voices that are marked and assigned to the "brown" girl become internalized or appropriated.

Bibliography

Abu-Lughod, L. 1991. Writing against Culture. In *Recapturing Anthology,* edited by R. G. Fox, pp. 137–62. Santa Fe, N.M.: School of American Research Press.

Alba, R., and V. Nee. 1997. Rethinking Assimilation Theory for a New Era of Immigration. *International Migration Review* 31(4): 826–74.

Alba, R., and V. Nee. 2003. *Remaking the American Mainstream: Assimilation and Contemporary Immigration.* Cambridge, Mass.: Harvard University Press.

Alexander, M. 1993. *Fault Lines.* New York: Feminist Press at the City University of New York.

Alexander, M. 1996. *The Shock of Arrival: Reflections on Postcolonial Experience.* Boston: South End Press.

Altheide, D., and M. Johnson. 1994. Criteria for Assessing Interpretive Validity in Qualitative Research. In *Handbook of Qualitative Research,* edited by N. K. Denzin and Y. S. Lincoln, pp. 485–99. Thousand Oaks, Calif.: Sage.

Amit, V. 2000. Introduction: Constructing the Field. In *Constructing the Field: Ethnographic Fieldwork in the Contemporary World,* edited by V. Amit, pp. 1–18. London: Routledge.

Anthias, F. 1998a. Evaluating "Diaspora": Beyond Ethnicity? *Sociology* 32(3): 557–80.

Anthias, F. 1998b. Rethinking Social Divisions: Some Notes towards a Theoretical Framework. *Sociological Review* 46(3): 505–35.

Anthias, F. 2001. New Hybridities, Old Concepts: The Limits of "Culture." *Ethnic and Racial Studies* 24(4): 619–41.

Anzaldua, G. 1987. *Borderlands/La Frontera*. San Francisco: Spinsters/Aunt Lute.

Appadurai, A. 1996. *Modernity at Large: Cultural Dimensions of Globalization*. Minneapolis: University of Minnesota Press.

Ashcroft, B., G. Griffiths, and H. Tiffin. 1995. General Introduction. In *The Post-Colonial Studies Reader*, edited by B. Ashcroft, G. Griffiths, and H. Tiffin, pp. 1–4. New York: Routledge.

Aukrust, V. G. 2001. Agency and Appropriation of Voice: Cultural Differences in Parental Ideas about Young Children's Talk. *Human Development* 44: 235–49.

Bahri, D. 1996. Coming to Terms with the "Postcolonial." In *Between the Lines: South Asians and Postcoloniality*, edited by D. Bahri and M. Vasudeva, pp. 137–64. Philadelphia: Temple University Press.

Bahri, D., and M. Vasudeva. 1996. Introduction to *Between the Lines: South Asians and Postcoloniality*, edited by D. Bahri and M. Vasudeva, pp. 1–32. Philadelphia: Temple University Press.

Bakhtin, M. M. 1981. Discourse in the Novel. In *The Dialogic Imagination: Four Essays by M. M. Bakhtin*, translated by Caryl Emerson and Michael Holquist. Austin: University of Texas Press.

Bakhtin, M. M. 1984. *Problems of Dostoevsky's Poetics*. Minneapolis: University of Minnesota Press.

Bakhtin, M. M. 1986. *Speech Genres and Other Essays*. Austin: University of Texas Press.

Bammer, A. 1998. The Dilemma of the "But": Writing Germanness after the Holocaust. In *Borders, Exiles, Diasporas*, edited by E. Barkan and M. D. Shelton, pp. 15–31. Stanford, Calif.: Stanford University Press.

Barkan, E. 1995. Race, Religion, and Nationality in American Society: A Model of Ethnicity—From Contact to Assimilation. *Journal of American Ethnic History* 14: 38–101.

Basch, L., N. Glick Schiller, and C. Szanton Blanc. 1994. *Nations Unbound: Transnational Projects, Postcolonial Predicaments, and Deterritorialized Nation-States*. Amsterdam: Grodon and Breach.

Becker, H. 1962. *Through Values to Social Interpretation: Essays on Social Contexts, Actions, Types, and Prospects*. New York: Greenwood Press.

Behar, R. 1995. Introduction: Out of Exile. In *Women: Writing Culture*, edited by R. Behar and D. A. Gordon, pp. 1–29. Berkeley: University of California Press.

Behar, R., and D. A. Gordon, eds. 1995. *Women: Writing Culture*. Berkeley: University of California Press.

Berry, J. W. 1980. Acculturation as Varieties of Adaptation. In *Acculturation: Theory, Models and Some New Findings*, edited by A. Padilla, pp. 9–25. Boulder, Colo.: Westview Press.

Berry, J. W. 1985. Psychological Adaptation of Foreign Students in Canada. In *Intercultural Counseling*, edited by R. Samuda and A. Wolfgang, pp. 235–48. Toronto: Hogreffe.

Berry, J. W. 1990. Cultural Variations in Cognitive Style. In *Bio-Psycho-Social Factors in Cognitive Style*, edited by S. Wapner, pp. 289–308. Hillsdale, N.J.: Erlbaum.

Berry, J. W. 1997. Immigration, Acculturation and Adaptation. *Applied Psychology: An International Review* 46: 5–68.

Berry, J. W. 1998. Acculturative Stress. In *Readings in Ethnic Psychology*, edited by P. B. Organista, K. M. Cren, and G. Marin, pp. 117–22. New York: Routledge.

Berry, J. W., U. Kim, T. Minde, and D. Mok. 1987. Comparative Studies of Acculturative Stress. *International Migration Review* 21: 491–511.

Berry, J. W., U. Kim, S. Power, M. Young, and M. Bujaki. 1989. Acculturation Attitudes in Plural Societies. *Applied Psychology* 38: 185–206.

Berry, J. W., and D. Sam. 1997. Acculturation and Adaptation. In *Social Behavior and Applications*. Vol. 3 of *Handbook of Cross-Cultural Psychology*, edited by J. W. Berry, M. H. Seagull, and C. Kagitçibasi, pp. 291–326. Needham Heights, Mass.: Allyn & Bacon.

Bhabha, H. 1994. *The Location of Culture*. New York: Routledge.

Bhachu, P. 1993. Identities Constructed and Reconstructed: Representations of Asian Women in Britain. In *Migrant Women: Crossing Boundaries and Changing Identities*, edited by G. Buijs, pp. 96–114. New York: Berg.

Bhatia, S. 2001. Social Acts, Class and the Construction of Personhood in Indian Families. *Early Education and Development* 12: 433–54.

Bhatia, S. 2002a. Acculturation, Dialogical Voices and the Construction of the Diasporic Self. *Theory and Psychology* 12: 55–77.

Bhatia, S. 2002b. Orientalism in Euro-American and Indian Psychology: Historical Representation of "Natives" in Colonial and Postcolonial Contexts. *History of Psychology* 5: 376–98.

Bhatia, S. 2003. Is "Integration" the Developmental End Goal for All Immigrants? Redefining "Acculturation Strategies" from a Genetic-Dramatistic Perspective. In *Dialogue and Development*, edited by I. Josephs and J. Valsiner. Stamford, Conn.: Ablex.

Bhatia, S. 2004. Culture, Hybridity, and the Dialogical Self. Cases from the South Asian Diaspora. *Mind, Culture and Activity* 11(3): 224–42.

Bhatia, S., and A. Ram. 2001a. Locating the Dialogical Self in the Age of Transnational Migrations, Border Crossings and Diasporas. Commentary on H.J.M. Hermans's *The Dialogical Self: Toward a Theory of Personal and Cultural Positioning, Culture and Psychology* 7: 297–309.

Bhatia, S., and A. Ram. 2001b. Rethinking "Acculturation" in Relation to Diasporic Cultures and Postcolonial Identities. *Human Development* 44: 1–17.

Bhatia, S., and A. Ram. 2004. Culture, Hybridity and the Dialogical Self: Cases from the South-Asian Diaspora. *Mind, Culture and Activity* 11(3): 224–41.

Bhattacharjee, A. 1992. The Habit of Ex-Nomination: Nation, Woman and the Indian Immigrant Bourgeoisie. *Public Culture* 5: 19–44.

Bochner, A. 1997. It's about Time: Narrative and the Divided Self. *Qualitative Inquiry* 3: 418–39.

Bourdieu, P. 1994. *Language and Symbolic Power.* Translated by G. Raymond and M. Adamson. Cambridge, Mass.: Harvard University Press.

Brah, A. 1996. *Cartographies of Diaspora: Contesting Identities.* New York: Routledge.

Bruner, J. 1986. *Actual Minds, Possible Worlds.* Cambridge, Mass.: Harvard University Press.

Bruner, J. 1990. *Acts of Meaning.* Cambridge, Mass.: Harvard University Press.

Buijs, G. 1993. Introduction to *Migrant Women: Crossing Boundaries and Changing Identities,* edited by G. Buijis, pp. 1–20. Oxford: Berg.

Burke, K. 1966. *Language as Symbolic Action: Essays on Life, Literature and Method.* Berkeley: University of California Press.

Camilleri, C., and H. Malewska-Peyre. 1997. Socialization and Identity Strategies. In *Basic Processes and Human Development.* Vol. 2 of *Handbook of Cross-Cultural Psychology,,* edited by J. W. Berry, P. R. Dasen, and T. S. Saraswathi. 2nd ed., pp. 41–67. Needham Heights, Mass.: Allyn & Bacon.

Caputo, V. 2000. At "Home" and "Away": Reconfiguring the Field for Late Twentieth-Century Anthropology. In *Constructing the Field: Ethnographic Fieldwork in the Contemporary World,* edited by V. Amit, pp. 19–21. London: Routledge.

Cassirer, E. 1955. *Mythical Thought.* Vol. 2 of *The Philosophy of Symbolic Forms.* New Haven, Conn.: Yale University Press.

Chambers, I. 1994. *Migrancy, Culture, Identity.* London: Routledge.

Chang, G. H. 1999. Writing the History of Chinese Immigrants to America. *South Atlantic Quarterly* 98: 135–42.

Chow, R. 1993. *Writing Diaspora: Tactics of Intervention in Contemporary Cultural Studies.* Bloomington: Indiana University Press.

Chow, R. 1994. Where Have All the Natives Gone? In *Displacements,* edited by A. Bammer, pp. 125–51. Bloomington: Indiana University Press.

Clifford, J. 1986. Introduction: Partial Truths. In *Writing Culture: The Poetics of Ethnography,* edited by J. Clifford and G. E. Marcus, pp. 1–26. Berkeley: University of California Press.

Clifford, J. 1994. Diasporas. *Cultural Anthropology* 9: 302–38.

Clifford, J., and G. E. Marcus, eds. 1986. *Writing Culture: The Poetics of Ethnography.* Berkeley: University of California Press.

Cohen, R. 1995. Rethinking "Babylon": Iconoclastic Conceptions of the Diasporic Experience. *New Community* 21(1): 5–18.

Cohen, R. 1997. *Global Diasporas: An Introduction.* Seattle: University of Washington Press.

Conquergood, D. 1991. Rethinking Ethnography: Towards a Critical Cultural Politics. *Communication Monographs* 58: 179–94.

Cornell, S., and D. Hartman. 2004. Conceptual Confusions and Divides: Race, Ethnicity, and Study of Immigration. In *Not Just Black and White: Historical and Contemporary Perspectives on Immigration, Race, and Ethnicity in the United States,* edited by N. Foner and G. M. Frederickson, pp. 23–41. New York: Russell Sage.

Culler, J. 1982. *On Deconstruction: Theory and Criticism after Structuralism.* Ithaca, N.Y.: Cornell University Press.

Dasgupta, M. 2006. *Unruly Immigrants: Rights, Activism and Transnational South Asian Politics in the United States.* Durham, N.C.: Duke University Press.

Dasgupta, S. D. 1998. Introduction to *A Patchwork Shawl: Chronicles of South Asian Women in America,* edited by S. D. Dasgupta, pp. 1–17. New Brunswick, N.J.: Rutgers University Press.

DasGupta, S., and S. D. Dasgupta. 1998. Sex, Lies, and Women's Lives: An Intergenerational Dialogue. In *A Patchwork Shawl: Chronicles of South Asian Women in America,* edited by S. D. Dasgupta, pp. 111–28. New Brunswick, N.J.: Rutgers University Press.

Day, J., and M. B. Tappan. 1996. The Narrative Approach to Moral Development: From the Epistemic Subject to Dialogical Selves. *Human Development* 39: 67–82.

de Certeau, M. 1984. *The Practice of Everyday Life.* Berkeley: University of California Press.

Denzin, N. K., and Y. S. Lincoln. 1994. *Handbook of Qualitative Research.* Thousand Oaks, Calif.: Sage.

Edwards, D., and J. Potter. 1992. *Discursive Psychology.* London: Sage.

Emerson, R. M., R. I. Fretz, and L. L. Shaw. 1995. *Writing Ethnographic Fieldnotes.* Chicago: University of Chicago Press.

Espín, O. M. 1999. *Women Crossing Boundaries: A Psychology of Immigration and Transformations of Sexuality.* New York: Routledge.

Fabricant, C. 1998. Riding the Waves of (Post) Colonial Migrancy: Are We All Really in the Same Boat? *Diaspora* 7(1): 21–51.

Faist, T. 2000. Transnationalization in International Migration: Implications for the Study of Citizenship and Culture. *Ethnic and Racial Studies* 23(2): 189–222.

Fogel, A. 1993. *Developing through Relationships.* Chicago: University of Chicago Press.

Foner, N. 1997. What's New about Transnationalism? New York Immigrants Today and at the Turn of the Century. *Diaspora* 6(3): 355–75.

Frankenberg, R., and L. Mani. 1993. Cross Currents, Cross Talk: Race, "Post-coloniality" and the Politics of Location. *Cultural Studies* 7: 292–311.

Ganguly, K. 1992. Migrant Identities: Personal Memory and the Construction of Selfhood. *Cultural Studies* 6(1): 27–49.

Gans, H. J. 1979. Symbolic Ethnicity: The Future of Ethnic Groups and Cultures in America. *Ethnic and Racial Studies* 2(1): 1–20.

Gans, H. J. 1992. Second-Generation Decline: Scenarios for the Economic and Ethnic Futures of the Post-1965 American Immigrants. *Ethnic and Racial Studies* 15(2): 173–92.

Geertz, C. 1973. *The Interpretation of Cultures.* New York: Basic Books.

George, R. M. 1997. "From Expatriate Aristocrat to Immigrant Nobody": South Asian Racial Strategies in the Southern Californian Context. *Diaspora* 6(1): 27–59.

Gergen, K. 1985. The Social Construction Movement in Modern Psychology. *American Psychologist* 40(3): 266–75.

Gergen, K. 1994. *Realities and Relationships: Soundings in Social Construction-ism.* Cambridge, Mass.: Harvard University Press.

Gibson, M. 1988. *Accommodation without Assimilation: Sikh Immigrants in an American High School.* Ithaca, N.Y.: Cornell University Press.

Gilroy, P. 1987. *There Ain't No Black in the Union Jack.* London: Hutchinson.

Glick Schiller, N. G. 1997. The Situation of Transnational Studies. *Identities* 4(2): 155–65.

Glick Schiller, N. G., L. Basch, and C. Szanton Blanc. 1995. From Immigrant to Transmigrant: Theorizing Transnational Migration. *Anthropological Quarterly* 68: 48–63.

Glick Schiller, N. G., and G. E. Fouron. 2001. *Georges Woke up Laughing: Long-Distance Nationalism and the Search for Home.* Durham, N.C.: Duke University Press.

Goodall, H. L. Jr. 2000. *Writing the New Ethnography.* New York: AltaMira Press.

Gordon, Milton. 1964. *Assimilation in American Life: The Role of Race, Religion and National Origin.* New York: Oxford University Press.

Grewal, I. 1994. The Postcolonial, Ethnic Studies, and the Diaspora: The Contexts of Ethnic Immigrant/Migrant Cultural Studies in the U.S. *Socialist Review* 24(4): 45–74.

Grosofuguel, R., and H. Cordero-Guzman. 1998. International Migration in a Global Context: Recent Approaches to Migration Theory. *Diaspora* 7(3): 351–69.

Guba, E. G., and Y. S. Lincoln. 1994. Competing Paradigms in Qualitative Research. In *Handbook of Qualitative Research,* edited by N. K. Denzin and Y. S. Lincoln, pp. 105–18. Thousand Oaks, Calif.: Sage.

Gudykunst, W., and M. H. Bond. 1997. Intergroup Relations. In *Social Behavior and Applications.* Vol. 3 of *Handbook of Cross-Cultural Psychology,* edited by

J. W. Berry, M. H. Segall, and C. Kagitçibasi. 2nd ed., pp. 119–61. Needham Heights, Mass.: Allyn & Bacon.

Gupta, A., and J. Ferguson. 1992. Beyond "Culture": Space, Identity, and the Politics of Difference. *Cultural Anthropology* 7: 6–23.

Gupta, A., and J. Ferguson. 1997. Culture, Power, Place: Ethnography at the End of an Era. In *Culture, Power, Place,* edited by A. Gupta and J. Ferguson, pp. 1–29. Durham, N.C.: Duke University Press.

Gutiérrez, R. A. 1999. Hispanic Diaspora and Chicano Identity in the United States. *South Atlantic Quarterly* 98: 203–16.

Hall, S. 1990. Cultural Identity and Diaspora. In *Identity, Community, Culture and Difference,* edited by J. Rutherford, pp. 222–37. London: Lawrence and Wishart.

Hall, S. 1991a. The Local and the Global: Globalization and Ethnicity. In *Culture, Globalization, and the World-System: Contemporary Conditions for the Representation of Identity,* edited by A. D. King, pp. 19–39. Albany: State University of New York Press.

Hall, S. 1991b. Old and New Identities, Old and New Ethnicities. In *Culture, Globalization, and the World-System: Contemporary Conditions for the Representation of Identity,* edited by A. D. King, pp. 41–68. Albany: State University of New York Press.

Hall, S. 1993. Culture, Community, Nation. *Cultural Studies* 7(3): 349–63.

Halonen, J. S., and J. W. Santrock. 1996. *Psychology: Contexts of Behavior.* Dubuque, Iowa: Brown and Benchmark.

Hammersley, M. 1992. *What's Wrong with Ethnography? Methodological Explorations.* London: Routledge.

Hanks, W. 1996. *Language and Communicative Practices.* Boulder, Colo.: Westview Press.

Hannerz, U. 1992. *Cultural Complexity.* New York: Columbia University Press.

Harré, R., and G. Gillett. 1994. *The Discursive Mind.* Thousand Oaks, Calif.: Sage.

Hasnat, N. 1998. Being "Amreekan": Fried Chicken versus Chicken Tikka. In *A Patchwork Shawl: Chronicles of South Asian Women in America,* edited by S. Das Das Gupta, pp. 33–45. New Brunswick, N.J.: Rutgers University Press.

Hegde, R. S. 1998. Swinging the Trapeze: The Negotiation of Identity among Asian Indian Immigrant Women in the United States. In *Communication and Identity across Cultures,* edited by D. V. Tanno and A. Gonzalez, pp. 34–55. Thousand Oaks, Calif.: Sage.

Helweg, A. W., and U. Helweg. 1990. *An Immigrant Success Story: East Indians in America.* Philadelphia: University of Pennsylvania Press.

Hermans, H. J. M. 1996. Voicing the Self: From Information Processing to Dialogical Interchange. *Psychological Bulletin* 119: 31–50.

Hermans, H. J. M. 2001. Mixing and Moving Cultures Require a Dialogical Self. *Human Development* 44: 24–28.

Hermans, H. J. M., and H. J. G. Kempen. 1993. *The Dialogical Self: Meaning as Movement.* San Diego: Academic Press.

Hermans, H. J. M., and H. J. G. Kempen. 1998. Moving Cultures: The Perilous Problems of Cultural Dichotomies in a Globalizing Society. *American Psychologist* 53: 1111–20.

Hermans, H. J. M., H. J. G. Kempen, and R. J. P. van Loon. 1992. The Dialogical Self: Beyond Individualism and Rationalism. *American Psychologist* 47: 23–33.

Hernandez, D. J. 1999. Children of Immigrants, One-Fifth of America's Children and Growing: Their Circumstances, Prospects, and Welfare Reform. Master lecture presented at the biennial meeting of the Society for Research in Child Development, Albuquerque, N.M.

Hofstede, G. 1980. *Culture's Consequences: International Differences in Work-Related Values.* Beverly Hills, Calif.: Sage.

Holland, D. C. 1997. Selves as Cultured: As Told by an Anthropologist Who Lacks a Soul. In *Self and Identity: Fundamental Issues,* edited by Richard D. Ashmore and Lee Jussim, pp. 160–90. New York: Oxford University Press.

Hutnyk, J., and S. Sharma. 2000. Music and Politics—Introduction to Special Issue. *Theory, Culture and Society* 17: 55–63.

Hymes, D. 1990. Toward Ethnographies of Communication: The Analysis of Communicative Events. In *Language and Social Context,* edited by P. P. Giglioli, pp. 21–44. London: Penguin.

Jensen, J. M. 1988. *Passage from India: Asian Indian Immigrants in North America.* New Haven, Conn.: Yale University Press.

Jessor, R. 1996. Ethnographic Methods in Contemporary Perspective. In *Ethnography and Human Development: Context and Meaning in Social Inquiry,* edited by R. Jessor, A. Colby, and R. A. Shweder, pp. 2–14. Chicago: University of Chicago Press.

Jessor, R., A. Colby, and R. A. Shweder, eds. 1996. *Ethnography and Human Development: Context and Meaning in Social Inquiry.* Chicago: University of Chicago Press.

Johnson, J. M. 2001. In-Depth Interviewing. In *Handbook of Interview Research: Context and Method,* edited by J. F. Gubrium and J. A. Holstein, pp. 103–19. Thousand Oaks, Calif.: Sage.

Josephs, I. 1998. Constructing One's Self in the City of the Silent: Dialogue, Symbols and the Role of "As-If" in Self-Development. *Human Development* 41: 180–95.

Josephs, I. 2002. "The Hopi in Me": The Construction of a Voice in the Dialogical Self from a Cultural Psychological Perspective. *Theory and Psychology* 12: 161–73.

Kagitçibasi, C. 1997. Individualism and Collectivism. In *Social Behavior and Applications.* Vol. 3 of *Handbook of Cross-Cultural Psychology,* edited by J. W.

Berry, M. H. Seagull, and C. Kagitçibasi, 2nd ed. Needham Heights, Mass.: Allyn & Bacon.

Kalita, S. M. 2003. *Suburban Sahibs: Three Immigrant Families and Their Passage from India to America*. New Brunswick, N.J.: Rutgers University Press.

Kastoryano, R. 1999. Muslim Diaspora(s) in Western Europe. *South Atlantic Quarterly* 98: 191–203.

Kearney, M. 1995. The Local and the Global: The Anthropology of Globalization and Transnationalism. *Annual Review Anthropology* 24: 547–65.

Khan, S. 1998. Sexual Exiles. In *A Patchwork Shawl: Chronicles of South Asian Women in America*, edited by S. D. Dasgupta, pp. 62–71. New Brunswick, N.J.: Rutgers University Press.

Khandelwal, M. S. 2002. *Becoming American, Being Indian: An Immigrant Community in New York City*. Ithaca, N.Y.: Cornell University Press.

Kibria, N. 1998. *Becoming Asian American: Second-Generation Chinese and Korean American Identities*. Baltimore: Johns Hopkins University Press.

Kibria, N. 2002. *Becoming Asian American*. Baltimore: Johns Hopkins University Press.

Kiesinger, C. E. 1998. From Interview to Story: Writing Abbie's Life. *Qualitative Inquiry* 4(1): 71–95.

Kivisto, P. 2001. Theorizing Transnational Immigration: A Critical Review of Current Efforts. *Ethnic and Racial Studies* 24(4): 549–77.

Knowles, C. 2000. Here and There: Doing Transnational Fieldwork. In *Constructing the Field: Ethnographic Fieldwork in the Contemporary World*, edited by V. Amit, pp. 54–70. London: Routledge.

Kondo, D. 1996. The Narrative Production of "Home," Community, and Political Identity in Asian-American Theater. In *Displacement, Diaspora and Geographies of Identity*, edited by S. Lavie and T. Swedenburg, pp. 97–118. Durham, N.C.: Duke University Press.

Koshy, S. 1998. Category Crisis: South Asian Americans and Questions of Race and Ethnicity. *Diaspora* 7(3): 285–319.

Koshy, S. 2001. Morphing Race into Ethnicity: Asian Americans and Critical Transformations of Whiteness. *Boundary* 2, 28(1): 153–94.

Kumar, A. 2000. *Passport Photos*. Berkeley: University of California Press.

LaFromboise, T., L. K. Coleman, and J. Gerton. 1998. Psychological Impact of Biculturalism: Evidence and Theory. In *Readings in Ethnic Psychology*, edited by P. B. Organista, K. M. Cren, and G. Marin, pp. 123–55. New York: Routledge.

Lavie, S., and T. Swedenburg. 1996. Introduction: Displacement, Diaspora, and Geographies of Identity. In *Displacement, Diaspora and Geographies of Identity*, edited by S. Lavie and T. Swedenburg, pp. 1–26. Durham, N.C.: Duke University Press.

Leonard, K. I. 1992. *Making Ethnic Choices: California's Punjabi Mexican Americans*. Philadelphia: Temple University Press.

Lessinger, J. 1995. *From the Ganges to the Hudson: Indian Immigrants in New York City.* Boston: Allyn & Bacon.

Levitt, P. 2001. *The Transnational Villagers.* Berkeley: University of California Press.

Levitt, P., and M. C. Waters. 2002. *The Changing Face of Home: The Transnational Lives of the Second Generation.* New York: Russell Sage Foundation.

Lipsitz, G. 1998. *The Possessive Investment in Whiteness: How White People Profit from Identity Politics.* Philadelphia: Temple University Press.

López, H. I. F. 1996. *White by Law: The Legal Construction of Race.* New York: New York University Press.

Lowe, L. 1996. *Immigrant Acts.* Durham, N.C.: Duke University Press.

Mahalingam, R. 2003. Essentialism, Culture and Power: Rethinking Social Class. *Journal of Social Issues* 59(4): 733–49.

Mahalingam, R. 2006. Cultural Psychology of Immigrants: An Introduction. In *Cultural Psychology of Immigrants,* edited by R. Mahalingam, pp. 1–12. Hillsdale, N.J.: Erlbaum.

Mahalingam, R., and J. Haritatos. 2006. Cultural Psychology of Gender and Immigration. In *Cultural Psychology of Immigrants,* edited by R. Mahalingam, pp. 259–73. Hillsdale, N.J.: Erlbaum.

Maira, S. M. 2002. *Desis in the House: Indian American Youth Culture in New York City.* Philadelphia: Temple University Press.

Maira, S., and R. Srikanth. 1996. Introduction to *Contours of the Heart: South Asians Map America,* edited by S. Maira and R. Srikanth. New York: Asian American Writers' Workshop.

Malinowski, B. 1948. *Magic, Science and Religion, and Other Essays.* New York: Natural History Press.

Mani, L. 1994. Gender, Class, and Cultural Conflict: Indu Krishnan's "Knowing Her Place." In *Our Feet Walk the Sky,* edited by South Asian Women's Descent Collective, pp. 32–36. San Francisco: Aunt Lute Press.

Marcus, G. E. 1995. Ethnography in/of the World System: The Emergence of Multi-Sited Ethnography. *Annual Review Anthropology* 24: 95–117.

Marcus, G. E. 1998. *Ethnography through Thick and Thin.* Princeton, N.J.: Princeton University Press.

Marcus, G. E., and M. M. J. Fischer. 1986. *Anthropology as Cultural Critique.* Chicago: University of Chicago Press.

Mathew, B. 2005. *Taxi! Cabs and Capitalism in New York City.* New York: New Press.

Mazumdar, S. 1989. Racist Responses to Racism: The Aryan Myth and South Asians in the United States. *South Asia Bulletin* 9(1): 47–55.

McIntosh, P. 1997. White Privilege and Male Privilege: A Personal Account of Coming to See Correspondences through Work in Women's Studies. In *Critical White Studies: Looking behind the Mirror,* edited by R. Delgado and J. Stefancic, pp. 291–99. Philadelphia: Temple University Press.

Mead, M. 1960. *Coming of Age in Samoa: A Psychological Study of Primitive Youth for Western Civilization.* New York: Mentor Books.

Mohanty, C. T. 1991. Cartographies of Struggle: Third World Women and the Politics of Feminism. In *Third World Women and the Politics of Feminism,* edited by C. T. Mohanty, A. Russo, and L. Torres, pp. 2–47. Bloomington: Indiana University Press.

Moraga, C., and G. Anzaldua. 1983. *This Bridge Called My Back: Writings by Radical Women of Color.* New York: Kitchen Table Press.

Morris, P. 1994. *The Bakhtin Reader.* New York: Edward Arnold.

Mukherjee, B. 1981. An Invisible Woman. *Saturday Night,* March, pp. 36–40.

Narayan, K. 1993. How Native Is a "Native" Anthropologist? *American Anthropologist* 95: 671–85.

Nicolopoulou, A., and J. Weintraub. 1998. Individual and Collective Representations in Social Context: A Modest Contribution to Resuming the Sociocultural Developmental Psychology. *Human Development* 41: 215–35.

Nonini, D., and A. Ong. 1997. Chinese Transnationalism as an Alternative Modernity. In *The Cultural Practices of Modern Chinese Transnationalism,* edited by A. Ong and D. Nonini. New York: Routledge.

Okhirio, G. 1994. *Margin and Mainstreams: Asians in American History and Culture.* Seattle: University of Washington Press.

Okley, J. N. 1996. *Own or Other Culture.* New York: Routledge.

Okley, J. N., and H. Callaway, eds. 1992. *Anthropology and Autobiography.* New York: Routledge.

Olson, D. 1998. Institutions Are Real but Internalization Is Not. *Human Development* 41: 236–38.

Omi, M., and H. Winant. 1994. *Racial Formation in the United States: From the 1960s to the 1990s.* New York: Routledge.

Ong, A. 1999. *Flexible Citizenship: The Cultural Logics of Transnationality.* Durham, N.C.: Duke University Press.

Ortner, S. 1984. Theory in Anthropology since the Sixties. *Society for Comparative Study of Society and History* 26: 126–66.

Packer, M., and M. Tappan, eds. 2001. *Cultural and Critical Perspectives on Human Development.* Albany: State University of New York Press.

Portes, A. 1996. Introduction: Immigration and Its Aftermath. In *The New Second Generation,* edited by A. Portes, pp. 1–7. New York: Russell Sage Foundation.

Portes, A. 1997. Immigration Theory for a New Century: Some Problems and Opportunities. *International Migration Review* 4: 799–825.

Portes, A. 1999. Conclusion: Towards a New World: The Origins and Effects of Transnational Activities. *Ethnic and Racial Studies* 22.

Portes, A., L. Guarnizo, and P. Landolt. 1999. Introduction: Pitfalls and Promise of an Emergent Research Field. *Ethnic and Racial Studies* 22.

Portes, A., and R. Rumbaut. 2001. *Legacies: The Story of the Immigrant Second Generation.* Berkeley: University of California Press.

Portes, A., and M. Zhou. 1993. The New Second Generation: Segmented Assimilation and Its Variants among Post-1965 Immigrant Youth. *Annals of American Academy of Political and Social Science* 530: 74–98.

Prashad, V. 2000. *The Karma of Brown Folk*. Minneapolis: University of Minnesota Press.

Prashad, V. 2001. *Everybody Was Kung Fu Fighting: Afro-Asian Connections and the Myth of Cultural Purity*. Boston: Beacon Press.

Purkayastha, B. 2005. *Negotiating Ethnicity: Second-Generation South Asian Americans Transverse a Transnational World*. New Brunswick, N.J.: Rutgers University Press.

Radhakrishnan, R. 1996. *Diasporic Mediations: Between Home and Location*. Minneapolis: University of Minnesota Press.

Raj, D. S. 2003. *Where Are You From? Middle-Class Migrants in the Modern World*. Berkeley: University of California Press.

Rangaswamy, P. 2000. *Namaste America: Indian Immigrants in an American Metropolis*. University Park: Pennsylvania State University Press.

Richards, G. 1997. *"Race," Racism and Psychology: Towards a Reflexive History*. London: Routledge.

Rogoff, B. 1990. *Apprenticeship in Thinking: Cognitive Development in Sociocultural Activity*. New York: Oxford University Press.

Rogoff, B., J. Mistry, A. Göncü, and C. Mosier. 1993. *Guided Participation in Cultural Activity by Toddlers and Caregivers*. Monographs of the Society for Research in Child Development 58(7, serial no. 236).

Rong, X. L., and J. Prissele. 1998. *Educating Immigrant Students: What We Need to Know to Meet the Challenge*. Thousands Oaks, Calif.: Corwin Press.

Rosaldo, R. 1993. *Culture and Truth: Remaking of Social Analysis*. Boston: Beacon Press.

Rubin, J. R., and I. S. Rubin. 1995. *Qualitative Interviewing: The Art of Hearing Data*. Thousand Oaks, Calif.: Sage.

Rudrappa, S. 2004. *Ethnic Routes to Becoming American: Indian Immigrants and the Cultures of Citizenship*. New Brunswick, N.J.: Rutgers University Press.

Rumbaut, R. 2002. Severed or Sustained Attachments? Language, Identity, and Imagined Communities in the Post-Immigrant Generation. In *The Changing Face of Home*, edited by P. Levitt and M. C. Waters, pp. 43–95. New York: Russell Sage Foundation.

Rushdie, S. 1991. *Imaginary Homelands: Essays and Criticism 1981–1991*. London: Granta.

Safran, W. 1991. Diasporas in Modern Societies: Myths of Homeland and Return. *Diaspora* 1(1): 83–99.

Sagar, P. 1996. Postcolonial Theory. In *A Dictionary of Cultural and Critical Theory*, edited by M. Payne, pp. 422–25. Cambridge, Mass.: Blackwell.

Said, E. W. 1979. *Orientalism*. New York: Vintage Books.

Said, E. W. 1993. *Culture and Imperialism*. New York: Knopf.

Said, E. W. 1999. *Out of Place: A Memoir.* New York: Knopf.

Sampson, E. 1993. *Celebrating the Other: A Dialogic Account of Human Nature.* Boulder, Colo.: Westview Press.

Schieffelin, B. B., and E. Ochs, eds. 1986. *Language Socialization across Cultures.* Cambridge: Cambridge University Press.

Segall, M. H., W. J. Lonner, and J. W. Berry. 1998. Cross-Cultural Psychology as a Scholarly Discipline: On the Flowering of Culture in Behavioral Research. *American Psychologist* 53: 1101–10.

Sharpe, J. 1995. Is the United States Postcolonial? Transnationalism, Immigration, and Race. *Diaspora* 4(2): 181–97.

Shome, R. 1996. Postcolonial Interventions in the Rhetorical Canon: An "Other" View. *Communication Theory* 6: 40–59.

Shome, R., and R. S. Hegde. 2002. Postcolonial Approaches to Communication: Charting the Terrain, Engaging the Intersections. *International Communication Association* 12(3): 249–70.

Shotter, J. 1993. *Conversational Realities: The Construction of Life through Language.* London: Sage.

Shukla, S. 2003. *India Abroad: Diasporic Cultures of Postwar America and England.* Princeton, N.J.: Princeton University Press.

Shweder, R. A. 1996. True Ethnography: The Lore, the Law, and the Lure. In *Ethnography and Human Development: Context and Meaning in Social Inquiry,* edited by R. Jessor, A. Colby, and R. A. Shweder, pp. 15–52. Chicago: University of Chicago Press.

Smith, R. C. 2000. How Durable and New Is Transnational Life? Historical Retrieval through Local Comparison. *Diaspora* 9(2): 203–33.

Stacey, J. 1988. Can There Be a Feminist Ethnography? *Women Studies International Forum* 11(1): 21–27.

Stacey, J. 1991. Can There Be a Feminist Ethnography? In *Women's Words: The Practice of Oral History,* edited by S. B. Gluck and D. Patai, pp. 111–20. New York: Routledge.

Suárez-Orozco, M. M., and C. Suárez-Orozco. 2001. *Children of Immigration.* Cambridge, Mass.: Harvard University Press.

Tavris, C., and C. Wade. 1997. *Psychology in Perspective.* 2nd ed. New York: Addison-Wesley.

Taylor, S. J., and R. Bogdan. 1998. *Introduction to Qualitative Research Methods: A Guidebook and Resource.* 3rd ed. New York: Wiley.

Todorov, T. 1984. *Mikhail Bakhtin: The Dialogical Principle.* Translated by W. Godzich. Minneapolis: University of Minnesota Press.

Tölöyan, K. 1996. Rethinking Diaspora(s): Stateless Power in the Transnational Moment. *Diaspora* 5: 3–35.

Trujillo, N. 1998. In Search of Naunny's Grave. *Text and Performance Quarterly* 18: 344–68.

Valsiner, J. 1998. *The Guided Mind.* Cambridge, Mass.: Harvard University Press.

Valsiner, J. 2000. Making Meaning out of Mind: Self-less and Self-ful Dialogicality. Paper presented at the First International Conference of the Dialogical Self, University of Nijmegen, Netherlands, June.

Valsiner, J. 2002. Forms of Dialogical Relations and Semiotic Auto-Regulation within the Self. *Theory and Psychology* 2: 251–65.

van der Veer, P. 1992. Introduction: The Diasporic Imagination. In *Nation and Migration: The Politics of Space in the South Asian Diaspora,* edited by P. van der Veer, pp. 1–16. Philadelphia: University of Pennsylvania Press.

Van Maanen, J. 1988. *Tales of the Field: On Writing Ethnography.* Chicago: University of Chicago Press.

Vertovec, S. 1999. Conceiving and Researching Transnationalism. *Ethnic and Racial Studies* 22(2): 447–62.

Vertovec, S. 2001. Transnationalism and Identity. *Journal of Ethnic and Migration Studies* 27(4): 573–82.

Visweswaran, K. 1994. *Fictions of Feminist Ethnography.* Minneapolis: University of Minnesota Press.

Visweswaran, K. 1997. Diaspora by Design: Flexible Citizenship and South Asians in U.S. Racial Formations. *Diaspora* 6(1): 5–39.

Warner, W. L., and L. Srole. 1945. *The Social Systems of American Ethnic Groups.* New Haven, Conn.: Yale University Press.

Waters, M. C. 1990. *Ethnic Options: Choosing Identities in America.* Berkeley: University of California Press.

Waters, M. C. 1999. *Black Identities: West Indian Dreams and American Realities.* New York: Russell Sage Foundation.

Werbner, P., and T. Modood. 1997. *Debating Cultural Hybridity.* London: Zed Books.

Wertsch, J. V. 1991. *Voices of the Mind: A Sociocultural Approach to Mediated Action.* Cambridge, Mass.: Harvard University Press.

Wertsch, J. V. 1998. *Mind as Action.* New York: Oxford University Press.

Westen, D. 1997. *Psychology: Mind, Brain and Culture.* New York: Wiley.

Whorf, B. 1956. *Language, Thought and Reality,* edited by J. Carroll. Cambridge, Mass.: MIT Press.

Zhou, M. 1997. Growing Up American: The Challenge Confronting Immigrant Children and Children of Immigrants. *Annual Review of Sociology* 23: 69–75.

Index

About the Author

Sunil Bhatia is an associate professor in the Department of Human Development at Connecticut College, New London, Connecticut.